# Dreams of the Burning Child

David Lee Miller

# Dreams of the Burning Child

*Sacrificial Sons and the Father's Witness*

Cornell University Press    *Ithaca and London*

First published 2003 by Cornell University Press

Printed in the United States of America

Epigraph from *Father Fox's Pennyrhymes* used by permission of
HarperCollins Publishers. Text copyright © 1971 by Clyde Watson.

Library of Congress Cataloging-in-Publication Data

Miller, David Lee, 1951–
    Dreams of the burning child : sacrificial sons and the father's
witness / David Lee Miller.
        p. cm.
Includes bibliographical references and index.
    ISBN 0-8014-4057-2 (cloth : alk. paper)
    1. Fathers and sons in literature.   2. Death in literature.   3.
Literature—History and criticism.   4. Child sacrifice.   I. Title.
    PN56.F37 M55 2002
    809'.933520431—dc21                              2002007037

Cornell University Press strives to use environmentally responsible
suppliers and materials to the fullest extent possible in the publishing
of its books. Such materials include vegetable-based, low-VOC inks
and acid-free papers that are recycled, totally chlorine-free, or partly
composed of nonwood fibers. For further information, visit our
website at www.cornellpress.cornell.edu.

Cloth printing     10  9  8  7  6  5  4  3  2  1

To the Miller men,
John Y, John P, Truman, and Sam,
with love.

A father had been watching beside his child's sickbed for days and nights on end. After the child had died, he went into the next room to lie down, but left the door open so that he could see from his bedroom into the room in which his child's body was laid out, with tall candles standing round it. An old man had been engaged to keep watch over it, and sat beside the body murmuring prayers. After a few hours' sleep, the father had a dream that *his child was standing beside his bed, caught him by the arm and whispered to him reproachfully, "Father, don't you see I'm burning?"* He woke up, noticed a bright glare of light from the next room, hurried into it and found that the old watchman had dropped off to sleep and that the wrappings and one of the arms of his beloved child's dead body had been burned by a lighted candle that had fallen down on them.

—Freud, *The Interpretation of Dreams*

The firstborn of your sons you shall give to me.

—Exodus 22:29

Gallop, oh gallop down Vinegar Lane,
Gallop, oh gallop, oh gallop again!
Hedges and ditches and fence-posts beware,
I've seventeen children, but none I can spare.

—Clyde Watson, *Father Fox's Pennyrhymes*

# Contents

# Preface

I have three sons, so of course family and friends have assumed for years that in choosing the topic for this book I followed the adage "Write about what you know." My approach has been just the reverse, however. Friendship, love, and family relations are all mysterious matters, and I believe that the father-son bond in Western cultures enfolds a few mysteries of its own. Freud thought he had plucked out the heart of this mystery with his "discovery" of the Oedipus complex—probably the last century's most influential piece of literary criticism. But I have not sought out fathers and sons in order to confirm a theory, demonstrate a thesis, or apply a method, nor have I thought to dwell safely in the realm of the domestic and the familiar. Rather I would say the topic found me, and I have tried, in the piecemeal and belated fashion typical of criticism, to understand it strictly in self-defense.

At first I thought this book was going to be the history of a topos, or of two related topoi, the sacrificial son and the *puer senex* (boy/old man). Only after long and variously frustrated struggles to articulate an understanding of these figures did I recognize that the book's unifying subject is what they have in common: the father's witness, a gaze that constructs its objects according to the demands of patriarchy. Even then, the difficulties of defining my topic seemed daunting, to say the least. Anthropology, classical studies, biblical studies, theology, art history, psychoanalysis, and gender theory all contribute in fundamental ways to an understanding of cultural practices of representing boys. Even within literary study, the topic seems to have no respect for cultural, political, or historical boundaries. My argument takes in major instances from classical epic, early modern drama, the nineteenth-century novel, the postcolonial novel, the lyric, the funeral elegy, sacred scripture, and the theoretical discourse of psychoanalysis. It reaches out as well to draw examples from painting, sculpture, photography, and architecture into a discussion that ranges from the *aqedah* (the binding of Isaac) to Jacques Lacan's *Four Fundamental Concepts* and Chinua Achebe's *Things Fall Apart*. I often felt while working on this book that I, too, might fall apart before managing to speak competently about so many different texts, periods, and media. Specialists will inevitably challenge some of my readings, but it will be enough if this book can establish the power of explanation that I claim for its central concerns, even if that power should seem not to be perfectly realized in every detail of the argument.

It must also be conceded that the range of what I ignore is greater than the scope of what I include. By far the most frequent challenge posed (in manifold guises) by audiences responding to parts of this book has been the "What about X?" query. The variable in this equation may stand for Greek epic, tragedy, and theogony; for Latin authors outside of Virgil and Statius ("You should look at Ausonius"); for most of medieval European culture and almost all non-European culture; for early modern and modern texts in French, Spanish, German, and other European literatures outside England; for North and South American literatures; for film and popular culture; and of course for the bulk of English literature. It may stand as well for daughter-sacrifice ("What about Iphigenia? Antigone? Jephthah's daughter?"), Shakespeare's heroines ("What about Desdemona and Cordelia?"), or Victorian representations of the deaths of beautiful women. The first person to offer such a remark was Susan Snyder, who told me, upon learning over lunch one day that I was researching the *puer senex* topos, "Oh, you really must read *Dombey and Son*." I was a young man then, and believed her. Before long I would learn to quote Roberto Duran, the legendary Panamanian fighter who achieved immortality by crying, "¡No más! ¡No más!"

The logic of my argument provides no answer to the "What about X?" question, which I can only invite the questioners to pursue—hoping, of course, to persuade them that they should do just that.

I would like to thank the John Simon Guggenheim Memorial Foundation and the University of Kentucky College of Arts and Sciences for the combined support that enabled me to spend a year researching this book in 1994–95, and the National Endowment for the Humanities for the stipend that gave me a head start in the summer of 1994. Several short-term fellowships from the Folger Shakespeare Library have aided my research and writing as well; I am grateful for the working environment provided by the staff and readers of the Folger. Closer to home, Terri Brown and the rest of the staff at the University of Kentucky's W. T. Young Library have been consistently helpful over the years. Early on my work was supported by the Hudson Strode Program in Renaissance Studies at the University of Alabama; more recently I have benefited from the generous support of the Department of English, the College of Arts and Sciences, and the vice-chancellor for research at the University of Kentucky.

No chapter of this book has appeared elsewhere in its present form, but some material from previously published essays has been rewritten. Chapter 5 recasts "Writing the Specular Son: Jonson, Freud, Lacan, and the (K)not of Masculinity," which appeared in *Desire in the Renaissance: Psychoanalysis and Literature,* edited by Regina Schwartz and Valeria Finucci and published in 1994 by Princeton University Press. A section of this chapter also appears in slightly different form as "All Father: Ben Jonson and the Psychodynamics of Authorship," in *Parenting and Printing in Early Modern England,* edited by Douglas Brooks (Ashgate, forthcoming). Parts of "The Father's Witness: Patriarchal Images of Boys," *Representations* 70 (spring 2000), have been incorporated into chapters 1, 3, and 6; thanks are due to the University of California Press for permission to adapt this material. A few pages from chapter 1 are combined with parts of the *Representations* essay in "The Father's Witness: Sacrifice and Subjectivity in the Elizabethan Theater," a lecture delivered on March 23, 2000, at the Massachusetts Center for Renaissance Studies in Amherst, Massachusetts, and published by the Center later that year as "Occasional Publication No. 3." The introduction appeared with minor alterations in a special issue of *American Notes and Queries* (winter 2002) featuring work by members of the English Department at the University of Kentucky.

I have been fortunate in my advisers and professional role models. For years of friendship, advice, and support that have meant a great deal to me, I would like to thank Harry Berger Jr., Richard Helgerson, Arthur Kinney, Elizabeth Meese, Stephen Orgel, and Ann Lake Prescott. Margaret Ferguson, Stephen Greenblatt, Bernhard Kendler, Peter Stallybrass, and Randolph Starnes also gave counsel and support when it counted most. Kara Lee Miller, director of academic services at National University, has inspired me by her example for as long as I can remember, if not longer.

To name the friends and colleagues who read and commented on parts of this study, often more than once, as it took shape over the years is to count a long list of blessings. Virginia Blum, Douglas Brooks, William Campbell, Christopher Canaan, Patrick Cheney, Ann Baynes Coiro, Margareta de Grazia, Richard Halpern, Philip Harling, Linda Gregerson,

Richard Greissman, Kenneth Gross, John D. Kilgore, Theodore Leinwand, David Leverenz, Dana Nelson, Robert Newsome, David Riggs,
Theodore Schatzki, Louis J. Swift, Harold Weber, and Stephen Wheeler
offered valuable suggestions and encouragement. I will always be grateful
for the time, energy, and interest these friends have given me. The uniden-
tified reader for Cornell University Press, too, suggested some final revi-
sions that significantly improved the manuscript. I have also enjoyed the
advice and assistance of some very talented graduate students: Lisa
Broome-Price, Anne Beebe, Sean Morris, Jeff Osborne, and Jeannie
Provost. Noam Flinker, Thomas Kovacs, and Patricia Harris Stäblein
helped me puzzle over texts in Hebrew, German, and Latin.

Opportunities to present work in progress to faculty and students at
other universities are especially valuable. I would like to thank Harry
Berger Jr., director of a 1994 Summer Research Institute at the Folger
Shakespeare Library; James Broaddus and his colleagues at Indiana State
University, hosts of the Joseph S. Schick lecture; Patrick Cheney, at Pennsylvania State University; Ann Baynes Coiro, at Rutgers University; Scott
Cook, then at Tulane University; Alexander Dunlop, at Auburn University; Patricia Fumerton, at the University of California, Santa Barbara; Anthony Grafton, director of the Shelby Cullom Davis Center for Historical
Studies at Princeton University; Arthur Kinney, director of the Massachusetts Center for Renaissance Studies, and his colleagues in the English Department at the University of Massachusetts, Amherst; Gary Taylor, director of the Hudson Strode Program at the University of Alabama; and Paul
Yachnin, at the University of British Columbia. For the opportunity to
present parts of this work at professional meetings, I am grateful to Douglas Brooks, Pamela Royston Macfie, and Stella P. Revard.

For twenty years now, Greg Jay's enthusiastic friendship and intellectual
passion have been generous and inspiring gifts, without which my ideas of
literary study would not be the same. Marshall Grossman's extraordinary
grasp of this project has yielded many valuable contributions to the argument, while his gifts in the art of table talk have been a steady source of
consolation and delight. For her companionship over the years, for the
shared pleasures of raising our boys, and for her willingness to take on
added responsibility, delaying her own work while I was preoccupied with
mine, my wife, Lynn Pruett, deserves more acknowledgment than is possible here. That will have to be my next project.

DAVID LEE MILLER

*Lexington, Kentucky*

# Dreams of the Burning Child

# Introduction: The Body of Fatherhood

The motif of filial sacrifice is the most striking feature shared by the canonical texts of English literature, along with their classical and biblical antecedents. Why is this so? Why do Western patriarchies so persistently imagine sacrificing their sons?

This question cannot be answered in the abstract, solved, like an equation, with the right theoretical proof. It is historical, although framed so broadly as to be almost unanswerable in purely historical terms. While postmodern literary and cultural studies are increasingly political, their historicism tends to be local, remaining notably skeptical of "master narratives" that sweep across material differences in language, custom, economic organization, family structure, and institutional context. What can be the object of a study that crosses millennia? My answers are speculative but I take the question seriously. The cultural breadth and historical insistence of the motif are precisely what have to be accounted for. To ask about its recurrence in spite of so much change is a way of asking about its power. What could enable this cultural fantasy and the ensemble of practices that support it to reproduce and mutate like a virus? Why does it haunt the most intimate spaces of personal subjectivity even as it invades the most public spaces of Western culture—the book, the altar, the museum, the theater? What has the sacrificial son meant to the melancholy patriarchies of the past, and to what extent does this fantasy still determine their meaning for us today?

In this book I address such questions by describing what must surely be Western culture's oddest couple, the deified father and the sacrificial son. In doing so I assume, as my initial questions imply, that the rule of fathers requires such offerings. One reason may be that blood sacrifice meets in a special way the more general need of any social order for powerful forms of self-representation. The historical importance of literature and other art forms owes much to the fact that imaginary unities—nations, estates, lineages, regimes—exist primarily in, and as, visual or verbal representations of themselves. But how is a patriarchal and patrilineal society to represent its specifically father-centered character? Paternity is not naturally visible; unlike maternity, it has no distinct bodily form. Patrilineal patriarchy therefore turns what might be a neutral or insignificant empirical fact— the invisibility of biological fatherhood—into a structural crisis. This form of socially constructed authority, unlike others that might exist, generates a demand for representations of an object that *does not exist* and cannot be visualized: the body of fatherhood.

According to one theory, rituals of blood sacrifice compensate for the formal embarrassment of fatherhood's inability to represent itself. Karen E. Fields, summarizing the work of the anthropologist Nancy Jay, explains the connection:

> Turning the lens toward ancient Greek, Israelite, and Roman sacrifice, toward Tallensi, Nuer, Hawaiian, and Ashanti sacrifice, Nancy Jay shows how, in unrelated settings, sacrificial ritual enacts patrilineal descent. The important idea is not simply that patrilineal descent is widely associated with sacrifice, the affinity that Robertson Smith noticed, but that patrilineal descent is socially organized and publicly achieved. Thus: Roman descent was established not by birth but by participation in the sacrificial cult. The Tallensi told their ethnographer that clan ties were a consequence of sacrificing together. The Nuer defined patrilineal kin as those who shared the meat of sacrifice. Demosthenes won a probate suit for a man whose patrilineal right to inherit was contested by demonstrating that, years before, no one had contested the man's placing of a sacrifice upon the clan altar. And so on and so on. Kinship through the male line is not a biological relation which people merely acknowledge or of which they only need remind themselves in ritual. It is a social relation. Patrilineal kin know they are kin *because* they sacrifice together; they become patrilineal kin by so doing. To so create social and religious paternity is precisely to transcend a natural relation. (xii)[1]

---

1. I prefer Jay's approach to the more established theories of Girard and Burkert, both of which offer myths of origin that are themselves sacrificial ideologies, as Jay observes in her chapter "Theories of Sacrifice" (131). Girard claims to identify the origin of all social and cultural difference, indeed of meaning itself, despite the logical impossibility of doing so from within the sphere of difference created by that origin. The resulting argument is not only deeply unappealing in its sheer hubris; it is also universalistic and reductive in a way that ultimately impoverishes analysis. A good example of both the value and the limitations of this approach is Bandera's "Sacrificial Levels": Girard's theory enables Bandera to recognize that a Lucretian critique of sacrificial religion is implicit in Virgil's *Aeneid*, and this is a major contribution to modern understanding of the poem; but his reading soon flattens out into

Blood sacrifice appears in this view as a technology of representation, a way to make paternity spectacular and so to foster its social reality.

Jay's account opposes sacrifice to the maternal power of childbirth, but it doesn't require that we see these practices as evidence for some primal dread of the female body. I take it for granted that whatever values or affects may attach to bodies, to their functions and differences, these are not primordial but socially created. The invisibility of fatherhood may be natural, but the structural crisis to which this invisibility leads is socially produced: the body of fatherhood doesn't exist in nature, but it is *missing* only from patriarchal culture. In principle this distinction is simple enough, but it has far-reaching consequences for our ways of thinking about gender and kinship. The critique of classical psychoanalysis reminds us that Freud's theory of castration anxiety makes sense only because its view of the female body is already male, already phallic. To take this imaginary scene as the origin of phallic masculinity is therefore circular. I make a similar point about the maternal body. In fact, my argument links the fatherly body to the female genitals in a way that, if counterintuitive, is nevertheless quite logical: *both* are culturally determined "absences" that cannot sensibly be posited as origins of the values that determine them. Each takes the body of the other as a point of contrast: the swelling of the maternal belly determines the nothingness of fatherhood just as that of the penis defines what Hamlet calls the "no-thing" between a maid's legs. But these contrasts are neither natural nor universal. They belong to the cultural grammar of social systems that privilege fatherhood and therefore need to symbolize it. Only within such systems could the existence of unpregnant men or penisless women be imagined as a source of psychic trauma.

Jay's theory of blood sacrifice is fundamental to my argument, but it leaves open two crucial questions: why should there be *human* sacrifice, and what is the special significance of sacrificing a *son*? These are not questions to be answered at once and then dismissed. The scandal of human

---

an allegorizing demonstration that the poem illustrates the theory. Burkert offers a succinct summary of his own myth of origins: "I have attempted to derive sacrificial ritual from Paleolithic hunting" ("Ritual Killing" 164). The problem with this theory is simple: as Jay observes with equal succinctness, "Hunter-gatherers do not sacrifice" (131). Jonathan Z. Smith makes the same observation: "The Paleolithic indications for sacrifice are dubious. I know of no unambiguous instances of animal sacrifice performed by hunters. *Animal sacrifice appears to be, universally, the ritual killing of a domesticated animal by agrarian or pastoralist societies*" (197, emphasis in original). Finally, and for my purposes most crucially, both theories are vitiated by the gender blindness that leads them, in Jay's words, to "present sacrifice in terms of a universal human nature, including gender relations determined by biologically given male violence" (133). As a result, "human evolution" emerges in both theories as "the achievement of males only" (132).

sacrifice has troubled both theology and anthropology. One long-standing interpretation of the *aqedah* (the binding of Isaac) takes this episode from the Book of Genesis as enjoining the substitution of animals for human sacrificial victims—a reassuring but untenable response to the text, as Jon D. Levenson has argued.[2] Virgil's *Aeneid*, by contrast, opens and closes with a reversal of this pattern, substituting human victims for the animals that *would* have been sacrificed, had sanctioned rituals not been disrupted by conflict.[3] Anthropological theory has almost always stressed one or another logic of substitution as central to the economy of sacrifice; if animal victims are surrogates for the humans who offer them, then the possibility of reversing this substitution inheres in the system itself. This remains true, as Joseph Conrad reminds us, even for a culture in which "enlightened" Christian sacraments have long since replaced blood sacrifice. "All Europe contributed to the making of Kurtz," says Marlow, the narrator in Conrad's *Heart of Darkness*. But somewhere along the way that leads from "The International Society for the Suppression of Savage Customs" to the depths of the Congo, Kurtz's "nerves went wrong, and caused him to preside at certain midnight dances ending with unspeakable rites which—as far as I reluctantly gathered from what I heard at various times—were offered up to him—do you understand?—to Mr. Kurtz himself" (50–51). Whatever else may be signified by Kurtz's notorious last words ("The horror! The horror!"), they acknowledge the persistence of something unspeakable in the dark heart of European Christianity, something that Marlow gathers reluctantly and can't quite bring himself to say. "If then the light in you is darkness, how great is the darkness!" (Matthew 6:23).

But why should this horror take sons as its special objects? In classical, Hebrew, and Christian cultures, the son offered in sacrifice provokes worship, fascination, and dread. The son in these traditions acts as a complement to the father, as his ideological reflector, and, ultimately, as an index of the contradictions inherent in fatherhood under patriarchy. He is thus at once the father's mirror and his undoing. On one hand, a son is indispensable "proof" of fatherhood, for only the male heir can extend the patriline. On the other hand, his existence provokes the crisis of fatherhood's uncertainty, for there is no way to *see* that any particular boy springs from this man rather than that one, or indeed from any man at all.

2. See *The Death and Resurrection of the Beloved Son*: "The cumulative evidence against the ubiquitous idea that the *aqedah* opposes child sacrifice and substitutes an animal cult is overwhelming" (113). Levenson traces the lingering of the sacrificial motif in beloved-son narratives from Isaac to Jesus.

3. Philip Hardie offers this observation in the best account of sacrifice in the *Aeneid* and its Latin successors; see *The Epic Successors of Virgil* 19–20.

If the fatherly body existed, it would join the male progenitor to his heirs; since it does not, they can be joined only disjunctively, through the testimony of the mother-wife and in the abstract, corporate "body" of the lineage-group. In the words of Fields, again, "Kinship through the male line . . . is a social relation." But if blood sacrifice in some mysterious way substantiates the otherwise merely notional patriline, displaying its reality in the opened body of the victim, then *filial* sacrifice goes to the heart of this mystery, forcing its paradox to the breaking point by offering up, in the firstborn son, the very body that *creates* fatherhood in the full patriarchal and patrilineal sense. The father who sacrifices a son—especially a firstborn son or, even more so, an only son—would seem to be destroying along with that son the very paternity the ritual is supposed to create.[4] How can fatherhood thrive on what appears to be self-destruction? I argue that the binding of Isaac, which sets forth this paradox so unforgettably, forces its contradiction to a crisis resolved by the deification of fatherhood in Yahweh. As a prototype of filial sacrifice, Isaac embodies in radical form both the structural dilemmas of the filial relation and their narrative resolution.

Sacrificial sons are a special instance of the practice of representing boys. Like blood sacrifice in ritual cultures, literary and artistic images of boys have regularly sought to compensate for the natural invisibility of fatherhood. In this sense all boys become "sons," called upon to signify a generic identification with the fatherly ideal. For this reason, they almost always bear traces of the topos that Ernst Robert Curtius names the *puer senex,* or boy/old man (98–107). This affinity between the sacrificial son and the *puer senex* is a major theme in *Dreams of the Burning Child.* Its most complete statement comes in chapter 4 with Dickens's little Paul Dombey, a quaintly "old-fashioned" boy who succumbs to figurative progeria, rushed into the grave by his father's impatience for him to grow up.[5] But as I show in chapter 2, the conjunction of these figures is already prefigured in Virgil's *Aeneid,* where the "elderly boy" first emerges as the trope of dynastic historicism.

The father who corresponds to these boys is often imagined gazing down on the scene of sacrifice or, in the case of Dickens's Mr. Dombey,

4. Robert Con Davis argues in *The Paternal Romance* that the sacrificing father "usurps (or attempts to usurp) God's position and ends up negating paternity over three generations, culminating in an act of theocide" (101). I argue the reverse: the contradiction between divine and human paternity *sustains* God's fatherhood by destroying that of the human father—which is then reestablished as an extension of God's.

5. "Old-fashioned" is a dialect term meaning precocious (*Oxford English Dictionary*, new ed. [*OED*] 3); for a discussion of the meanings this phrase accumulates in the novel, see Malcolm Andrews, *Dickens and the Grown-up Child* 125–34. For the notion that Paul suffers from progeria, see Terry J. Box, "Young Paul Dombey."

looking on from the shadows, feeling at once proprietary and excluded. In the *Iliad,* Priam watches helplessly from the walls of Troy, lamenting his own destruction in the fate of Hector; Zeus, too, looks down weeping on the fate of Sarpedon, but does not dare to intervene. The *Aeneid* is filled with sons who die *ante ora parentum,* before their fathers' eyes.[6] Christianity avoids this scene. Jesus does ask from the cross why God has forsaken him, but neither the Gospels nor the iconographic tradition shows the Father looking down to behold his son's suffering; that is the role of the Virgin Mother in *pietàs.* The exception is a set of Calvinist texts in the sixteenth century, retellings of the Passion that describe a vengefully sadistic God presiding over the Crucifixion.[7] In general, however, to be a father in the literary tradition is to bear witness to the destruction of the son, and to see in his death at once the essence and the destruction of fatherhood itself. Shakespeare's *Hamlet* is so resonant in part because of the way it doubles and reverses this ancient motif, staging the father's destruction for the son and the son's destruction for the theater audience. Shifting the pathos of old Priam's death onto his sorrowing queen, the Player's speech in act 2 treats the witness of the gods as a question: *Do they see? Do they care?* In response Hamlet links this wrenching appeal to equally mysterious questions about the power of dramatic empathy: "What's Hecuba to him, or he to [Hecuba], / That he should weep for her?" (2.2.558–59). The emotional force of this scenario carries through the pathetic death scenes of Dickens's child martyrs to the dream of the burning child in Freud, where the question of the father's witness emerges once again with arresting force: *"Father, don't you see I'm burning?"* (547–48).

The notion of witnessing proves central to my understanding of how fathers are linked to sons. This is a crucial point, for the object of this book is not a figure, a topos, or even a tradition. It is not empirical at all, for what I take up are historically diverse responses to the *absence* of an empirical "body" for fatherhood. Repeatedly, I have found that to grasp

---

6. *Os* means "mouth"; the word for "eyes" is *oculis.* The figurative or transferred use for "sight" is common, as Lewis and Short (*Harper's Latin Dictionary*) attests, but as Marshall Grossman has pointed out to me, the word probably also carries the sense of "countenance," and as the root of *oratio,* it glances at the father's or the son's *pleading* for clemency. M. Owen Lee, *Fathers and Sons in Virgil's "Aeneid,"* comments on the use of this phrase as a leitmotif in the poem. He sees the death of Pallas in book 10 as exemplary: "We have in the death of Pallas a summary [of] and comment on the *Aeneid* itself, which is the story of a hero who went to fulfill his destined role in history with his father on his shoulders and his son at his side, and whose eventual success, never reached in the compass of the poem, is dependent on the sacrificial deaths of many surrogate sons" (6–7).

7. See Debora Kuller Shuger, "The Death of Christ," in *The Renaissance Bible* 89–127. I return to this point in chapter 3.

these responses it is necessary to trace in texts and works of art the implied cultural transactions in which they are caught up. These transactions involve exchanges of meaning and desire within a symbolic economy of witnessing. For this reason the horizon my argument looks toward must, in principle, be a plausible literary and cultural genealogy for this economy, even though I can realistically expect only to sketch the genealogy while illustrating in some detail what it might mean to analyze the economy's workings.

Patrilineal patriarchies recruit sacrificial victims as visible stand-ins for the fatherly body; post-sacrificial cultures represent filial sacrifice and display the images of boys for much the same purpose. "Witnessing" proves crucial to all these transactions because although the spectacle can be observed, its connection to the patriline cannot. Dismembering an animal and burning its flesh do not supply the kind of evidence we get from DNA samples. (Nor does scientific testing establish fatherhood as an object of belief. It may establish fatherhood as a scientific fact, but only by reaffirming science itself as the ultimate object of belief, one that depends on an experimental economy of witnessing.) Ritual, then, secures the patriline only for a witnessing community that already in some sense "knows" patrifiliation to be what the sacrifice "means." This knowledge takes intuitive form as a perception—one you may inhabit or view from without, depending on whether you stand inside or outside the community in question. This condensing of a whole system of social relations into a highly charged perception is what distinguishes witnessing from empirical seeing. Unless such a synthetic perception is already laid up in the community's store of shared intuitions, ritual actions will be powerless to transform the still-warm flesh of a sacrificial victim into visible proof of the kinship system and the gods who authorize it.

Sacrifice in a strict anthropological sense is not a prominent feature of the works I consider. The *aqedah* is a narrative of averted human sacrifice, the death of Jesus a political execution reinterpreted as sacrificial; the battlefield deaths of Greek and Roman warrior-sons are sacrifices in metaphor only, while the deaths of Shakespeare's Hamlet and Mamillius and Dickens's little Paul Dombey extend the notion further. The cultural functions of these works, however, may be seen to elaborate the purposes that anthropological theory ascribes to sacrifice. Rituals not only make descent through the father visible; they also articulate the structure of kinship and locate the participant in that structure. The most ambitious literary texts take as their objects of representation social and political systems built on patricentric kinship relations, weighing the religious and historical dimensions of social order against its personal costs. They, too, tend to situate their viewers or readers socially; but at the same time they also reflect on the technologies employed by their cultures to "interpellate" the social subject. In this sense, such works are not only post-sacrificial, they are *meta*-sacrificial: they open up for scrutiny the role played by sacrificial myth in organizing the repertoire of fantasies that guide desiring subjects toward their places in the social order.

I demonstrate this proposition in readings of major works by Virgil, Shakespeare, and Dickens. Surrounding and informing these chapters are discussions of many other texts and artifacts, but for extended treatment I have singled out works distinguished by their cultural prestige, historical duration, and emotional resonance, written by authors whose careers have shaped the idea of literature so forcibly that they come, through a kind of metalepsis, to stand for it. Their status is not immutable, as the example of Virgil shows: his poetry helped lay the foundations for classical, medieval, and modern European culture, but since the nineteenth century his centrality has diminished so far that many of these observations no longer apply to him in quite the same way as they once did. Shakespeare and Dickens are popular icons yet; in their aura we seek a reassuring convergence of highbrow prestige and universal appeal. They also personify for our "official" culture the belief that the human imagination is a radically creative genius or indwelling spirit. They thus stand for both the shaping spirit and its artifacts, linking the artwork to its vital human origins in a wishful denial of its commodification. The idea of the great artist assures us, through this powerful tautology, that truth and beauty are fully intended and fully available in the literary masterwork, the utmost expression of our will to be human.

A second reason for my choice of authors has to do with the historical predicaments to which they were responding. Anthropological models imply that ritual practices should be most efficacious in stable settings, yet their modern history is one of crisis, conflict, and disruption. In this book I try to gain some perspective on the *longue durée* of Western culture by zeroing in on epochal shifts in the social and political order. Virgil's *Aeneid* stands poised between the civil wars that brought an end to the Roman Republic and the consolidation of power under Caesar Augustus near the end of the first century B.C.E. Shakespeare's plays respond to the consolidation of political power under the Tudors, to economic changes fostered by the early period of mercantile capitalism, and to the bloody culture wars triggered by the splitting of the religious community in the English Reformation—developments that were crucial in different ways to the emergence of the professional theater in London at the end of the sixteenth century. The novels of Charles Dickens captured the attention of Victorian England just as publishing was undergoing its own industrial revolution, driven by the steam-powered press and the mass production of paper. At the same time, England was struggling to absorb the broader economic shocks of industrialization and the political repercussions of the French Revolution, while the evangelical revival of the late eighteenth and early nineteenth centuries was losing momentum to a new wave of Enlightenment skepticism, fostered by the growing prestige of experimental science and by such prophets of secular culture as Carlyle and Arnold.

Virgil, Shakespeare, and Dickens have been taken up as holy places of humanism—not just canonical but hypercanonical, in the sense that the very idea of a literary classic draws on their enduring prestige. They also offer powerful and original renditions of the underlying myth of filial sacrifice, reformulating it in the aftermath of global shocks to the social order. Is there a connection? Have these works become hypercanonical *because* they respond to crisis—the Roman civil wars, the Reformation, the combined French and Industrial Revolutions—by reinventing the repertoire of sacrificial gestures, re-centering the symbolic economies of their cultures around the quintessential myth of patriarchy? Such a hypothesis cannot become a theory in the strong sense because it isn't provable, but I pursue it as speculation. If there *were* a connection between these authors' iconic status in the official culture and the force with which their major works reconceive economies of filial sacrifice, what would the connection be? If we align these authors according to such a supposition, how are we led to view them? Is the result a plausible and enlightening description of their work?

In pursuing this speculation we must not oversimplify the larger narrative in which these moments of crisis arise. To speak of *a* symbolic economy is an expository convenience, for at any given moment there are many cultural venues, all depending on local custom and circumstance. The effort to consolidate or impose a common culture in fact belongs to the project of empire- or nation-building, and it proceeds against the resistance of the provinces. Even within the culture of the court or metropolis, different institutions foster different practices and engage differently with state power, market forces, and the range of tastes associated with learned, elite, or popular audiences. As the term *economy* implies, there are established patterns of production and circulation for cultural artifacts, conventional transactions through which meanings are exchanged and pleasures generated. But as the term also implies, these systems are open-ended and dynamic, subject to contingency and thriving on innovation. It is for this reason, I believe, that sacrificial narrative and symbol are so crucial. They are prominent because they are potent, whether one's goal is to establish a canon or transform it, to break in or to break out.

Many of the books and authors I discuss are connected by specific lines of transmission, and thus may be seen as part of an active tradition. Virgil systematically imitates Homer, and Shakespeare places *Hamlet* in this epic patriline with the Player's speech of act 2. He had almost certainly read and translated book 2 of the *Aeneid* in grammar school; he would also have known Sackville's verses on the death of Priam in the "Induction" to *A Mirror for Magistrates* and Marlowe's treatment of the scene in *Dido, Queen of Carthage*. Dickens, of course, knew Shakespeare's plays intimately both as a reader and as a theatergoer, but there is probably a more important, if less direct, link between the two authors by way of the evangelical tradition. I argue that in *Hamlet* and *The Winter's Tale* Shakespeare is responding as powerfully to the Reformation, exemplified in John Foxe's *Acts and Monuments,* as he is to classical epic or popular romance. Dickens, as is well known, takes over his child martyrs from latter-day evangelical works such as the *Cheap Repository Tracts,* late eighteenth-century descendants of Foxe's martyrology.[8] Sigmund Freud, finally, was an enthusiastic reader of both Virgil and Shakespeare. He takes the epigraph to *The Interpretation of Dreams* from book 7 of the *Aeneid,* alluding to the infernal *furor* that enters the poem through Allecto and overtakes Aeneas himself in the end; and he broaches the Oedipus complex by pairing his reading of Sophocles' play with an equally forceful interpretation of *Hamlet.*

Specific, demonstrable connections of this sort are only part of the history this book describes, however; some of the most striking patterns that emerge are of a different sort. *Dombey and Son* offers many examples of such patterns, for without apparently trying to do so, Dickens has encompassed a virtual encyclopedia of the figures and motifs associated with filial sacrifice. In part, no doubt, this achievement reflects his prodigious appropriation of the ideal known to classical and humanist rhetoricians as amplification, for which Dickens had economic as well as artistic motives. But the expansive impulse by itself could scarcely enable an author to reproduce a detailed, well-ordered anthology of traditional themes and figures that he does not appear to have studied.

Take the *puer/puella senex* topos, for example. *Dombey and Son* is typical of Dickens in its proliferation of elderly boys, childish old men, girlish old women, and maternal girls. No previous writer works this motif so exhaustively as he has done. Since Dickens, like Shakespeare, was a popular artist who lacked a university education, criticism has tended to underestimate the range and sophistication of his reading. But even if we acknowledge his familiarity with Latin literature, the multiplication of old-young and young-old characters in his work probably does not suggest that he

---

8. John R. Knott discusses Foxe's centrality for the nonconformist tradition, and for the Protestant model of heroic suffering generally, in *Discourses of Martyrdom.*

was deeply moved by Virgil, or preoccupied with the late classical authors studied by Curtius. On the contrary, allusions to the Romans in *Dombey and Son* are consistently facetious, casting this "fierce people" as the persecutors of oppressed schoolboys wracked by declamations and declensions.

*Dombey and Son* is also marked by striking parallels to *The Winter's Tale:* in each, the dynastic heir is destroyed by his father's obsession; the mother is falsely branded with adultery; and the daughter is first cast out but then recovered from beyond the seas, redeeming the blasted patriarch and mending his broken dynasty through marriage to a new heir (Gager 12–13). We know that Dickens was close to William Macready, the preeminent Shakespearean actor of the day, and saw Macready's influential performance as Leontes. Yet in spite of Dickens's predilection for mimicking Shakespearean turns of phrase, *Dombey and Son* contains no verbal reminiscence of *The Winter's Tale*. The plays that echo in the text are *Macbeth*, *Hamlet*, and *Antony and Cleopatra*. In short, there is no direct evidence that Dickens modeled his novel on the play. Both in his use of the *puer senex* motif and in his transformation of Shakespeare's romance plot, he appears, rather, to have re-created narrative and figurative patterns inherent in the symbolic economy that links fathers and sons. He seems to have rediscovered these venerable topics in his own idiom, in pursuit of his own artistic purposes.

Of all these recurring topics, by far the most compelling is the burning child. Its arresting figure appears in the sacrificial children of Hebrew scripture, in Virgil's Ascanius with his halo of fire, and in Statius' lament at the funeral pyre of his adopted son, as he watches "the cruel flames creep over the fresh down of the dead boy" (V.v.20–21). We encounter the burning child again in a gruesome episode from Foxe's *Book of Martyrs*, illustrated by a notorious woodcut, and in "the pretty Babe all burning bright" of Robert Southwell's Christmas poem. It returns in *The Winter's Tale*, where Shakespeare's Leontes at the height of his madness orders Antigonus to "see" the infant Perdita "instantly consum'd with fire" (2.3.134); and it returns in Milton's haunted recollection of Moloch, the "children's cries unheard, that passed through fire / To his grim idol" (*Paradise Lost* 1.395–96). Toward the end of the eighteenth century, this same figure reappears in the consumptive child martyrs of evangelical melodrama, burning with their providential fevers. These lurid children, "passed through fire" to the Christian God, pass the fires of imaginary martyrdom on to their literary heirs—children such as Dickens's little Paul Dombey, toasting by the hearthside "as if his constitution were analogous to that of a muffin" (49). Last in this series is the dream of the burning child recounted by Freud, my source for the title of this book.

Patterns like this one, too insistent to be accidental yet clearly not the result of conscious imitation, call for a different order of explanation. I return to this issue in chapter 6; for now I simply want to note how resourcefully my topic eludes capture by any of the histories (or historicisms) it takes in. Defying such boundaries, the motif of filial sacrifice leads to a range of materials, "literary" in the broad sense, from the last chapter of Freud's dream book to the first book of the Hebrew scriptures. This backward chronology is more apt than it may initially seem, for the sacrificial son and the *puer senex* are figures of temporal reversal. The reversal is not arbitrary, although motivations for it may vary. Paradoxically, temporal reversal is intrinsic to historicism itself as a belated and retrospective mode of knowing, a point which the ur-historicist Virgil initially (and conclusively) demonstrates. It also embodies the wish that time might really run backward, as it does for the souls of the dead in Plato, Virgil, and Spenser.

We know that in this world, the whirligig of time brings in his revenges, turning sons into fathers and fathers into dust. But as Hamlet says to Polonius, "Yourself, sir, shall grow old as I am, if like a crab you could go backward" (2.2.202–4). The syntax of this assertion is out of joint; propping the confidence of *shall* upon the counterfactual whimsy of *if you could,* it reverses and dismantles the if-then logic of normative predication. Does this make it an exceptional, perhaps meaningless utterance, or might it somehow be normative on a more rarified level? Language, like the unconscious and unlike the aging process, always does move in both ways at once, predicating a past and a future on which the hypothesis or fantasy of its presence depends.[9] In writing as in dreams, incompatible temporalities collide; the sacrificial son, not only a creature of the unconscious but also an essentially literary thing, is imbued with fantasies of writing as a way out of death. For this reason, he occupies a special relation to the modern concept of authorship, as I argue in chapter 5. It has often been observed that our cultural ideal of authorship is both implicitly masculine and implicitly divine: the canonical author is a male parthenogeneticist, embodying his fictional universe in a godlike solitary act and then pronouncing it good. But to grasp the full import of this commonplace, it is necessary to remember that the link in our culture between masculinity and godhead is filial sacrifice. The cost of deification is very high.

The core of this book, in chapters 2 through 4, considers Virgil's *Aeneid,* Shakespeare's *Hamlet* and *The Winter's Tale,* and Dickens's

---

9. For a more detailed demonstration of this point, see my essay "Spenser and the Gaze of Glory."

*Dombey and Son.* In each case I try not only to interpret a literary text but also to describe that text's engagement with a symbolic economy of sacrificial witnessing. Chapter 1 surveys the broader context to which these discussions belong. It illustrates the general proposition that cultural artifacts tend to encode (and so to perpetuate) specific economies of witnessing, and it introduces the narrative, rhetorical, and pictorial motifs that characterize the sacrificial son and related figures in biblical, classical, and iconographic traditions. The three chapters on works by hypercanonical authors are followed by the fifth chapter's speculations about a sacrificial subtext underlying the concept of authorship. In chapter 6 I turn back to the sacrificial son's uncanny ubiquity, reconsidering the challenges it presents to historicist explanations.

In all of the following chapters I approach the materials under discussion as a textual critic, taking cues from anthropology and psychoanalysis for the practice of literary study. The focus is on narrative and symbolic motifs in English literature along with its classical and biblical antecedents; my treatment of works in other media, whether painting, sculpture, photography, or architecture, reflects the methods of literary interpretation. Without attempting a comprehensive survey of the topic, I nevertheless do try to understand its historical persistence and cultural centrality. Accordingly I have chosen (at the risk of hyperextending my scholarly expertise) to offer a very broad, if necessarily selective, range of discussion. Readers are asked to follow lines of speculation that run from Abraham and Isaac through the Gospels of the New Testament and Michelangelo's first *Pietà* to Chinua Achebe's *Things Fall Apart,* from Virgil's *Aeneid* through Shakespeare to Charles Dickens, and from Ben Jonson's poem "On My First Sonne" to Sigmund Freud's *The Interpretation of Dreams* and Jacques Lacan's *The Four Fundamental Concepts of Psychoanalysis.* At the same time, many of these speculations wind through episodes of close textual analysis and historical argument, for I hold that ideas have not really been explored until they are tested against complexities of circumstance and subtleties of figuration.

My hope is that readers of this book will want to explore its ideas further, testing and revising them in the study of other subjects. Work of this kind is by no means disinterested, though its motives may vary. One of them, I suppose, is the long-term project of detaching scholarship itself from the ideological structures of patriarchy and patriliny. This may be more difficult than it seems, for we are always ambiguously caught up in the texts we analyze—no less in deploring what we take to be their politics than in admiring their cunning or their beauty. As I suggest in chapter 6, criticism bears an intriguing resemblance to the Freudian model of mourning, with its gradual and imperfect reconstruction of one's relation to a lost object. In terms of this analogy, the project to which I should like to imagine this book contributing might be thought of as a collective work of mourning. It would be an academic work of mourning for the dead body of patriarchy; for although it was never alive, never even there at all, I believe we are still somehow its subjects.

I defiled them through their very gifts in making them offer
by fire all their firstborn, that I might horrify them;
I did it that they might know that I am Yahweh.
                                        —Ezekiel 20:26


## The *Aqedah*

Whether practiced, commemorated, narrated, or otherwise depicted, sacrifice may be understood as a social technique for the manufacture of
God. As gift giving, it substantiates Him through the symbolic economy
of the gift.[1] Specific kinds of gifts establish His character: if giving a child
makes God a progenitor, then giving the firstborn son makes Him a patriarch. This gift has reciprocal effects as well, binding the members of the
social group in specific ways to each other and to the God they manufacture. (Etymologically, *religion* means tying a knot.) Lévi-Strauss argues
that the totem in tribal cultures articulates the system of classification on
which social organization depends, and Jay shows that sacrifice works in a
complementary way to secure subordinations internal to the clan and to
articulate these with larger structures; sacrifice installs paternity as the cornerstone of social organization. The measure of who you are, it says to
each member of the group, is your relation to the still point of fatherhood.

This book focuses on one set of relations among the many that filial sacrifice sustains: the knots that bind father and son. This is not an exclusive

1. The most important study of gift giving as a system of exchange remains Mauss; for an
assessment of its influence and place in the field, see the foreword by Mary Douglas to the
1990 Norton edition. The standard summary of this seminal work stresses that every gift im-
poses the obligation to reciprocate. The creation of reciprocal ties is important to my account, as the next sentences indicate, but gift exchanges with an invisible deity as opposed to
a human social group have the added function of substantiating the deity. On the Bible's use
of the sacrificial body to "confer the force and power of the material world on the noumenal
and unselfsubstantiating," see Scarry 181–243.

focus because mothers are conceptually as well as biologically necessary to the making of fathers and sons: like all terms of relation, these depend on one another for their meaning. Nevertheless, I intend to stress the importance of the father–son bond in the cultural reproduction of masculinity. Studies of masculine identity have tended to concentrate on its defensive and reactionary elements; with varying subtlety, such work has perpetuated the tendency of first-phase feminism to caricature the masculine subject as an anxious oppressor. Meanwhile, studies of gender seeking to correct the preeminence of the phallus in psychoanalytic theory have turned to the pre-Oedipal mother, and therefore stress the male child's "separation" anxiety. While granting the fundamental importance of such work, I note that it sees masculinity as essentially defensive in part because it assumes either femininity or maternity as a reference point for defining masculine identity. Yet the pre-Oedipal mother and child form an idealized, implicitly romanticized couple no less fictional than the Freudian *ménage* they replace.[2]

I do not propose to re-essentialize masculinity. All gender identities are highly artificial. Partly for this reason, they are also in an important sense untenable. Perhaps it makes biological sense to say that one "is" a man or a woman, but masculinity and femininity are not things we can "be." The fact that we do have core gender identities, fixed in infancy, means that from the start our sense of ourselves is built on contradiction. We lead our lives trying to *be* something that is not an essence but an ensemble of cues and protocols of imaginary unity. The contradictions are compounded for fatherhood by the prestige accorded the role. One term among others in a system of reciprocal relations, fatherhood is also supposed to anchor the system to which it belongs. Symbolically it is at once the origin, foundation, and summit of the family, the tribe, the nation, and the church. No member of a class can stand outside the class to which it belongs; no human person can be the Father. Figures of patriarchal authority, however, are presumed by definition to speak from the place and in the name of this absolute fatherhood.

The impossibility of embodying such a function is precisely what requires its personification as a deity. God the Father is indispensable to patrilineal patriarchy. Since he cannot exist it is necessary to invent him; since he has no body it is necessary to substantiate him; and since, being socially manufactured, he is vulnerable to history it is necessary to sustain him. Hence the importance of Jay's argument that ritual sacrifice creates patriliny. This simple but powerful thesis yields an original, wholly persua-

2. For a shrewd critique of object-relations theory's reliance on the mother-child couple, see Blum chapter 3.

sive analysis of the Abraham legend from Genesis, in which Jay unearths the traces of a suppressed contest between matrilineal and patrilineal structures of descent and inheritance. Semitic tradition, she notes, is endogamous because marriage from within the patriline solves the structural problem of "how to maintain unilineal descent from fathers while recognizing descent from mothers" (98). But this solution "conceals a conflict"; it produces a "latent bilateral structure" that leaves unresolved the question "Whose is the son?—the mother's or the father's?" (99–100). The binding of Isaac "restores him to patriliny": "Isaac, on the edge of death, received his life not by birth from his mother but from the hand of his father as directed by God" (102).

The importance of Jay's argument about the "descent conflict" played out in the patriarchal narratives can hardly be overstated. Yet because of its focus on the contest between matriliny and patriliny, this argument tends to obscure the conflict *within* paternity that primarily interests me here. If the social function of blood sacrifice is to reinforce patrilineal descent, then *child* sacrifice presents something of a scandal, since it tends to do away with the descendant: it establishes symbolic paternity only by destroying the evidence of fatherhood. Of course in the *aqedah,* this contradiction is finessed: Isaac is not sacrificed, but, as Jay puts it, "receive[s] his life . . . from the hand of his father as directed by God." Yet this way of describing the scene tends to consolidate Abraham with Elohim. This may accurately describe the ritual, but the *aqedah* is not a ritual—it is a *story about* ritual. This story and its narrative context repeatedly emphasize the contradiction at the heart of human fatherhood. They do so as part of a narrative dynamic distinct from the social practice of sacrifice, having a different aim—not just to evince patriliny, but to link human paternity to the sublime object of patrilineal ideology: the symbolic function of absolute fatherhood.

The Abraham story reminds us, pointedly and repeatedly, that a father who sacrifices his child undoes his own paternity. The story of Abraham emerges from a recitation of the generations of Shem, and it lays great stress on Sarai's barrenness, which interrupts the fecundity of the paternal line and stands in stark contradiction to the Lord's promise that he will make Abram (as he is first called) "a great nation." This promise, though often repeated and elaborated, goes unfulfilled for twenty-five years. At the end of the first ten, Abram and Sarai resort to surrogate motherhood, procuring a son they call Ishmael from Sarai's maid Hagar. When God renews his promise in the twenty-fourth year, first Abraham and then Sarah (as they are now renamed) find the idea ludicrous, since at this point their respective ages are ninety-nine and eighty-nine. Isaac, named for the laughter with which his parents come to regard God's promise, is withheld until Abraham's hundredth year. Meanwhile, Abraham's long wait for fatherhood is set off by God's recurrent assertion of it as his own prerogative. The terms in which their covenant is first announced, in Genesis 12:1–2, specifically require that Abraham *replace* his human father, Terah, with the Lord: "Now the Lord said to Abram, 'Go from your country and your kindred and your father's house to the land that I will show you. And I will make of you a great nation.' "[3] Twice in their wanderings Abraham out of fear resigns his rights in Sarah to strangers, instructing her to tell first Pharaoh and later Abimelech that he is her brother, not her husband. In contrast, the mark of circumcision, instituted as the sign of the covenant in chapter 17, carves the Lord's prerogative into every male body in the house of Abraham, reminding each human father under the covenant that the penis is his to use only because it belongs ultimately to the Father.[4]

Between Isaac's birth and his binding, Abraham is forced to send Ishmael and Hagar into the wilderness. When God then demands that Abraham give *Isaac* back, the story forces to a crisis point the central and prolonged conflict between paternity and childlessness that had seemed, with Isaac's birth, to be resolved. The man God has promised to make a mighty progenitor, father not just to a son but also to a "multitude of nations," must by his own hand undo his long-deferred paternity. The story thus uses the motif of filial sacrifice to push the essential and reiterated contradiction of fatherhood to its furthest point.[5] God makes Abraham a progenitor—*the* progenitor of Israel—on the paradoxical condition that Abraham sacrifice his status as a father, affirming in the most absolute way that Isaac and the generations enfolded within him belong not to Abraham, but to God. Like the ritual of circumcision and the absurdity of Isaac's birth, the arbitrariness of his binding and release insist on God's fatherhood at the expense of Abraham's. Isaac is a gift that always still belongs to the giver.

The *aqedah*'s narrative strategy turns the impossibility of fatherhood

---

3. Biblical quotations, except where otherwise noted, refer to Metzger. (My chapter epigraph is quoted from Greene 175).

4. Eilberg-Schwartz argues that circumcision "symbolized the fertility of the initiate as well as his entrance into and ability to perpetuate a lineage of male descendants" (143). He also critiques—usefully—much of the scholarship opposed to this view. The book's introduction offers a well-reasoned defense of anthropological approaches to the study of Judaism and (by extension) Christianity.

5. Kristeva asserts, incorrectly I think, that "the biblical text does away with sacrifice, particularly human sacrifice: Isaac is not offered to God" (111). Cf. Levenson: "The mythic-ritual complex I have been calling 'child-sacrifice' was never eradicated: it was only *transformed*" (43). Likewise E. O. James: "The conviction that the god of Israel demanded the sacrifice of their first-born male offspring was so deeply laid that it was always liable to recur" (70).

into a source of strength. It does this by substituting for the human father's incapacity his absolute submission to the principle he cannot embody. Once substantiated by the human father's complete self-cancella-
tion *as father,* the principle of absolute paternity, personified as God, can
reauthorize his status; it does so, of course, by retroactively defining this
unquestioning obedience as just what qualifies Abraham for fatherhood,
now seen, like Isaac and the penis, to be at once God's gift and his exclusive possession. Abraham's naming follows the same logic. His name is
not really his, for it means "exalted father," a descriptive phrase proper to
the Almighty. God returns it to him in Genesis 17:5 by way of a pun,
adding a pleonastic *ha* to make *av-ram* sound like the Hebrew for *father
of a multitude.*[6] In much the same way the covenant, the knot that binds
the human father to his deified counterpart, makes the sheer contradiction
of the concept that they share work to sustain each in the impossibility of
his being.

The *aqedah* not only makes its point through narrative logic but also
proves it emotionally, building up pity and horror and then suddenly releasing them. In *Fear and Trembling* Kierkegaard's persona, Johannes *de
silentio,* asks why Abraham did not go alone to Mount Moriah and sacrifice himself in place of Isaac. It's a good question—one that must have occurred also to the fourteenth-century Jewish commentator Bachya ben
Asher, who wrote, "If Abraham had had a hundred bodies, it would have
been suitable to give them all up for the sake of Isaac, but this act was not
like any other, this trial was not like any other, and nature cannot bear it,
nor the imagination conceive it."[7] Evidently the intolerability of the story
is its point: if Abraham sacrificed himself, he would win sympathy and admiration but not horror (from the Latin *horrere,* to tremble). The thought
of killing Isaac arouses more pathos. The emotion it leads to is not quite
tragic—not only because the killing is averted but also because the feelings it arouses, even in prospect, are not pity and terror but pity and horror. We can be terrified by what a protagonist like Oedipus does or suffers
unknowingly; we are horrified by what a protagonist like Abraham *intends
to do.* "Then Abraham reached out his hand and took the knife to kill his
son" (22:10). We are meant not to empathize with Abraham but to recoil
from his incomprehensible will.

Aristotle describes the denouement of a tragic plot as purging pity and
terror, but the *aqedah* rather converts than purges the emotions it arouses.
The narrative form of the Abraham story has been unlike Aristotelian
tragedy from the beginning, for its necessity, far from the formally consis-

6. Buttrick et al., I.15, s.v. "Abraham. Etymology"; see also Albright.
7. Bachya ben Asher, *Commentary on the Torah,* qtd. and trans. Levenson 128.

tent causal sequence of the ideal tragic plot, derives from the arbitrary im-position of an inscrutable will. As the crisis and denouement of this con-sistently unmotivated plot, the episode called the *aqedah* is an epiphany of arbitrariness: Abraham's test turns out to have been a freshly imposed condition for the fulfillment of a promise made and reiterated decades be-fore. *Denouement* means the untying of a knot, but the denouement of Genesis 22 is a tightening of the knot that binds Abraham to God: "And the angel of the Lord called to Abraham a second time from heaven, and said, 'By myself I have sworn, says the Lord: Because you have done this, and have not withheld your son, your only son, I will indeed bless you, and I will make your offspring as numerous as the stars of heaven and as the sand that is on the seashore'" (15–17). This reaffirmation of an am-plified covenant corresponds to a conversion of affect: pity and horror, wrought to extremity, are, like Isaac himself, released—only to be bound again to the power that releases them. (*I did it that they might know that I am Yahweh.*) The new form into which they are bound is the *aqedah*'s ver-sion of filial piety: love as a modulation of fear, gratitude flowing from an abrupt sense of relief.[8]

The form of the Abraham story suggests that it *should* produce such a conversion of affect, and its history suggests that it often has. But this will hold true only for readers already prepared to identify with the principle of fatherhood. As Jay points out, such an identification prevented genera-tions of biblical scholars from recognizing the "descent conflict" in the patriarchal narratives: "Biblical scholars have not recognized this descent conflict," she observes, "because they bring to the stories a presupposition of established certainty of patrilineal descent not to be found in the text" (101). Her reading of Genesis demonstrates that at least one other per-spective is inscribed within the story along with the effort to subordinate it. So too, in a more general way, the story signals the pressure of other perspectives, whether seen or unforeseen. This pressure can be felt, I think, in the episode of Abraham's and Sarah's laughter, which seems to catch *El Shaddai* offguard. Why do you laugh, he demands of Abraham, don't you think I can do what I say? Sarah, knowing what is good for her, tries first to conceal her laughter and then to deny it. The incident has an unmistakable touch of burlesque: Sarah is hiding behind a tent flap, eaves-dropping on the men. When *El Shaddai* overhears her laughing and talk-ing to herself, he demands—not of Sarah, but of Abraham—Why did she laugh? Sarah, caught in the act, protests: Who, me? I didn't laugh! And

8. Eilberg-Schwartz argues that the substitution of animals for humans in ritual sacrifice is perceived to be "efficacious" because it "instills in actors the feeling that they should also be sacrificed. The fact that God does not require this of them reminds them of the divine ca-pacity to forgive human failure (Exod. 34:7)" (135).

the Almighty argues with her: Oh yes you did, you laughed, I heard you. Isaac is the child of this laughter; but on the road to Mount Moriah, nobody laughs.

*El Shaddai* is, among other things, "he who makes one wait"—a hundred years for a son, four hundred years for release from bondage (Lacan, "Introduction" 92). In the laughter of Abraham and Sarah, the story acknowledges that too much waiting can wear down the covenant with God. History is not just the providential unfolding of the promised generations of the chosen; it is also a principle of attrition, the never quite conquered resistance of a different response. This is one reason the narrative pattern of mortifying and exalting the "beloved son" keeps replaying itself in biblical narrative until its decisive transformation in the Gospels.[9] The historicity of the absolute Father, his vulnerability to difference and delay, is implicit as well in the reiteration of the covenant. In the Abraham narrative alone God repeats his promise eight times. After the climax of this series in the *aqedah*, it is repeated five more times by human actors— first by Abraham himself, and then (four times, in a more general form) by his steward, who sees the errand to fetch Rebekah as a test of the Lord's continued love for his master. Such tireless reiteration is only partly explained as a gradual unfolding of the covenant in its various aspects as a pledge of territory, offspring, protection, power, prosperity, and abiding status. The repetition must also reflect an impulse to keep testing the covenant, an inkling that no matter how often ratified, it remains susceptible to laughter, curiosity, and disbelief.

## The Gospel Narratives: "I Desire Mercy, Not Sacrifice" (Matthew 9:13)

The binding of Isaac clarifies the contradiction of fatherhood as a symbolic category. It does so, however, by making this contradiction a source of power, forcing it to an emotional crisis that tightens the knots of religion and social order. The story achieves this clarity by combining starkness with extremity. The gospel accounts of Jesus could hardly be more different: in contrast to the anonymous voice, narrative economy, and linear sequence of Genesis, the books of Matthew, Mark, Luke, and John are a tour de force of postmodernism. Their multiplication of fictionalized narrators creates a fragmented and recursive story line and a collage of dis-

9. Levenson provides an informative account of these narratives as symbolic transformations of the sacrifice of the firstborn son, constituting "a strange and usually overlooked bond between Judaism and Christianity" (x). My remarks on the "beloved son" throughout this chapter are indebted to his study.

continuous styles, dialects, and forms (pericope, parable, homily, diatribe) marked by the opaqueness of their central character and by the persistent, highly self-conscious thematization of both the reader and the act of narration. In spite of these contrasts in form, style, and technique, however, the story of Jesus is recognizable as a transformation of the "beloved son" paradigm introduced with Isaac and repeated with variations in the careers of Jacob and Joseph. The decisive feature of this transformation is that, compared with the *aqedah*, the Jesus story shifts dramatic interest from father to son, and in doing so transfers the emotional burden of the crisis from the horror of what the father intends to the pity of what the son endures.

Other changes also are part of this complex transformation. In various ways, the four Gospels restate the contradiction between human and absolute fatherhood, which cannot be more intense than it is in the *aqedah*, but does become more insistent and more openly declared. At the same time, the Gospels tend to withdraw the father (both human and divine) from the narrative, bringing forward in his stead the figure and perspective of childhood. Where Genesis repeatedly stresses the Father's appropriation of female procreativity, the Gospels transfer the pathos of women's vulnerability and children's innocence onto the figure of the Son. Partly for this reason, a strong anti-authoritarian strain runs through the Gospels, which sharpen the opposition between secular powers and the regency of heaven rather than, like Genesis, instituting a covenant between them. Finally, the Gospels take up the motif of elevating the younger son (neither Isaac, Jacob, nor Joseph is actually a firstborn) as a model for their own textual relation to the Hebrew scriptures—and again, in a more abstract form, for the act of delayed interpretation that generates their narrative.

Matthew opens the New Testament with a genealogy showing the Messiah to be lineally derived from King David and the patriarch of the covenant. A second genealogy given by Luke (3:23–38) lays more stress on the common humanity of Jesus than on his royalty, tracing him all the way back through Adam to God. Luke's version also differs in several particulars from Matthew's, most strikingly in that it unfolds as a list not of fathers but of sons. Thus not only does Luke's account begin where Matthew's ends, with Jesus, it also reverses each relation along the way: whereas Matthew begins "Abraham was the father of Isaac," Luke says Isaac was "the son of Abraham." This purely formal reversal is not substantive, like the difference between the genealogies when they branch off from one another in the age of kings. Yet in making the last first, Luke does enact the central and repeated impulse by which the Gospels challenge the primacy of earthly fathers. He does the same thing more dramatically by prefacing the whole list with a parenthetical disclaimer: "Jesus being the son (as was thought) of Joseph. . . ." This parenthesis in effect short-circuits the whole list, reminding us before we begin its fifteen verses, comprising seventy-five generations, that the last name in the series, "God," is also the first and in essence the only one.

Matthew does not address the contradiction between Jesus' human paternity and his virgin birth, but in all three synoptic Gospels Jesus himself insists on it. He confounds the Pharisees by demanding how, if Christ is the son of David, David can refer to him in Psalm 110 as his Lord. Since in other parts of the Gospels Jesus accepts the title "Son of David" (and even refers to it in the cleansing of the temple as "perfect praise"), his rhetorical question to the Pharisees seems meant to insist on the contradiction, not to resolve it by denying his human lineage. The opening chapter of John goes further, in keeping with the tendency throughout the fourth gospel to elaborate the character of Jesus in metaphysical terms. Recasting the first verses of both Genesis and Matthew, John's genealogy places the Logos at the creation "in the beginning," and goes on to assert that the same Logos gives all believers the power to become "children of God" (John 1:12).

Such passages take the contradiction of fatherhood to an extreme by turning it into a negation, and by extending the negation of human paternity from Jesus to all his followers, children of God and *not* of human flesh. Yet in doing so the fourth gospel extends a motif already evident in the first three. In Matthew and Luke, Jesus tells a would-be disciple who asks for leave to bury his father, "Let the dead bury their own dead" (Matthew 8:22; Luke 9:60); he tells the Twelve Apostles, again in Matthew and Luke, that he brings not peace but a sword, "to set a man against his father" and all the other members of the household against one another, adding that whoever loves either parents or children more than him "is not worthy of me" (Matthew 10:34–37; Luke 12:51–53). All three synoptic Gospels report that Jesus is rejected at Nazareth by those who know him only as Joseph the carpenter's son; in Matthew he bluntly commands the crowds, "Call no one your father on earth, for you have one Father—the one in heaven" (23:9); and he tells "great multitudes" in Luke that the cost of discipleship is hatred of father, mother, children, brethren, sisters, and self (14:26).

The fourth gospel identifies Jesus with the absolute Father so completely he can say, "Before Abraham was, I am" (John 8:58). This identification combines the rejection of human fatherhood with the tendency to withdraw the father (human or divine) from an active role in the sacrificial narrative. In Genesis the Almighty often intervenes to direct the course of events, but the synoptic Gospels introduce him only twice, at the baptism and the transfiguration. Neither time is God seen; only his voice is heard, confirming Jesus (in an echo of the *aqedah*) as his "beloved son" (Levenson 200). These manifestations disappear from John's account, replaced by the assertion that "No one has ever seen God" (1:18). The Logos, whom John and his listeners have seen, somehow both *is* and *is with* this invisible God, substituting for him but not replacing him—much as the ram in Genesis substitutes for Isaac (acceptable "in his stead") but does not replace him (acceptable only *after* Isaac is "not withheld").[10] This logic justifies the Son as the Father's only manifestation, and thus as the exclusive means of access to him: "No one comes to the Father except through me" (14:6).

Like God, the human father is withdrawn as an active presence in the Gospels. After Luke's version of the Nativity, for example, Joseph for the most part simply disappears from the story. Where Jesus' family does intrude—seeking him in the temple, trying to get through a crowd to reach him—they are brought in to be repudiated, but in these scenes Joseph is either absent or overshadowed by Mary. Human fatherhood may be rhetorically denied any number of times, but when the denial of family bonds occurs as a dramatic event the burden shifts to her. And yet when Jesus denies his mother and brothers, he is still devaluing relations that derive from human fatherhood in favor of those that derive from the absolute Father: "My mother and my brothers," he says, "are those who hear the word of God and do it" (Luke 8:21). Joseph is not a strong enough presence to be denied in the flesh, but the symbolic centrality of his fatherhood is confirmed even in his retreat from the story.

As the father is withdrawn and the mother brought forward to be denied, the figure of the human child gains a striking new prominence—almost as if the *aqedah* were being retold from Isaac's point of view. Luke, with his full-dress manger scene, gives this motif its fullest treatment, but it emerges throughout the synoptic Gospels in some of their most memorable scenes and sayings. In the Sermon on the Mount, Jesus instructs the multitude to love their enemies "so that you may be children of your Father in heaven" (Matthew 5:45). Together with the injunction against judging (7:1), such rhetoric enjoins listeners to surrender the imaginary position of fatherhood in order to take up that of childhood, as in the Lord's Prayer. When Jesus appeals to the emotions of human fatherhood ("Is there anyone among you who, if your child asks bread, will give a

10. Levenson notes the distinction between replacement and substitution in the *aqedah*, and argues that "the evolutionary view [the idea that the Isaac story illustrates a progress in which animal sacrifice replaces human sacrifice] misses the crucial point: deprive the sacrifice of the *child* of all preciousness in the eyes of the deity, and the sacrifice of the *animal* becomes pointless" (22).

stone?"), it is to transfer these emotions by analogy to God, turning the human listener back into a child (Matthew 7:9–11). Throughout the Gospels Jesus draws on the emotional power of the child as a vivid image of dependency, vulnerability, and innocent truth: "Jerusalem, Jerusalem, the city that kills the prophets and stones those who are sent to it! How often have I gathered your children together as a hen gathers her brood under her wings, and you were not willing!" (Matthew 23:37); "Let the little children come to me, do not stop them; for it is to such as these that the kingdom of God belongs" (Mark 10:14); "Truly I tell you, unless you change and become like children, you will never enter the kingdom of heaven. Whoever becomes humble like this child is the greatest in the kingdom of heaven. Whoever welcomes one such child in my name welcomes me" (Matthew 18:3–5). *This* child: in an episode reported by all three synoptic Gospels, Jesus responds to his disciples' rivalry over which of them is the greatest by setting a human child before them like a prop. His gesture epitomizes the rhetorical strategy of the Gospels.

The Messiah's frequent association with women (Mary Magdalen, the woman taken in adultery, and others) also belongs to this group of narrative strategies, for it allows the Gospels to stress forgiveness in place of judgment while borrowing the women's vulnerability and humility. Like the innocence of the child and the protective feelings it arouses, these values, gathered to the sacrificial figure, heighten the pathos of his eventual suffering and death. The withdrawal of the Father from the story makes it possible, meanwhile, to finesse the element of horror. The agony in the garden of Gethsemane leaves no doubt that Jesus' suffering and death are required by his heavenly Father, but the anger stirred by these events is drawn off onto human betrayers, persecutors, and judges who are far more present to the imagination.[11]

This displacement of anger onto human figures may be compared to the repudiation of family ties, shifted to the mother as a symbol of bodily connectedness. The conversation between Jesus and Nicodemus in John 3:1–10 exemplifies this strategy as it opposes the Spirit to the mother's womb, which stands for all flesh in contrast to the disembodied freedom of the wind: "The wind blows where it chooses, and you hear the sound of it, but you do not know where it comes from or where it goes. So it is

---

11. Compare Scarry's resonant description of the crucifix as a weapon without a handle: "The cross, unlike many weapons, has only one end: there is not a handle and a blade but only the blade, not a handle and a lash but only the lash. Though like any other weapon it requires an executioner, the executioner's position is not recorded in the structure of the weapon itself" (213). This feature of the cross is crucial to the ideological sleight of hand whereby God manages to occupy both the highly visible position of the victim and the unseen role of executioner.

with everyone who is born of the Spirit" (3:8). John's systematic redefin-
ition of filial relations through the metaphor of rebirth is easily derived
from Luke 8:21, which defines the disciples as Jesus' family because they
are related to him through "the word of God." In this symbolic economy,
connections formed on the basis of the Father's Word replace connections
based on the natural body identified with the mother. Joseph's presence as
a human father would weaken this pattern, which derives human family
bonds from the father only insofar as they are already symbolic, defined by
his name and lineage, but stigmatizes them in the mother insofar as they
are bodily and natural. The same economy extends into modes of presentation: the repudiation of human family ties in their paternal aspect is carried out rhetorically, but the repudiation of these same ties in their maternal aspect is made vivid in the body of the story.

This combination of maneuvers appears in the New Testament partly as
a way of accommodating a severe dichotomy between body and soul, flesh
and spirit. This dichotomy, imported from Greek philosophy, is alien to
the Hebrew scriptures and at most latent in the synoptic Gospels, but in
John and in the writings of Paul it assumes an overriding importance (Boyarin, "'This We Know to Be the Carnal Israel'"). Withdrawing the Father as a dramatic presence in the story is a powerful way of dissociating
him from the body to build up his standing as a symbolic category; the
withdrawal also creates a space into which the mother can be brought forward to represent the flesh. But the Father's gain in symbolic standing
comes at the cost of vividness and imaginative reality, the narrative equivalents of bodily presence.

The New Testament's extraordinary solution to this problem is a radical
transformation of the *aqedah,* taken from the heart of Genesis and turned
inside out. The two characters who were distinctly subordinate in that
story, the human mother and the human son, are brought forward into
the narrative space left empty by the father's withdrawal, and there they
divide between them the contradiction intrinsic to the privileged category
of fatherhood. If the mother absorbs the negative values associated with
the body the Father has abandoned, the Son restores all the vividness and
pathos the Father has lost in the process: the human child is brought forward not to replace the heavenly Father but to compensate for his invisibility. So in the person of Jesus and in the image of the "little ones" he repeatedly invokes, the gospel story makes up in pity and righteous anger
what it has surrendered in the way of horror. Mark describes *this* economy
of substitution with perfect clarity: "Whoever shall welcomes one such
child in my name welcomes me, and whoever welcomes me welcomes not
me but the one who sent me" (9:37). When John insists on the identity of
the Father and the Son while maintaining that "the Son can do nothing

on his own" (5:19), he is again carrying the symbolism of the synoptic Gospels to its logical conclusion, binding the emotions released by Jesus' sacrifice to the figure whose law made that sacrifice necessary: the absolute Father, whose perfect self-consistency would be thrown into contradiction if the human inability to sustain the law of his being were seen to result from its sheer impossibility. This strategy exemplifies the New Testament's version of filial piety: horror diffused by the veiling of its object; and love as a transformation of mourning, replacing the lost human son with a resurrected god who is, mysteriously, his transcendent Father's twin.

## Narrative, Rhetoric, and Image: "The Father and I Are One" (John 10:30)

By allowing the transcendent Father to be immanent only as the Son, the New Testament sets up the filial relation as contradiction: Father and Son are at once opposite and identical. This contradiction is irreducible, but there are any number of narrative, rhetorical, and pictorial means of transforming it—from the resonant, grammatically incoherent declaration "Before Abraham was, I am" to the labyrinths of Trinitarian theology. The histories of European painting and statuary offer an extraordinary range of responses to the challenge of visualizing this contradictory relation, while literary history offers a comparable range of responses to its narrative and rhetorical complexities. These responses are by no means confined to religious works, for the central paradoxes of Hebrew and Christian myth persist within secular culture just as powerfully as pagan elements stayed on in the religious culture of medieval and early modern Europe. Such influences may be most powerful when least visible.

One form the contradiction takes is temporal, for if the absolute Father is eternal, the Son's body moves through a sequence of days and years. The Gospels take advantage of this disjunction to challenge the priority of Hebrew scripture, insisting at every opportunity on reversals of sequence and priority (the first shall be last, the least shall be greatest) because they seek to reverse their own belatedness. John, as usual, takes the motif to its conceivable limit, rewriting the first sentence of Genesis to assert Jesus himself as a beginning that preceded the creation of the heavens and the earth. The synoptic Gospels pursue a less extreme version of this strategy by taking from Genesis the narrative motif of the younger son preferred before his elder brothers. The firstborn son is traditionally designated as heir to patriarchal status, and it is the firstborn to whom God several times lays claim in Exodus (13:2, 13:11–15, 22:29). But in the "beloved son" narratives Isaac displaces Ishmael, Jacob displaces Esau, and Joseph displaces a full dozen of his elders. Jesus has no elder brother, but he is nevertheless the narrative as well as genealogical descendant of these upstart siblings, whose elevation repeatedly demonstrates God's indifference to the priorities of temporal sequence.

The Gospels resume this motif generally in the Messiah's claim that he at once fulfills and supersedes the covenant of Abraham and Moses, specifically in Luke's account of John the Baptist. Luke begins with Elizabeth and Zechariah, reprising in an obvious way the keynotes of the Abraham story: Elizabeth is barren, the couple is "advanced in years," and Zechariah is at first incredulous when Gabriel comes to foretell the miraculous birth of a son. When Mary is visited with similar news, she goes immediately to the house of Zechariah, where John prophesies the advent of the Messiah by leaping in Elizabeth's womb. John thus takes the place of the elder brother that Jesus cannot have, identifying this elder brother with Isaac and by extension with the covenant of Abraham. His symbolic mission is to personify the Hebrew scriptures' recognition that he who comes after is preferred before.

The Gospels turn temporal disjunction to narrative advantage in yet another way through their selective combining of foreshadowing and hindsight. Luke, who gives the fullest treatment of Christ's infancy and childhood, fills his account with portents, but collectively the Gospels lay more stress on the repeated failure of everyone, even the disciples—sometimes *especially* the disciples—to understand the true nature and mission of the savior. This motif is strongest in Mark, who treats Jesus' identity as a carefully guarded secret. But even John, who diverges strikingly from the synoptic Gospels by having Jesus claim openly and repeatedly to be "one" with God, preserves this structure of delayed recognition. It is, in fact, essential to all versions of the story that Jesus be misrecognized (otherwise he would never be persecuted) and that he be recognized (otherwise the good news would not be proclaimed). So the pattern is repeated many times, although John again makes it most explicit: "His disciples did not understand this at first; but when Jesus was glorified, then they remembered that these things had been written of him and had been done to him" (12:16). All four Gospels assume the perspective of a recognition at once younger and older than the story itself; their dramatic tension is generated by the ways in which this recognition is kept continually present and yet continually out of sync with the story.

Another form of the filial contradiction is erotic, for if the Son in some sense *is* the Father then his mother must also be his daughter and his wife. The incest taboo (which Lacan in a French pun calls the *nom du Père*, the name-and-no of the Father) is presumably meant to ward off just such a collapse of sexual and familial categories into polymorphous paradox. But in its strong form, the identity of father and son erases the distinctions that organize the patriarchal family, again courting crisis for the sake of vividness. Christian theology manages the crisis by replacing the mother in the Trinity with an implicitly male Spirit, and by sublimating the structure of human sexual relatedness in its celebration of a mother who can be her son's daughter and spouse because she remains in all her relations a virgin.

The problem with such solutions is that of the New Testament's invisible Father: disembodying human relations drains them of imaginative power. To invoke the Virgin in the words, for example, of Giovanni Battista Strozzi the Elder—"O His only spouse, daughter, and mother"—is poetically effective because of the clash this phrasing sets up among the carnal associations of its terms.[12] The theology that explains how Mary can be daughter and spouse to her own son clears away the sexual and generational scandal of such imagery and therefore cannot match its compression and rhetorical appeal. The transcendent Father depends for his historical survival on representation, but representation inevitably manifests his incoherence. He endures by continually courting the dangers of representation and then mustering its resources to turn the risk to advantage.

If narrative and rhetoric have ways of drawing contradiction into crisis and then reattaching the emotions it kindles to the absolute Father, what about visual art? How does a painter, for example, give visual form to the idea that baby Jesus embodies the eternal Father? The conventions of iconography supply one means. A system of cross-referencing allows any scene from the life of Christ to include citations to others as well as, by typological extension, to corresponding scenes from any part of biblical history. Such conventions reorganize linear time according to an eternal pattern, and since repudiating sequentiality is their purpose, they tend to cluster at its extremes: asserting the coexistence of beginning and end is an emphatic way of denying time's reality. So Nativity scenes allude regularly to the Crucifixion, Crucifixion scenes to the circumcision, pietàs to the Nativity. As Richard Crashaw writes of the circumcision, "These cradle-torments have their towardness." Quoting this line, Leo Steinberg comments, "Like Renaissance paintings of the brooding Christ Child, Crashaw's poem foreshortens duration. . . . Christ's death is conceived as wholly infolded in his miracle birth" (61).

What Steinberg calls "the familiar prolepses in Renaissance scenes of the Infancy—their stark allusions to the Passion and Resurrection"—may lie in some easily missed detail—the infant's genitals screened, for example,

12. From a poem composed for Baccio Bigio's copy of the St. Peter's *Pietà*, located in the church of Santo Spirito, Florence. Qtd. in Hartt 83.

by two strands of rosary beads draped over one another to form a cross. This motif links the circumcision to the Crucifixion. Its counterpart appears in various fifteenth- and sixteenth-century crucifixions, pietàs, and entombments that look backward to the circumcision, "guid[ing] the trickle of gore," as Steinberg says, "from the breast back to the groin—a blood hyphen between commencement and consummation" (58 and n66).

The most powerful realization of this interplay between foreknowledge and recollection is also among the most deeply implicit. The crucified body in Michelangelo's first *Pietà* (figure 1), sprawled helpless across the mother's lap, evokes a Nativity scene with Madonna and Child—except that this Mary, firm-breasted and impossibly young, is clearly not yet a mother, though already bereaved.[13] Ignoring conventional iconographic pointers, Michelangelo simply assumes the freedom to which they point, using this freedom to synthesize a tableau with a narrative impossibility that is the source of its emotional power. Mary's slender torso and limbs, her breasts, accentuated by the band that crosses between them, and the flawless beauty of her face awaken a delicate eroticism. The composition shuttles us forward and backward in time, blending the prenuptial sexuality of Mary's youth with the nurturing tenderness of her maternity even as it infantilizes the eroticism thus aroused, recalling the sleeping baby in the recumbent corpse. The curious gesture of the Christ figure's descending right hand, for example, recalls a Nativity motif in which the infant grasps his mother's robe (figure 2); without this quiet reference, the adult hand reaching down to finger a fold of drapery between the Virgin's parted knees could seem indelicately sexual. This already complex erotic synthesis gathers still other nuances from the ways in which Christ's body is not only infantilized but also feminized: limp, open, punctured, thighs parted in a motif reminiscent of Leda, this body surrenders itself to very different kinds of regard (Davila and Foss).

The pathos of glimpsing the infant in the corpse is inverted with real

13. The conventional association of the pietà with the Nativity is attested by de Tolnay, who explains that Michelangelo bypassed the treatment most popular among his Italian contemporaries in favor of "another, older type created independently in Italy and Germany at the beginning of the fourteenth century. It is the type of the lone Virgin, who, like a seated Madonna, holds her Son on her lap. The basic idea of this type is the representation of the moment in which the Virgin with the body in her arms recalls the time when she fondled the Christ Child, a scene which the medieval mystics, both in Italy and in the Northern lands, described in moving words" (*Youth* 91). Michelangelo departs strikingly from convention in his anachronistic portrayal of Mary, "in contrast to all earlier Pietàs where the Virgin with her grief-furrowed countenance is represented as a matron" (92). Slightly different accounts of the provenance of the "older type" are given in Weinberger 68–69 and de Tolnay, *Michelangelo* 10.

**Figure 1.** Michelangelo, *La Pietà*, St. Peter's Basilica, Vatican State. Copyright Alinari / Art Resource, New York, N.Y.

**Figure 2.** Giovanni di Marco, called Dal Ponte, "Virgin and Child with Angels." Florence, early fifteenth century. Reproduction by permission of the Syndics of the Fitzwilliam Museum, Cambridge, England.

**Figure 3.** Parmigianino, *Madonna of the Long Neck,* Uffizi, Florence, Italy. Copyright Alinari / Art Resource, New York, N.Y.

precision in Parmigianino's *Madonna of the Long Neck* (figure 3). An oddly oversized baby Jesus reclines across his mother's lap in a posture imitated from the *Pietà,* but transposed so that the head rests on her left arm, not her right. The Son's right hand reaches up, now, rather than down, to touch the Virgin's robe, but the arrangement of the fingers is an exact quotation. This creates an odd effect, for in reappropriating this gesture Parmigianino is not just imitating the *Pietà;* he is self-consciously citing *its* imitation of the Nativity. The result is a highly stylized rendering in which the Nativity seems to recall, as well as to anticipate, the tableau of mourning—the two scenes wound together so intimately now that each seems to be at once the future and the past of the other. In the process, the pathos of Michelangelo's sculpture is reversed along with its temporal perspective. Parmigianino gives us God's view of the infant as already dead, meanwhile distancing Mary from her suspiciously cadaverous child by the exaggerated arch of the neck from which she coolly peers down. The viewer shares this distance. Where the *Pietà* folds the gaze into its center, wrapping it in the subtle play of eroticized sorrow and beatific passivity, the *Madonna* estranges itself from the emotions of the passion narrative, cultivating the divine perspective as an alienation effect.

The corresponding element of the *Pietà* is the imperturbable downcast gaze of its Madonna (figure 4). The Italian word *pietà* means both pity and piety.[14] The horror of seeing the Crucifixion as intended by the Father would drive pity *against* piety. This is surely why we have no image of God as the grieving Father. Since God in his aspect as law requires the sacrifice and in his aspect as love sponsors the resurrection, to show him anthropomorphically struck with grief would be shocking evidence of a rift in God himself between love and law. The fatherly counterpart to the *pietà* is rather the visionary Throne of Grace, which typically shows Christ next to God, held or standing erect and pointing to the wound in his side (Steinberg 106–7 and figs. 122–23, 243–46). Pity is shifted onto Mary, again brought forward to fill a representational space from which the Father has withdrawn, though the Gospels nowhere authorize this scene. On their authority the figure bearing Jesus' crucified body should be

---

14. On the tension between senses of duty and compassion in the medieval Italian *pietà,* see Ball, "Theological Semantics." The term's ambivalence in troubadour verse may be relevant to the equally nuanced eroticism of Michelangelo's sculpture: "Although *mercey* and *pietat* fluctuate semantically between the material or sexual sense of 'reward' and the spiritual sense of 'pity' in the troubadours," writes Ball, "the former seems to tend toward the material and the latter toward the spiritual" (250 n. 2). The sense of hesitant erotic entanglement "tending toward" the spiritual seems analogous to the effects of the *Pietà.*

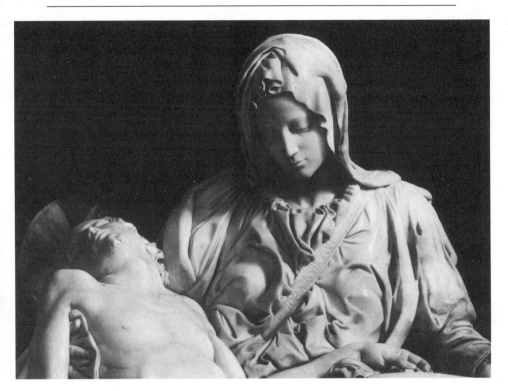

**Figure 4.** Michelangelo, *La Pietà*, detail, St. Peter's Basilica, Vatican State. Copyright Alinari / Art Resource, New York, N.Y.

Joseph of Arimathea, but the *pietà* motif follows the symbolic economy of the narrative rather than its literal detail. Mary supplements the Father, filling the gap between law and desire where his grief should be. Michelangelo captures the ambiguity of this role by reversing precedent and *not* showing Mary's grief: the impassivity of her demeanor in his *Pietà* registers not maternal sorrow—"since the Middle Ages the fundamental theme of all Pietàs"—but a peace that can belong only to God (de Tolnay, *Youth* 91–92).

Even as the Virgin's downcast look draws the gaze to her lap, her submissive tranquility refers us upward to its transcendent source and object. The counterpart to her impassive features is the ambiguously expressive gesture of her left hand. If Mary's face refers us outside the representational space of the sculpture to its point of disappearance in the divine, this "speaking hand" breaks the invisible frame of the scene in the opposite way, soliciting the witness of a human audience otherwise wholly excluded from the intimacy of the moment.[15] Face and hand together declare a contradictory middle ground between spectacle and invisibility; they designate the endpoints of a movement that carries us into the scene only to refer us to an inexpressible beyond. The work of the *Pietà* is precisely to sustain this movement as a process of emotion, sublimating the eroticized pity aroused by beautiful sorrow into pious contemplation of an unseen God.

## The Masculine Masquerade

The religious typology informing Renaissance art and literature refers history to eternity. From within time it signifies radical freedom from temporal sequence, a freedom attributed to God and assumed by the artist in a work like the *Pietà*. Michelangelo evokes the temporal contradictions of Jesus' dual identity indirectly, laying him across the lap of a strangely young mother as if reflecting his timelessness in her. This oblique handling of temporal paradox is part of the sculpture's remarkable decorum. But what if this fold in time were not displaced or merely signified? What if temporal contradiction were directly embodied in a single image?

The result might look something like figure 5. In this untitled photomontage from around 1915, the body of a small boy perches on one corner of a chair much too large. The toy sailboat resting on one leg is balanced, in the symmetry of the composition, against an incongruous, grandfatherly head, gazing blandly from behind its spectacles as if unaware of its predicament. The boat and sailor suit represent the allegorical voyage of life—the distance, so to speak, between this head and the body that supports it. Only the flicker of a smile, fainter even than the Mona Lisa's, hints that the head in its wisdom may be amused by its toy boat and toylike body.

Deliberately absurd, this image parodies the impulse to cherish precocious adulthood that has governed literary and artistic representations of children since Virgil first praised Ascanius for being "thoughtful, responsible / Beyond his years."[16] Curtius gives this figure a name: the *puer senex,* or elderly boy. The elderly boy has an antitype, the *senex puer* (think of

15. I take the phrase "speaking hand" from Gould; cf. Dixon: "Michelangelo has made Mary into an altar. The incomparably lovely and enigmatic gesture of her left hand becomes more intelligible: she is offering the body, as Eucharist, to the faithful" (94). The hand was broken at an early date and restored in the eighteenth century; I assume the restoration to be accurate, but my remarks apply to the statue as we know it.
16. *Ante annos animumque gerens curamque uirilem* (Virgil [P. Vergili Maronis], *Aeneidos* 9.311; in English, Virgil, *Aeneid,* 9.436–37).

**Figure 5.** "Boy with Man's Head," photomontage by Purdy, c. 1915. R. P. Kingston Collection, by permission of the owner.

Polonius, or Charles Dickens's Harold Skimpole), and each of these has a sister, the *puella senex* and the *senex puella*. The *puer senex,* though, appears far more frequently than the others do. After Virgil it becomes a topic of praise for writers in the rhetorical tradition of late antiquity when they want to grace a youthful subject with a high-toned allusion. As they work their variations on the topic these writers also stylize it, polarizing its synthesis of youth and maturity to create a more striking image—not just a youth mature beyond his years, but a prodigy displaying in a child the wisdom of a graybeard.

The nearly anonymous Boston photographer, surnamed Purdy, who created this montage is a modern inheritor of the *puer senex* tradition, which in highly sentimentalized form passes through William Wordsworth and Dickens and into Victorian popular culture. Like the rhetoricians who were his remote antecedents, Purdy takes the components of the figure to opposite extremes. But as parody, his image has a disconcerting edge, turning the compliment around to expose the adult audience for whom it was always, finally, intended. By taking the rhetorical "figure" literally, that is, Purdy uncovers the transaction implicit in it, the unspoken address to an adult witness who is both the speaker's audience and the child's model. Purdy's composite image skewers convention by flushing this witness out of hiding, revealing that the "space" in which he hides is a reflective surface, at once the child's face and his persona.

Earlier examples from the tradition illustrate complex forms of the transaction that Purdy has compressed into a single unsettling image. An entry from the *Tatler,* published by Richard Steele in 1709, offers a revealing instance. Thomas Betterton, seventy years of age but still the most celebrated Shakespearean actor of the day, is praised for the remarkable feat of playing prince Hamlet. In almost the same breath, a little boy named Jerry is commended for responding so ardently to the performance:

> I was going on in reading my Letter, when I was interrupted by Mr. *Greenhat,* who has been this Evening at the Play of *Hamlet.* "Mr. Bickerstaff," said he, "had you been to Night at the Play-house you had seen the Force of Action in Perfection. Your admir'd Mr. *Betterton* behav'd himself so well that tho' now about Seventy he acted Youth; and by the prevalent Power of proper Manner, Gesture and Voice, appear'd through the whole *Drama* a Youth of great Expectation, Vivacity and Enterprize. The Soliloquy where he began the celebrated sentence of *To be, or not to be;* the Expostulation where he explains with his Mother in her Closet; the noble ardor after seeing his Father's Ghost, and his generous Distress for the Death of *Ophelia;* are each of them Circumstances which dwell strongly upon the Minds of the Audience, and would certainly affect their Behaviour on any parallel occasions in their own Lives. Pray, Mr. *Bickerstaff,* let us have Virtue thus repre-

sented on the Stage with its proper Ornaments, or let these Ornaments be added to her in Places more sacred. As for my Part," said he, "I carry'd my Cousin *Jerry*, this little Boy, with me and shall always love the Child for his Partiality in all that concern'd the Fortune of *Hamlet*. This is entring Youth into the Affections and Passions of Manhood before-hand, and as it were antedating the Effects we hope from a long and liberal Education."[17]

In this passage there is an odd symmetry between little Jerry's introduction to manhood and the rejuvenation of Steele's "admir'd Mr. Betterton." It is as if the mysterious "Force of Action in Perfection" has somehow drawn them together. Taken a step further, the process might lead to just such a fantastic amalgamation as Purdy has visualized. But here the middle term that gathers youth and age into itself is not—apparently—the *puer senex*. It is Hamlet.

Little Jerry is "partial" to Hamlet; he enters the drama of manhood by vicariously taking Hamlet's part. But why should he want to be Hamlet? Because Mr. Greenhat does, and will always love Jerry for doing the same. The child seeks approval by imitating the grown-up "cousin" (his uncle, perhaps?) who "carries" him to the performance in more than one sense. If we ask, in turn, why Mr. Greenhat should want to be Hamlet, the answer lies in his self-gratifying pronouncements about the moral value of Shakespeare: "Pray, Mr. *Bickerstaff,* let us have Virtue thus represented on the Stage with its proper Ornaments." In Hamlet he can love an idealized image of himself, and by carrying his little cousin to this exemplary performance of virtue, he can flatter himself for doing what he calls his "Part" to promote "the Effects we hope from a long and liberal Education."

Mr. Greenhat's notion of virtue may strike us as odd. The *Tatler* essays, writes Brian Vickers, show Steele's "personal appropriation of Shakespeare to a new sentimental morality" (2.203). No doubt this appropriation also reflects the ego ideal of the medium. The coffeehouse newspaper aspires to model discriminating taste and behavior for a broadening public sector, and if there is a touch of self-regard in Mr. Greenhat's estimate of Hamlet, there may likewise be a touch of institutional vanity in the *Tatler*'s praise for the theater. But however we construe them, these circles of self-congratulation exercise remarkable transformative powers, reconceiving Hamlet's sexual violence toward Gertrude as "explain[ing] with his Mother in her Closet," and his egotistical rivalry with Laertes as "generous Distress" for the death of Ophelia.

17. *Tatler* no. 71, 20 September 1709; rpt. in Vickers 2:207–8.

The idealization that assimilates Hamlet's violence to the morality of a later age shows itself capable of even greater miracles when it assimilates Betterton at age seventy to an image of youthful expectation. It is almost as if the actor were making good on Hamlet's taunt to Polonius: the truth about old men's bodies should not be bluntly set down, "for yourself, sir, shall grow old as I am, if like a crab you could go backward." Later in the same scene Hamlet marvels at the transformative powers of make-believe:

> Is it not monstrous that this player here,
> But in a fiction, in a dream of passion,
> Could force his soul so to his own conceit
> That from her working all his visage wann'd,
> Tears in his eyes, distraction in his aspect,
> A broken voice, an' his whole function suiting
> With forms to his conceit? And all for nothing.
> (2.2.551–57)

Together these passages form a kind of Shakespearean matrix for Mr. Greenhat's account of the admired Betterton: is it not monstrous that this player here can, like a crab, go backward, forcing his soul so to his own conceit that forty years drop away from his visage? He works this miracle by suiting his whole function with forms to his conceit. Or as Steele puts it, "the prevalent power of proper Manner, Gesture and Voice" allows him to simulate the conventional ideal of manhood. This ideal is the "conceit" (notion or concept) the age saw in Hamlet—the image of virtue "with its proper Ornaments" that Mr. Greenhat, spokesman for "the Minds of the Audience," wants to see and wants to be. In itself this ideal may not be monstrous, but there is something disturbing in the way Betterton's rejuvenation is replayed inversely in little Jerry—as if, like the portrait of Dorian Gray, he were aging on the actor's behalf.

And yet whether monstrous or miraculous it is all, as Hamlet says, "for nothing." Betterton turns into "a Youth of great Expectation," a personification of energy and life subject to the effects of an imaginary future. However conceived, the "Affections and Passions of Manhood" will be just such a fiction, such a dream of passion. The *Tatler* passage shows how this dream sustains itself; it details the transactions by which culturally sanctioned "manhood" appropriates persons and is appropriated by them as a persona. Mr. Greenhat is especially concise in formulating the temporal paradox that allows the effects of culture to antedate their causes. He is no less explicit about how this paradox organizes the circulation of masculine self-love, forever pursuing its own image through a minuet of substitutions. The dream of manhood passes from dreamer to dreamer, from

Betterton to Mr. Greenhat to little Cousin Jerry. Each imitates the object of the others' desires, but the object itself is purely imaginary.

Moving further back in the tradition we see how this transaction may be embedded in the conventions of portrait painting. In a portrait by Sir Anthony Van Dyck, *Filippo Cattaneo, Son of Marchesa Elena Grimaldi* (figure 6), little Filippo postures manfully. Against the prevailing darkness of the background his left hand comes forward into the light, establishing itself and the face as highlights of the composition.[18] The hand appears to rest on the hilt of an unseen weapon, perhaps a dagger of the sort that Shakespeare's Leontes remembers from his childhood days, "muzzled, / Lest it should bite its master" (*The Winter's Tale* 1.2.156–57). The gesture is one of assurance, an impression reinforced by the projecting elbow that, in the postural conventions of the genre, signifies masculine self-assertion.[19] The bravado of the left hand is balanced by the right hand's retreat into shadow, grasping the leash of a spaniel that crouches submissively in the background. Gaze averted in contrast to the boy's forthright stare, this cowed pet testifies to its little master's authority.[20]

And yet, for all of Filippo's precocious mastery, we gaze down on this scene of petty triumph from a superior position; a ledge across the bottom of the foreground hints, meanwhile, that Master Filippo has been artificially elevated. Harry Berger shrewdly notes that "the foreshortened perspective produced partly by the tilted-up floor plane" in this painting "signifies a bird's-eye view" even as it "places the observer's eyes at the sitter's eye-level," so that "the face is not only brighter but bigger and nearer," and "the resultant fantasy of disproportion contributes to the pathos of infantile bravado."[21] In this way the picture solicits patronizing indulgence

18. Christopher Brown notes that during Van Dyck's stay in Italy the painter experimented repeatedly with effects of light and shadow. Most of his portraits in this period were painted "from dark to light . . . that is, Van Dyck adopted the Italian procedure of priming the canvas with a dark ground and laying the light pigments over it. The usual Flemish practice was the reverse" (82).

19. See Spicer on the masculine and implicitly military connotations of "the brandished male elbow" (101). Spicer notes that "in Anthony van Dyck's companion portraits of the small son and daughter of the Marchesa Cattaneo of 1623 four and a half year old Filippo is shown in the same protective pose as the adult males with their wives or families" (112).

20. Brown thinks the puppy's crouch means it "has just seen a cat or a mouse and is about to pounce" (94). I don't find the "invisible mouse" theory persuasive, but the portrait is dark enough that a halftone reproduction can scarcely convey the details on which these impressions depend.

21. Harry Berger Jr., e-mail communication. Berger also notes that the portraits of Filippo and his little sister Clelia are pendants. A more extended reading than I pursue would consider the implicitly conjugal themes of the pairing, noting the thinly veiled anatomical symbolism of the baby girl's portrait: the hands meeting at the waist hold an apple upside-down over the belly, its broken stem superimposed over the infant pudendum. On pair portraits as a marriage topos, see David R. Smith.

**Figure 6.** Sir Anthony van Dyck, *Filippo Cattaneo, Son of Marchesa Elena Grimaldi* (1623), Widener Collection, Photograph © 2002 Board of Trustees, National Gallery of Art, Washington, D.C.

from an adult viewer, a delegate like Steele's Mr. Greenhat of the social
world that produces the "little man." As we saw in the *Tatler* passage, the
affective economy of this world offers the grown-ups' love as the child's reward for simulating manhood, the lure that entices him "beforehand" into
a cultural masquerade that is to generational difference what drag is to sex.

Purdy's photomontage literalizes this masquerade as a mask. Its superimposed head lets us see in retrospect that Van Dyck's posturing child was
already a weirdly composite figure in whom the time is out of joint. The
affective exchange at the heart of this transaction involves an awkward
mixture of whimsy and seriousness: the child is loved at once for imper-
sonating a man and for not being one. His bravado is endearing because it
is not threatening, so the response it calls for is a complementary masquerade in which adult amusement, signifying complacency in the face of
a mock challenge, pretends admiration, deference, or fear. We cannot literally see this complacency in the portrait of Filippo, but once we acknowledge its implied presence we are prepared to regard the child's assumed bravado as a form of submission no less abject than the spaniel's
crouch. As masquerade, the little boy's lordly attitude subordinates his
newfound ability to recognize and assert himself as *me* to the social
world's demand for deferential flattery expressed as precocious masculinity. In this way the panache of a little Jerry or Filippo, as he steps (or is carried) forward into an imaginary future, marks his immature *me* as a
wanna-be *us*.

## Mocking and Mourning the Untimely Boy

The desire for flattery emerges early in the literary tradition of the *puer
senex*, and so does mockery of that desire. Among the first instances
cited by Curtius is a passage from the *Ars Amatoria* (1.177–228) that
parodies Virgil with Ovid's usual savvy. Like Purdy, Ovid uses exaggeration to achieve travesty. Recognizing both Ascanius and Marcellus in the
*Aeneid* as vehicles of praise for the Emperor Augustus, Ovid turns the
*puer senex* topos into what one modern translator calls "such ghastly political sycophancy in praise of the young Caesar [Augustus' grandson]
against the Parthians that I was tempted to leave out the whole passage." The same translator consoles himself with the "not so Roman
thought . . . that this was a most brazen example of Ovidian impu-
dence."[22] The passage is surely a joke: the speaker of the first *Ars* is chat-

22. Ovid [P. Ovidius Naso], *The Art of Love*, "Introduction" 7. The *puer* in question,
Gaius Caesar, died in the campaign.

tering along in his customary vein, advising the neophyte womanizer on the best places to pick up *puellae*, when all at once a new paragraph starts off on what seems a tangent: "Caesar is ready now to add to the world he has conquered . . . soon the far East will be ours." And in comes the *puer senex:*

> Now an avenger is here, in the early prime of his manhood,
> A captain ripe for the wars, hardly more than a boy.
> Cease, O timid souls, to judge the gods by their birthdays!
> When a Caesar is born, valor anticipates time.
> Heavenly genius[,] matured more quickly than years in their passing,
> Looks, with imperious scorn, on the slow tides of delay.
> Hercules, only a child when he strangled the snakes in his cradle,
> Proved to be more than a child, worthy descendent of Jove.
> Bacchus, who still is a youth, was hardly more than a baby
> When the Indian tribes dreaded his conquering wands.

> *ultor adest primisque ducem profitetur in annis*
>   *Bellaque non puero tractat agenda puer.*
> *parcite natales timidi numerare deorum:*
>   *Caesaribus virtus contigit ante diem.*
> *ingenium caeleste suis uelocius annis*
>   *surgit, et ignavae fert male damna morae:*
> *paruus erat, manibusque duos Tirynthius angues*
>   *pressit et in cunis iam Ioue dignus erat;*
> *nunc quoque qui puer es, quantus tum, Bacche, fuisti,*
>   *cum timuit thyrsos India uicta tuos?*

>                                                        (I.181–90)

The passage heaps excess upon excess, but Ovid lets the air out abruptly as the triumphal procession imagined for young Caesar unexpectedly brings us back to the main point: now *there,* says the poet-speaker, will be an *excellent* opportunity to pick up women—and having suspended his cruising just long enough to solicit the emperor, he is off again, advising the reader on ways to identify the floats and figures in the triumphal procession—or how to fake it, if necessary—so as to sound impressive. Clearly, he has been faking it all along.

Ovid's send-up of imperial encomium deftly turns flattery to mockery. At the other emotional extreme we find the funeral elegies of Statius, who evokes the *puer senex* in a lament for Glaucias, the favorite (*delicatus*) of Atedius Melior:

> Long have I sought distractedly, beloved boy, a worthy approach and prelude to thy praises. Here thy boyhood, standing on life's threshold, calls me, there thy beauty, there a modesty beyond thy years and honor and probity

too ripe for thy tender age. Ah! where is that fair complexion flushed by the glow of health.

*Iamdudum dignos aditus laudumque tuarum,*
*o merito dilecte puer, primordia quaerens*
*distrahor. hinc anni stantes in limine uitae,*
*hinc me forma rapit, rapit inde modestia praecox*
*et pudor et tenero probitas maturior aeuo.*
*o ubi purpureo suffusus sanguine candor.*

(Silvae II.i.36–41)

Statius takes up the motives of praise in a melancholy spirit close to Virgil's. By applying the *puer senex* topos specifically to military praise of Augustus Caesar's grandson, Ovid had been alluding not only to Ascanius, but also to Octavian's nephew and adopted heir Marcellus, whose mournful shade comes last in the procession of future Romans shown by Father Anchises in the underworld. The strange sadness of Marcellus marks him with the future anterior, for he appears to Aeneas both as he is, not yet born, and as he will have been for Virgil and the imperial family, already dead. We will return to this episode in the next chapter, but for now let us note that the praise of Marcellus in *Aeneid* 6 is in fact an embedded eulogy (Brenk). When Statius echoes the praises of Ascanius, he is, like Ovid, conflating the two boys, not because he celebrates the military valor of an imperial scion but because he is writing an elegy, consoling his patron Atedius Melior for the death of an adopted son.

In Statius, praise of the dead boy is once again directed beyond him to his patron, who is also the poet's. When the boy is really dead—not just invaded by the adult world, like Van Dyck's Filippo or Steele's little Jerry—he becomes an object of pathos rather than condescension. The same kinds of detail, stressing the incongruity of the childish masquerade, evoke poignancy now instead of amusement, as the poet in his distraction hesitates between the attributes of youth and age, unsure which to praise first—boyhood beauty, "standing on life's threshold," or "modesty beyond thy years." The hesitation signals a deeper ambivalence in the love that Statius seeks to console, drawn at once to the diminuendo of the child and to his gratifying impersonation of the adult who loves him. The elegy vacillates between cherishing Glaucias' innocent curls, prattling mouth, and sweet kisses—all *delicatus,* in the sense of dainty or tender—and lamenting the "hope of coming manhood, the longed-for glory of his cheeks, that beard thou oft didst swear by" (*o ubi venturae spes non longinqua uventae / atque genis optatus honos iurataque multum / barbara tibi?* II.i.52–54). Statius praises Melior for having always dressed the rapidly growing boy in clothes the right size, but rhetorically the elegy dresses him by turns as a baby and a "little man." Something about Glaucias suggests the word that Statius uses for his lament: *intempestus*, meaning both timeless and untimely (line 8).

Statius speaks of his *intempesta cano* when representing Melior as too frantic to bear consolation. He calls Glaucias *praerepti*, taken too soon (line 1), but the lament in its ambivalence shows that even when alive the boy was "taken too soon" by a deeply narcissistic masculine passion. This passion takes a revealing turn when, by way of a pun, the child's stammering speech (*blaesus*) marks him as having already been consolation for a previous loss, the death of Melior's adult male friend Blaesus (*mox ubi delicias et rari pignus amici / sensit et amissi puerem solacia Blaesi*, II.i.200–201). Like little Jerry, the *puer senex* is an untimely figure because something else, neither man nor boy, neither self nor other, is loved in and through him. In this something else, the polarity of youth and age turns endlessly, like a revolving door.

Statius returns to the *puer senex* topos in the lament for his father as well as that for his own adopted son. He had already linked the death of Glaucias to his father's funeral, stressing his empathy for Melior's grief by recalling how "swooning beside kindred flames I mourned, O Nature, what a father!" (*cum proprios gemerem defectus ad ignes /—quem, Natura!—patrem*, II.i.33–34). The elegy repeatedly and emphatically identifies the poet with his patron as *parantem similes comes* (lines 24–25), a comrade in the same predicament, and their solidarity is reaffirmed in the "kindred flames" (*gemerem ignes*) that reflect the patron's grief for his *delicatus* in the poet's remembered loss of his father. Statius tries to curb in Melior a frenzy he also feels: "thee too, as thou didst break through sobbing fathers and mothers that would stay thee, and didst embrace the pyre and prepare to swallow the flames, could I scarcely restrain, thy comrade in like case, and offended by restraining" (*teque patrum gemitus superantem et brachia matrum / complexumque rogos ignemque haurire parantem / vix tenui similes comes offendique tenendo*, II.i.23–25). This suicidal paroxysm is a powerful, resonant image: to enter the circle of masculine desire, it says, is to embrace the pyre of the father-son and swallow its equivocal fire. Once swallowed, this fire becomes a "kindred flame," binding fathers, mothers, children, and friends together in a love founded on mourning.

These twinned (*gemerem*) flames are mirrored again each time the circle widens. Remembering how his father's pyre "shed its red light upon my face," Statius thinks of *stellatus Ascanius* after Aeneas died (*ut mihi vultibus ignis / inrubuit; stellatus . . . Ascanius*, V.iii.31–32, 38–39). This complex allusion cools and distances the flames of the funeral pyre, reflecting them into starlight, but it also boldly reinterprets the *lumen* that crowns Ascanius in *Aeneid* 2.682, signifying his imperial destiny: the son, it implies, is crowned by the flames that consume his mortal father's body. The cooling distance of this allusion is reversed with precision when Statius, mourning his own adopted son, fastens with horrified immediacy on the memory of having "plunged into the fire a lad still marked with the tender bloom of youth, and seen the cruel flames creep over the fresh down of the dead boy" (*quisquis adhuc tenerae signatum flore iuventae / immersit cineri iuvenem primaque iacentis / serpere crudeles vitid lanugine flammas / adsit et alterno mecum clamore fatiscat*, V.v.18–21). The intensity of this image asks us as readers to take it in—to swallow its fire—and so to enter the circle of masculine desire founded on mourning: "whoever has plunged . . ." the passage begins, and it ends, "let him come and grow weary with me in alternate wailing." The flames are "kindred," then, in more than one sense. They bind mourners together as grief answers grief; they bind mourners to the dead as love feeds on loss, kindling "the Affections and Passions of Manhood" at the funeral pyre. To swallow this fire is a way of taking masculine communion: this is my body, these are my flames.

Mourning in these elegies goes deeper than grief, for as Statius engages feelings specific to the occasions of death he finds in them something essential to the structure of love. Why should the passions of masculinity have to be founded on mourning? Psychoanalytic theories of mourning, ego-formation, and gender have much to offer on the subject, and I return to them in chapter 5; but a first answer is suggested by the texts we have already examined. Abraham must renounce his identity as a father in order to possess it, and he must do this in and through his son's flesh. The divinity of the Gospels must renounce all bodily form in order to be the Absolute Father, and Jesus can reunite us to this disembodied father only by dying. These antinomies are not just theological paradoxes; they are the templates of masculine identity in a patriarchal culture. Parental roles and gender roles are by no means identical, but they are inseparable: when fatherhood is elevated to the symbolic status of law and made the structural principle of kinship, when motherhood is consistently denigrated as mere nature, bodily and mortal, then masculinity and femininity are similarly weighted. Feminism has demonstrated the debilitating consequences for women in a culture that defines them as their bodies; I would stress the debilitating consequences for men in a culture that defines them *against* their bodies. Their physicality is narrowed to the athletic and combative, where it is seen as aggressively competing for dominance: in sports as in physical combat, one is an agent, hence "masculine," when dominant; one is an object, hence "emasculated," in defeat.

Within such a cultural system, to be masculine means to mourn the loss of the erotic male body. We see this in Statius. Unlike the biblical God, the fathers and sons in his elegies are touchingly human and affectionate—they hug, kiss, play, and weep with grief—but their tenderness and physical intimacy are evoked under the aspect of death—remembered, wished for, but never present. The body of the father (for the son) and the body of the son (for the father) are always lost as objects of desire. Two of the three filial loves that Statius commemorates are adoptive, but this intensifies rather than weakens them; in a perverse way it makes them more "masculine." "Often," says the poet, "do alien or adopted children creep further into our hearts than our own kindred" (*interius nova saepe adscitaque serpunt / pignora conexis,* II.i.86–87). Both Melior and Statius adopted slave-boys born in their own households. In this respect, Roman and Hebrew patriarchies are much the same: ancient Mediterranean societies did not limit "such apparently self-evident kinship terms as 'son,' 'brother,' and 'eldest son' . . . to their biological referents," but used them to "define special juridical relationships, relationships that can be created artificially through various types of adoption and specification" (Frymer-Kensky 211).

The name, the covenant, the legal code—these, not the tissue of the body, are the ties that bind. Even Statius' natural father was also his schoolteacher and poetic mentor: he gave his son "not only sky and sea and land . . . the due and wonted gift of parents, but this glory of the lyre. . . . What was thy pride, so oft as I charmed the Latian fathers with my song, while thou wert present, a happy witness of thy own bounty!" (*nec enim mihi sidera tantum / aequoraque et terras, quae mos debere parenti, / sed decus hoc quodcumque lyrae primusque dedisti. . . . qualis eras, Latios quotiens ego carmine patres / mulcerem felixque tui spectator adesses / muneris!* V.iii.211–17). Both the poetic medium, then, and the deeply internalized relation to Virgil are bound up with the filial relation, linked in memory with the image of a poet-father's pride before an audience of fathers. This bond is indeed passionate, but it is passionately literary and passionately mournful. Like the piety of the Gospels, it is love as a transformation of mourning—a longing for something inaccessible even when it seems embodied in a living father or son, giving and receiving affectionate caresses.

## The Spectral Son: "Tell Him Thou Art Not Dead" (Statius, *Silvae* II.i.233)

The *puer senex* and the sacrificial son are variations on a type. I propose to call this type the "specular son" in honor of Purdy's humorous photomontage because, like a mirror, it gives back the father's reflection. But the specular son can also be a spectral son, returning from death to be-seech or accuse the father who made him a ghost. The two are as closely related as piety and horror: where we find one, the other is never far away, however masked, buried, or repudiated.

Statius invites the dead in his elegies to visit the slumbers of the living. To Glaucias he says, "Come hither . . . soothe thou his heart and forbid his tears to flow; make his nights glad with thy sweet converse and thy living countenance" (*Glaucia . . . tu pectora mulce, / tu prohibe manare genas noc-tusque beatas / dulcibus alloquiis et uiuis uultibus imple,* II.i.229–32). And to his father: "In the semblance of a dream teach me what thou wert ever wont to teach" (*somnique in imagine monstra / quae solitus,* V.iii.289–90). These are comforting presences. More alarming is the shade of Hector, come to warn the sleeping Aeneas that Troy is in flames around him. Ben Jonson reports a similar visitation by his firstborn son the night before he learned the boy had died. Even Shakespeare's Mamillius whispers a ghost story in his mother's ear—and as I argue later in more detail, he is covertly identified with the skull of Yorick, recalled from the graveyard scene in *Hamlet.* The "burning child" in Freud is another such specter.

Not all writers want to hear the voice of the spectral son. T. S. Eliot, re-viewing a book by Edmund Blunden on the poetry of Henry Vaughan, adopts a dismissive tone:

> It does not occur to Mr. Blunden that the love of one's childhood, a passion which he appears to share with Lamb and Vaughan, is anything but a token of greatness. We all know the mood; and we can all, if we choose to relax to that extent, indulge in the luxury of reminiscence of childhood; but if we are at all mature and conscious, we refuse to indulge this weakness to the point of writing and poetizing about it. We know that it is something to be buried and done with, though its corpse will from time to time find its way up to the surface.[23]

By the end of the passage Eliot's tone is very much at odds with the gothic image of childhood as a corpse rising from the grave in defiance of our most "mature and conscious" efforts to have done with it. Eliot's pseudo-aristocratic disdain for bourgeois sentimentality has its counter-part in his poetry, a world without children or laughter, as Northrop Frye once described it, but one well-populated with prematurely aged men.[24] Prufrock, Gerontion, and the speaker of Ash Wednesday are all elaborately

23. "The Silurist" 260–61; qtd. in Leah S. Marcus, *Childhood and Cultural Despair* 8.
24. "Eliot's earlier poetry is mainly satiric, and presents a world that may be summed up as a world without laughter, love, or children." Northrop Frye, *T. S. Eliot* 48. The missing children and their ghostly laughter come back from the grave briefly in the opening move-ment of "Burnt Norton" in *Four Quartets.*

wearied by the sadness of their own aging, and their self-pity is obtrusive enough to have wearied Edmund Wilson, too, who wrote in *Axel's Castle,* "I am made a little tired at hearing Eliot, only in his early forties, present himself as an 'agèd eagle' who asks why he should make the effort to stretch his wings" (130).[25] Henry Reed was provoked to parody, as the speaker of "Chard Whitlow" solemnly intones:

> Seasons return, and today I am fifty-five,
> And this time last year I was fifty-four,
> And this time next year I shall be sixty-two.
> (2–5)

Eliot's poetry refuses the voice of the spectral son by hearing it in reverse—for what is the ostentatious self-pity of his *pueri senes* but childhood nostalgia in denial?

In the chapters that follow, I ask what this apparition has meant to its witnesses over the centuries—where it gets such intensity, how it manages to be so public and yet so intimate, why it comes back in so many times and places, in so many forms. While surveying the breadth, variety, and consistency of the motif, I have tried to begin answering these questions. The specular son is the mirror of patriarchy as the spectral son is its ghost. Together they haunt us intimately, charged with the pathos of the deep loss that makes us men or women and that binds us together in families, societies, and cultures. To show the power and necessity of this haunting, I set this compound figure within the affective and symbolic economies that join it to responsive witnesses—demonstrating each time how it tightens the knots of an ideological system centered on the absolute father, but attending also to the note of derision in Sarah's laughter or Ovid's parody, the resistance glimpsed in Parmigianino's *Madonna* and in Purdy's photomontage.

   Despite the casual anachronism of my vocabulary of the emotions, the argument of this book looks toward both a critique of historicism and a conception of what it means for human subjects to be constituted historically. I neither posit a stable human essence nor deny that modern subjects

---

25. See also 114: "And as Eliot, lately out of Harvard, assumed the role of the middle-aged Prufrock and today, at forty, in one of his latest poems, 'The Song of Simeon,' speaks in the character of an old man 'with eighty years and no tomorrow'—so 'Gerontion' and 'The Waste Land' have made the young poets old before their time." They grow "prematurely decrepit," he explains, by imitation: "In London, as in New York, and in the universities both here and in England, they for a time took to inhabiting exclusively barren beaches, cactus-grown deserts, and dusty attics overrun with rats—the only properties they allowed themselves to work with were a few fragments of old shattered glass or a sparse sprinkling of broken bones."

have anything in common with each other or their predecessors. Instead, I assume that *nothing* is precisely what we do have in common: the nothing that dreams, selves, cultures, nations and their gods are made on. This is not the ontological abyss of nihilism but a distinctively human nothingness called forth by our capacity to symbolize. It persists not *instead* of something, like the philosopher's nothing, but beneath, within, behind, or beyond material things. Patriarchy, I argue, gives this nothing an ideologically specific determination as *the body of fatherhood*. It may take the form of Steele's elusive masculine ideal, reflected in Hamlet or Mr. Greenhat but identical with neither. It may wear a crown, for "the king," as Hamlet observes, "is a thing . . . of nothing"; in *The Winter's Tale* Leontes goes abruptly mad under the strain of being such a *nothing,* harping on the word as if it could annihilate the world.[26] In fact, it is not only a negating but also an immensely productive force. Such is the insight of Wallace Stevens's distinction between "the nothing that is not there and the nothing that is," or of Shakespeare's prescient turn of phrase in the speech of Prospero: we are such stuff, he says—not such as dreams are made *of,* but as they are made *on.* In discussing Statius, I described this stuff as a "something else," neither self nor other, that calls desire forth out of mourning and finds its most potent image in the mourner's desperate wish to swallow the flames of a funeral pyre. I think this swallowed fire is what makes us what we are: beings subject to history, such stuff as dreams of the burning child are made on.

26. The phrase quoted from *Hamlet* appears at 4.2.28–30; these observations about both plays are developed further in chapter 3. My argument is broadly indebted to Lacan's discussion of the scopic drive in *Four Fundamental Concepts* and his discussion of the phallus in "Desire." See also Lacan, "Introduction."

# Virgil's *Aeneid:*
# The History of a Wound

*tuane haec genitor per uulnera seruor*
*morte tua uiuens?*
                                    —*Aeneid* 10.848–49

## Why These Wounds?

On the night of its fall, the city of Troy is wrapped in sleep. Greek ships glide out from behind the island of Tenedos, while high in the citadel warriors drop from the wooden horse, overpower the sentries, and silently open the gates. Just at this threshold in time, when the city is entered but not yet destroyed, Hector appears to Aeneas in a dream,

> Gaunt with sorrow, streaming tears, all torn—
> As by the violent car on his death day—
> And black with bloody dust,
> His puffed-out feet cut by the rawhide thongs.
> Ah god, the look of him! How changed
> From that proud Hector who returned to Troy
> Wearing Achilles' armor, or that one
> Who pitched the torches on Danaan ships;
> His beard all filth, his hair matted with blood,
> Showing the wounds, the many wounds, received
> Outside his father's city walls.

> *in somnis, ecce, ante oculos maestissimus Hector*
> *uisus adesse mihi largosque effundere fletus,*
> *raptatus bigis ut quondam, aterque cruento*
> *puluere perque pedes traiectus lora tumentis.*
> *ei mihi, qualis erat, quantum mutatus ab illo*
> *Hectore qui redit exuuias indutus Achilli*

> *uel Danaum Phrygios iaculatus puppibus ignis!*
> *squalentem barbam et concretos sanguine crinis*
> *uulneraque illa gerens, quae circum plurima muros*
> *accepit patrios.*
>
> $(2.270–79)^1$

This is the spectral son, come back from the dead to show his wounds.

In the symbolism Virgil takes over from Homer, these wounds betoken the city's fate. In the *Iliad* both Priam and Andromachë foresee the conquest of Troy in Hector's fall, and the poem closes with his funeral, as if the city's destruction were indeed comprehended in his: "It was most like what would have happened if all lowering / Ilion had been burning top to bottom in fire" (22.410–11, trans. Lattimore). Hector returns because the sorrow of his death is culminating, now, in the burning of Ilion; the communal agony that began with his defeat will be completed with the blow that beheads Priam. At the moment of the dream this blow has already begun to fall: the sounds of destruction are rising in the dreamer's ear even as he lies sleeping, and something in him knows what they mean.

Hector's wounds announce the breaching of the walls he died defending; in this way they signal the violation of a *collective* body. From this point on, the dreamlike action of book 2 takes place inside an urban funeral pyre, the cremation of a primal body that is not Priam, or Hector, or the city alone but *Troy*, the imaginary form in which all three are incorporate. Because they "stand in" for the phantasmic wound that decapitates this primal body, Hector's wounds appear to the dreamer both as themselves and as the mysterious signs of a greater sorrow. The dream knows how they were inflicted: Hector's feet, for example, are bloated and cut because his body was tied with rawhide thongs to the back of Achilles' chariot. A story locates these wounds in time and links them to their causes. But what story can explain the apparition itself, or absorb the shock of the change from proud victor to bleeding corpse? Something remains unaccountable in "the look of him," something irreducible to known causes.

It is this other something that leaves the dreamer, who knows perfectly well how Hector's wounds were inflicted, nonetheless mystified by what he sees:

---

1. For the Latin I cite *Opera;* translations are generally from Fitzgerald. I give English and then Latin or vice versa as context suggests, but line references are always to the Latin text. On occasion I refer to other Latin editions or other translations, or modify Fitzgerald for greater literalness.

I seemed
Myself to weep and call upon the man
In grieving speech, brought from the depth of me:

"Light of Dardania, best hope of Troy,
What kept you from us so long, and where?
From what far place, O Hector, have you come,
Long, long awaited? After so many deaths
Of friends and brothers, after a world of pain
For all our folk and all our town, at last,
Boneweary, we behold you! What has happened
To ravage your serene face? Why these wounds?"

*ultro flens ipse uidebar*
*compellare uirum et maestas expromere uoces:*
*"o lux Dardaniae, spes o fidissima Teucrum,*
*quae tantae tenuere morae? quibus Hector ab oris*
*exspectate uenis? ut te post multa tuorum*
*funera, post uarios hominumque urbisque labores*
*defessi aspicimus! quae causa indigna serenos*
*foedauit uultus? aut cur haec uulnera cerno?"*
                                                    (2.279–86)

Here the dream touches an inner depth at which Aeneas knows nothing of cause and sequence—only the shock of sudden change and the ache of an interminable delay. Achilles kept Hector's body twelve days before returning it, but this is not the endless duration at which the dreamer marvels. Even now, confronting the body ravaged in defeat, Aeneas invokes the glorified hero: "Light of Dardania, best hope of Troy." Where, he asks, has *this* Hector been? What has befallen the imaginary figure whose overwhelming virility can still prompt the incredulous question "Why these wounds?"

Alive and in his glory, Hector embodied the house and lineage of Priam, "the power of Asia" (*regnatorem Asiae,* 2.557). His wounds in defeat prophesy the eclipse of that power in a horror that exceeds all others, for the fall of Troy annihilates the very thing that sacrifice seeks to create: the body, not just of father or son, but of the whole patriarchal kinship network that joins father to son and so defines an imperial people. This destruction has been sung and painted many times; the *Aeneid* suggests, further, that it *must* be represented: imperious even in its ashes, Troy *demands* that its history be compulsively told and retold. At the same time, Virgil implies that the fall of Troy resists or exceeds all explanations, much like the torn and bleeding form that rises before Aeneas in his dream. Behind the visible wounds that move and astonish the dreamer looms the greater wound to which they allude, a trauma as metaphysical as the body it destroys. This

greater wound can never quite coincide with a given event, or take its determined place in a narrative sequence; it is, to borrow a word from Statius,
untimely (*intempestus*).[2] Always both *not yet* and *already* there at the narrat-
able (historical) moment, it can enter the narrative only through a gap, the
eclipse of one temporality by another. Its repetitions—in the blow that beheads the imaginary body of patriarchy when Priam dies, or in the sacrificial
stroke that comes from Pallas in the poem's closing lines—are therefore
marked as disruptions in the story of physical bodies. In this they resemble
the dream of Hector, set on the threshold between wakefulness and sleep,
opening into an expanse of mourning and expectation that seems to belong
at once everywhere and nowhere in the story of Troy.

If the destruction of Troy is announced in this dream, its coup de grace
arrives with the death of Priam. Breaking through to the central courtyard of the royal palace, the Greek warrior Pyrrhus spears the king's son
Politës before his parents' eyes. Then, slipping in the boy's pooled blood,
he drags King Priam trembling "to the altar step itself" (*altaria ad ipsa*,
2.550), where he beheads him. Virgil closes the scene by shifting suddenly into a long view, drawing back in historical perspective to merge
Priam's corpse with the ruins of the burned-out city in a single memorable image:

> That was the end
> Of Priam's age, the doom that took him off
> With Troy in flames before his eyes, his towers
> Headlong fallen—he that in other days
> Had ruled in pride so many lands and peoples,
> The power of Asia.
> On the distant shore
> The vast trunk headless lies without a name.

> *haec finis Priami fatorum, hic exitus illum*
> *sorte tulit Troiam incensam et prolapsa uidentem*
> *Pergama, tot quondam populis terrisque superbum*
> *regnatorem Asiae. iacet ingens litore truncus,*
> *auulsumque umeris caput et sine nomine corpus.*
> (2.553–58)

The last line-and-a-half removes us abruptly from the viewpoint we have
shared with Aeneas on the palace roof, revealing behind his gaze the retrospect of empire. Troy is now a *litore,* or as Fitzgerald translates (exag-
gerating the effect), "a distant shore." The line incorporates Priam and his
fallen city in a single "vast trunk": the image of the dead body, transferred

2. For discussion of Statius' *intempesta cano,* see chapter 1.

from Priam to Troy-as-Priam, is displaced to the beach, decapitated, and
stripped of its name. This associative leap condenses in a single phrase the
father, the king, the city, the royal name, the towers, and the head of the
body. It is as if, in the interval between the stab wound Pyrrhus delivers to
Priam and the "trunk" left headless on the shore, another stroke has
fallen, decapitating the imaginary body in which all these things are comprehended.

The final lines of the poem disclose this metaphysical wound one last
time. Blinded by rage, Aeneas buries his sword in the suppliant Turnus,
founding the Roman empire with an act of savagery that violates central
values of Roman culture—*pietas, humanitas, parcere subiectis* (to spare the
conquered).[3] Aeneas calls the killing a sacrifice, saying the stroke comes
not from him but from his protégé, killed by Turnus: *"Pallas te hoc uulnere, Pallas / immolat et poenam scelerato ex sanguine sumit"* ("It is Pallas
who, with this wound, sacrifices you, Pallas / who from your polluted
blood exacts his due," 12.948–49; translation modified).[4] Aeneas had already seen Pallas as sacrificed, and responded—predictably, dreadfully—
by including human sacrifice among the boy's funeral rites. Now he imagines himself an extension of the dead boy, a weapon wielded to reverse the
ritual. Through me, says Aeneas, Pallas makes things even, exacting *poenam* (atonement-price) by sacrificing his sacrificer. But even as Aeneas
plunges his agency into the fantasy of the sacrificial son, Virgil holds them
slightly apart: *first* Aeneas speaks, *then* he delivers the blow "in fury."
When Aeneas says *hoc uulnere,* his demonstrative adjective points to a
wound not yet there, the wound as he imagines it. When the blow does
fall, the narrator speaks of the hero's seething (*feruidus,* 12.951) passion,
a fury his delusions of sacrificial purification seem only to confirm. The
gap between these moments shows, simply but crucially, that Aeneas, not
Pallas, slaughters Turnus, and it allows us to ask what the phrase *hoc uulnere* really refers to: what *is* this imaginary wound that precedes the actual
deathblow, that comes from Pallas and constitutes a sacrificial offering?

In the system of allusions that joins the *Aeneid* to the *Iliad,* Pallas corresponds to Patroclus, while Turnus, wearing a sword belt stripped from
Pallas in the field, corresponds to "that proud Hector who returned to
Troy / Wearing Achilles' armor." One answer, then, to the horrified question "Why do I see these wounds?" is that it will be Aeneas' fate to inflict

---

3. This is the most widely debated passage in the poem. My sense of it is especially indebted to Putnam's detailed and recurrent comments in *Virgil's Aeneid;* see also Burrow
48–51 on the difference between Homeric compassion, based on "a common store of grief,"
and the ethical inflection of Virgilian compassion, based on "shared moral and emotional
values" (49).

4. Fitzgerald interpolates a future tense: "This wound will come / From Pallas."

them on another Hector. Implicit in this answer, of course, is a much larger question: if the destruction of Troy is the horror that lies behind the dream of Hector, does that same destruction somehow inhere in the death of Turnus? If the stroke that kills him is, in turn, the act that founds Rome (Virgil uses the same verb, *condere*, to describe both), does this mean that the annihilation of Troy lingers and is somehow repeated in the birth of Rome?[5]

This question takes on resonance and urgency in the *Aeneid* because the narrative alludes not only to the events of Homer's *Iliad* but also to the civil wars that brought Octavian Caesar to power as Virgil was writing the poem. So, for instance, Priam's "vast trunk" lying headless and nameless on a distant shore is proverbially read as a reference to the death of Pompey. Too often, interpreters have used this historical allusion to explain away the striking shift in perspective that introduces it. Instead, we should recognize that far from obviating the complex resonance of the perspectival shift, the allusion to Pompey amplifies it, casting the Roman civil wars as a trauma that persists within Octavian's efforts to consolidate the empire just as the fall of Troy haunts Aeneas' efforts to found it. Owen Lee suggests that the *Aeneid* is haunted by the memory of "The Proscriptions," accounts of killings during the civil wars that regularly feature the deaths of fathers and sons. These are, he notes, mainly stories of Octavian's cruelty; the civil wars were fought as his revenge on all who killed his adoptive father, Julius Caesar (15–17). One way to sanctify such violence is to define it as sacrificial, as Aeneas does when he takes his revenge on Turnus. In many ways Virgil's poem seems to sanction the violence on which Octavian founded his regime, but it also works assiduously to disturb the sanction; rather than simply representing such violence as a sacrifice regrettably demanded by the gods, the *Aeneid* exposes the fury that animates military heroism, questions the rationalization of such fury as *pietas*, and implies that filial "sacrifice" may be profoundly sacrilegious.

The poem questions all these distinctions radically because it questions the difference on which they all depend, the difference between creating and destroying the body of empire. Unless those two acts can be distinguished, neither Rome nor its history will have been possible. In the narrative and symbolic form of the *Aeneid*, however, the creation and destruction of empire are repeatedly superimposed. This effect is achieved in a number of ways, but they are all finally linked to an underlying structure that is complex, powerful, and indirect. It doubles the narrative, continu-

---

5. Fowler remarks on the peculiarity of the verb *condit:* "Aeneas *ferrum aduerso sub pectore condit,* 'buries (founds, lays down) the iron in his adversary's chest' (12.950, recalling 1.5 *dum conderet urbem,* 'before he could found a city' and 1.33 *tanta molis erat Romanam condere gentem,* 'so weighty a task was it to found the Roman people')" (261).

ally referring events back to the *Iliad* and forward to contemporary history; but it also dislocates the narrative, disrupting the story of bodies and actions with a dimension of experience and a form of causality that defy representation yet demand recognition.

The poem begins *Arma uirumque cano*—in Dryden's unrivaled translation, "Arms and the man I sing." In this opening Virgil announces the unconscious subject of his poem, for the conjunction of man and weapon is *wound*. The *Aeneid* as I read it is the history not only of Rome, but also of this primal wound and the succession of butchered bodies in which it is repeated. But the *Aeneid* also asks through its very form whether there can *be* a history of something that is "untimely" in the complex sense that, for us, has accumulated in the Greek word *trauma*. The story Aeneas relates in book 2 is already depicted on the walls of Juno's temple in book 1 and is "now known throughout the world" (*iam fama totum uulgata per orbem*, 457). He retells the story in book 2 and reenacts it in books 11 and 12, each time revisiting the Homeric scene in which Achilles defeats Hector. The mural focuses on the narrative sequence within which Hector's death is understood: the unappeasable wrath of Minerva, the dragging of the corpse, the supplication of Priam. But the death *recurs* because it cannot be absorbed by this history. Hector's return in a dream reveals how profoundly his death persists as an event that is not only historical, and hence unique, but also traumatic, and hence unassimilable; repeated, but always out of sync. The last of its eruptions, in the death of Turnus, brings the narrative not to any satisfying closure or affirmation of achieved progress, but to a notoriously abrupt and disturbing end.

Book 2 offers Virgil's fullest rendering of what we may call the "primal scene" of his narrative—an image of patriarchy devastated in the most intimate way, and of this devastation as the traumatic origin of Roman history. The essence of the violation is not only the beheading of the patriarch, for it includes both the desecration of the ancestral altar and the inversion of natural order whereby the father witnesses his son's death. "You forced me to look on / At the destruction of my son," Priam cries accusingly, "defiled / A father's eyes with death" (*nati coram me cernere letum / fecisti et patrios foedasti funere uultus*, 2.538–39). Aeneas describes the scene to Anchises in similar terms, almost as if reciting the formula of some terrible ritual: "He kills the son before his father's eyes, / The father at the altars" (*natum ante ora patris, patrem qui obtruncat ad aras*, 2.663).

This formula repeats itself with variations throughout the first three books of the poem, in one abortive effort after another to rebuild Troy. First comes the settlement of the Aeneadae, abandoned when the muffled sobs of Polydorus reveal that the ground itself is polluted with the blood of Priam's youngest son. Then comes Pergamum, the result of a misinterpreted oracle, and again the ground is contaminated: things won't grow here; a plague kills crops and trees. The third failure to transcend this pollution of the ground is the settlement at Buthrotum. Here we encounter the most striking repetition yet of the traumatic primal scene. First Andromachë mistakes Aeneas for the ghost of Hector. Then, in recounting her own history, she relates the death of Pyrrhus, killed by a rival suitor for the hand of Hermionë:

> "But now Pyrrhus is dead. Orestes, hot
> With lust for her whom he thought stolen from him,
> And maddened by the Furies for spilt blood,
> Caught Pyrrhus unprepared and cut him down
> Before his father's altar."

> *"ast illum ereptae magno flammatus amore*
> *coniugis et scelerum furiis agitatus Orestes*
> *excipit incautum <u>patriasque obtruncat ad aras</u>."*
> (3.330–32, emphasis added)

The final words echo Aeneas' description of Pyrrhus at 2.663, *patrem qui obtruncat ad aras.* The fate of Priam and Politës has caught up with Achilles' son as if some cosmic mechanism were repeating itself in the events of human history.[6]

The untimeliness of the primal scene in Virgil is reflected not only in its repetitions but also in its reversals, as the wounds of father and son mirror each other. Priam denounces the killing of Politës as a *scelus,* or "atrocity" (535), because it violates natural sequence, yet this powerful sense of decorum is complicated again by the presence of Aeneas as witness. Not only does the son die before the father's eyes, the father also dies before the eyes of the son:

6. Pyrrhus is obviously not a child, but Petrini aptly summarizes the implications of the sacrificial pattern that includes the death of Pyrrhus: "The deaths of children in the *Aeneid* are not mere pathos, nor are they only individual losses and particular tragedies. They represent the loss of renewal, both in the time of the narrative and in republican Rome. No less than the civil wars or the proscriptions and bloodshed of the 40s, Rome's lost power of growth and lost hope of renewal are presented as symptoms of a systemic affliction, located by Virgil in Troy and in Rome's founding, and doomed to repetition; though the seemingly endless civil wars had finally ended, their ancestral causes remained and would someday produce the symptoms again" (9). In "Virgil and Tragedy," Hardie seeks to qualify emphasis on the emotional impact of these deaths, arguing that the recent critical emphasis on "suffering parents and children, exposed to the impersonal and inhuman structures of militarism and absolutism" is "a symptom of liberal humanism's interest in the individual subject" (314). There is much to be said for the contrasting emphasis he recommends, on "the *locus* of contesting roles within the structures of gender, household, and city," but my effort in this chapter is rather to combine these two emphases. The pathos of filial sacrifice is integral not just to liberal humanism, but also to the social structures of Roman patriarchy and the ideology that sustained them.

> I stood unmanned,
> And my dear father's image came to mind
> As our king, just his age, mortally wounded,
> Gasped his life away before my eyes.
> Creusa came to mind, too, left alone;
> The house plundered; danger to little Iulus.

> *obstipui; subiit cari genitoris imago,*
> *ut regem aequaeuum crudeli uulnere uidi*
> *uitam exhuluntem, subiit deserta Creusa*
> *et direpta domus et parui casus Iuli.*
>                                   (560–63)

Aeneas responds to Priam's death as if it were indeed a "primal scene," reading his own family into its patterns. The paths of association are clear enough: Anchises corresponds to Priam, Creusa to Hecuba and her daughters, Iulus to Politës. But what about Aeneas? To whom does he correspond?

As absent defender he is a Hector, asking himself, when he thinks of his family's danger, "What kept you so long?" The scene repeats *and* reverses itself through this anchoring identification. In a spectacle built on so many reversals—a son (Politës) killed before his father, then the father (Priam) killed by a son (Pyrrhus) whose father (Achilles) killed that father's son (Hector)—Aeneas finds himself caught up *as Hector* in the cycle that keeps these deaths revolving upon one another. Politës' death preceded Priam's, but Aeneas' imagination leaps first from father to father. He returns home to find Anchises plunged in despair, unwilling to leave, and responds by seeking his own death in combat, plunging back into the violent night like a mourner embracing the funeral pyre to swallow its flames. He imagines himself at this moment witnessing the violence of Pyrrhus all over again:

> "My dear mother,
> Was it for this, through spears and fire, you brought me,
> To see the enemy deep in my house,
> To see my son, Ascanius, my father,
> And near them both, Creusa,
> Butchered in one another's blood? My gear,
> Men, bring my gear."

> *"hoc erat, alma parens, quod me per tela, per ignis*
> *eripis, ut mediis hostem in penetralibus utque*
> *Ascanium patremque meum iuxtaeque Creusam*
> *alterum in alterius mactatos sanguine cernam?*
> *arma, uiri, ferte arma."*
>                                   (664–68)

It sounds briefly as if Aeneas might be calling for arms to defend his family, but that is not what the scene means to him, as his next words make clear: "The last light calls the conquered. / Give me back to the Greeks" (*"uocat lux ultima uictos. / reddite me Danais,"* lines 664–65). Give me back to the Greeks: what the primal scene means to Aeneas is, *I am Hector.* It was *as Hector* that he witnessed the scene in Priam's palace, not only because he saw his own father in Priam but also because he watched from a passive, dreamlike remove. *Quibus ab oris uenis?* he had asked in his dream: from what region have you come? The answer must be, *from the place of the dead.* This is the place from which Aeneas views Roman history in book 6, but it is also, in a sense, the place from which he views the primal scene in book 2. As he prepares to rejoin Hector, buckling on his armor in the face of Anchises' despair, it is his destination as well.

In the *Aeneid,* Virgil apprehends the question of Rome's being as the question of its ability through history to redeem a polluted origin that persists within each failed attempt to rebuild the fallen Troy.[7] The poem demonstrates exhaustively that empire carries this origin forward within itself as an irreducible contradiction, one it can neither overcome nor leave behind. This contradiction is formally expressed in the familiar tension between narrative progression and the circularity of the mirroring system that binds fathers and sons and structures the gaze of Virgilian historicism.[8] The most basic question this tension raises can be put quite simply: does Roman history progress, or does it end where it began, trapped in a pattern of compulsive repetition, endlessly reversed but never undone?

The scene in book 2 adds to this structure a sense of deeply compromised sacrificial witnessing. The death of Politës is an atrocity because it takes place *ante ora parentum,* before his father's eyes, and *ad aras,* at the altar. Both phrases are repeated at key moments in the text, for the killing of Priam and Politës belongs to an extensive pattern of botched or travestied sacrifices in the *Aeneid,* from the fraud of Sinon early in book 2 to the

---

7. See Bellamy for an extended discussion of Troy as the repressed origin of "a Rome that cannot be until, in Panthus' words to Aeneas, 'fuit Ilium,' or 'Troy has been'" (71). Quint also writes perceptively about "the repetition compulsion that the *Aeneid* locates at the heart of Roman experience" (52). Although I resist Quint's emphasis on repetition as therapeutic mastery, these two critical readings of the poem inform my argument throughout this chapter. Compare also Wofford on the "psychological paradigm for narrative, according to which a trauma, engendered by an unresolvable opposition that is narrated in a dream, comes to be understood retrospectively, if not quite healed" (14–15).

8. This claim marks a point of engagement with Quint's influential argument, which associates circularity with romance wandering as opposed to the teleological form of the epic plot. I am arguing that this teleological form itself depends on a temporal doubling and reversal that the poem explicitly associates with the form of the labyrinth. The following paragraphs develop the corresponding argument that repetition is not only compulsive but also "untimely," and hence unassimilable to narrative sequence.

death of Turnus in the closing lines.[9] Sinon presents himself as the victim of a fraudulent sacrifice rigged by Ulysses—escaped from the altar but now captive to the Trojans, and in any event long lost to his "poor old father" (2.87). This story provides the emotional basis of his appeal for sympathy—the "tall tale and fake tears" that, as Aeneas says, "captured us" (*captique dolis lacrimisque coactis*, 2.196). Aeneas makes this observation in the midst of his own sorrowful tale, destined if not intended to capture Dido, and the truth of his story in contrast to Sinon's perjury matters less than their common reliance on filial piety and sacrifice to achieve pathos.

These elements are repeated in the episodes that frame Sinon's story. When the twin serpents approach from Tenedos, Laocoön is "on the point of putting to the knife / A massive bull before the appointed altar" (*sollemnis taurum ingentem mactabat ad aras*, 2.202).[10] He breaks off because the serpents are devouring his sons before his eyes. Laocoön dies horribly, covered with venom and filth, "Sending to heaven his appalling cries / Like a slashed bull escaping from an altar, / The fumbled axe shrugged off" (*clamores simul horrendos ad sidera tollit: / qualis mugitus, fugit cum saucius aram / taurus et incertam excussit ceruice securim*, 2.222–24). The interrupted ritual is reversed in this simile, as the priest takes the victim's place. Ironically, the ritual is also completed—for Laocoön, unlike the bull (and unlike his counterpart Sinon), does not escape from the imaginary altar at which he is "sacrificed."

Sinon's fraudulent story about a fraudulent, unfinished sacrifice is thus followed, and seemingly confirmed, by a legitimate sacrifice, first interrupted and then finished as travesty. This interlacing of miscarried, fraudulent, and travestied sacrifices anticipates the slaughter-at-the-altar of Priam and Politës and, eventually, of Pyrrhus himself. The motif is repeated often: in the sacrifice of Athenian youth, for example, depicted among the carvings in Apollo's temple. It is resumed in the battles that conclude the poem, where one brutal killing after another is sardonically labeled a "sac-

9. E. L. Harrison, describing the fate of Laocoön as an "ironic reversal, whereby the sacrificing priest suddenly finds himself to be a victim," adds, "It is striking how often in Book 2 death seems to have sacrificial undertones. Not only does Laocoön die at an altar in the act of sacrificing, but even the simile introduced to illustrate his cries (223f.) keeps within the same framework of reference. The very first Trojan casualty we hear of, Coroebus, *diuae armipotentis ad aram procumbit* (425); and the last, King Priam himself, is slaughtered by Neoptolemus at the palace's central altar, which is already drenched with the blood of his son, Polites (550–53). And before all this the motif of human sacrifice forms the ominous basis of Sinon's lying tale (108ff.)" (54 and n. 38).

10. *Mactare*, the verb translated as "putting to the knife," is the word used by Apollo in book 9 to praise Ascanius after his first battlefield kill (see n. 33). There it means "glorify," but the irony latent in the passage becomes clear enough if we imagine saying that Laocoön is "on the point of glorifying" the bull he sacrifices to Neptune.

rifice." Agamemnon's son Halaesus dies on the same day his father does: "the day / The old man closed his glazing eyes in death / The Parcae took the son in hand, to be / Cut down, blood sacrifice, by Evander's spear" (*ut senior leto canentia lumina soluit, / iniecere manum Parcae telisque sacrarunt / Euandri,* 10.418–20). Halaesus is slain by Pallas, repeatedly described as wielding his own father's spear to deprive other parents of their sons—a pattern that reaches its inevitable conclusion when Turnus, before killing Pallas, declares, "I wish his father / Stood here to watch" (*cuperem ipse parens spectator adesset,* 10.443), and afterward, "In that state which his father merited / I send back Pallas" (*qualem meruit, Pallanta remitto,* 10.492). Evander isn't there to watch, but the great father Jupiter bears futile witness, explaining to the weeping Hercules that he cannot save Pallas, any more than he could save his own son Sarpedon at Troy. Aeneas "takes alive" (*uiuentis rapit,* 10.518) eight sons to be sacrificed at Pallas' funeral.[11] The Rutulian warrior Magus pleads for mercy in the name of filial piety, but Aeneas bends his head backward "still begging" and cuts his throat (10.536). Hemonidës, a priest dressed in the robes of his office, repeats the fate of Laocoön, becoming the sacrificial victim (*immolat,* 10.541) in a travesty of the sacred bloodletting at the altar.[12]

Roman culture conventionally regarded human sacrifice as barbaric, but if we didn't know this already we could infer it from the *Aeneid:* by the time we come to the closing passage in which Aeneas "sacrifices" Turnus in Pallas' name, the poem has accumulated an unmistakable image of inhuman *furor* (supposedly the opposite of *pietas*) as motivating the unholy filial sacrifice on which Roman history is founded—and by which it is sustained. What is more, it has identified this *scelus* with the advent of Rome, the moment in which, as Troy and King Priam go down in flames, the history that *will have been Roman* begins.[13] Through the poem's elaborate network of repetitions Virgil seems to find, lodged at the heart of empire, a deeply sacrilegious "sacrifice" that repeats the trauma it would undo.

11. Tarrant notes that since "Octavian was rumored to have sacrificed human victims to the shade of Julius Caesar after the siege of Perusia, the incident takes on an additional chilling resonance" (179). Wiltshire also makes this connection (26–27).

12. Hardie, *Epic Successors,* notes that the motif of substituting a human for an animal sacrificial victim is introduced with Laocoön and then reintroduced when Messapus kills Aulestes in book 12, offering the gods "a better victim" (12.296): "This, the first deliberate confrontation in the battle, is balanced by the last, that of Aeneas and Turnus: both are 'sacrificial.' . . . In Aeneas' final outburst of violence and anger the institutionally sanctioned sacrifice of animals is replaced with (substituted by) the more powerful sacrifice of a man. *Finis*" (20). See also Lyne on substitution as a function of the figurative language in the Laocoön episode (74–76).

13. This is not to deny that the Trojan remnant in its diaspora is still recognizably Trojan. But Troy's aftermath will be retroactively understood as a narrative about the quest for Rome—a quest that can only be stalled by too fixed an allegiance to the memory of Troy.

This sacrifice is enacted in the unholy ritual of empire, the death of the son *ante ora parentum*.[14]

The sacrificial son emerges as the poem's complex figure for this atrocity because he haunts the labyrinth that is Virgil's deep image of imperial history. David Quint argues that Virgil's historicism is principally linear, opposed to the wandering and regressive movement associated with romance: "Epic," he remarks, "loves a parade," and it stages history as a pageant through which "identity and power are transmitted across time in patrilineal succession" (31, 30). But parades are spectacles, and as such are always enfolded by a historical gaze. Virgil identifies the structure of this gaze with the Cretan Labyrinth, scene of the ritual sacrifice of Athenian sons. At its center, he discovers the contradiction of a patrilineal succession that feeds on its own descendants, offering them up before their fathers' eyes in the sacrilegious ceremonies of war. In this ritual, Virgil traces the way empire is precariously sustained by its annihilation of fatherhood (for the father dies as father in the death of the son). This is the contradiction that empire must master to sustain itself, like the Minotaur, on a diet of filial sacrifice.

## The Sacrificial Son and the Labyrinth of History

As a work of mourning for this endless destruction of sons, the *Aeneid* has been thought to sanctify their deaths. Traditionally the poem was seen as contributing to the Augustan transformation of piety from an ancestor cult to a state ideology centered on the deification of the emperor.[15] Modern American criticism keeps one eye trained on Virgil's critical distance from this ideology, but the distance is internal—related perhaps to the so-

---

14. "Before the eyes of his father"; Lee discusses this phrase as a "leitmotif" in the *Aeneid*. Feeney, surveying the state of scholarship on Roman ritual in *Literature and Religion*, relays some useful warnings—for example, that both "ritual" and "sacrifice" are modern concepts without precise equivalents in Latin or Greek—and draws what I take to be the appropriate conclusion: "Whatever theorizing went on about sacrifice was conducted in myth and poetry. And it goes without saying that poets were not concerned to elucidate the meaning of sacrifice exactly, but to put it to work in a system of meanings of another kind" (117–18). Bandera uses Girard to argue that in the *Aeneid* Virgil "discovered that even the most respectable sacrificial order is not only grounded on violence, but in fact made possible through violence" (233). Hardie, *Epic Successors*, offers a thoughtful and perceptive extension of Bandera's thesis, interpreting Virgil's epic and its Latin successors in terms of the Girardian notion of "sacrificial crisis" (19–57).

15. This is the view of Wagenvoort in his careful tracing of the philological transformations undergone by *pietas* (in relation to the associated terms *humanitas* and *religio*) during the transition from the republic to the monarchy (1–20). Burrow is perceptive in analyzing the opposed tendencies toward pity and piety contained within Virgilian *pietas* (34–51).

phisticated skepticism fostered by the urban culture of Rome and associated in different ways with Lucretius and Ovid.[16] Virgil's distinctive achievement in the process of forging an Augustan ideology was to have intensified this skepticism as well, heightening and transforming its negative force while binding it more integrally to imperial myth. This means that the venerable commonplace about Virgil's "melancholy" is accurate in a technical sense: if epic poetry is often a work of mourning, Virgil's epic is also a work of melancholia by Freud's definition, fixing an internal negation of the form it identifies with.[17]

That form is empire as the deification of the state; its negation is the specter of so many sons sacrificed to the gods of empire. Suetonius reports that when Virgil read the *Aeneid* before Augustus and Octavia, the emperor's sister fainted on hearing the eulogy for her dead son Marcellus.[18] Whether this story is true, its currency implies that even in antiquity such an imaginary scene of reading lay at the heart of the poem, as the eulogy for Marcellus lies near its center. Read in this way the *Aeneid* becomes a complex rehearsal of loss, summing up the sorrows of empire in the sacrifice of the chosen son.

The traditional understanding of such loss is well represented by C. M. Bowra. In "Some Characteristics of Literary Epic," Bowra argues that the definitive trait of the epic hero is his willingness to die: "It is because they are ready to make this last annihilating sacrifice that heroes are honoured. Compared with this even their courage and prowess are of secondary importance" (58). In a comment as perceptive as it is partial, he makes this point the key to the affective appeal of epic in general and of the *Aeneid* in particular:

> The great hero, Achilles or Roland, appeals to two deep impulses of the human heart, the desire for glory and the respect for sacrifice. Through the second the first is satisfied; the hero sacrifices his life and wins thereby an immortal glory. When this happens, the human state gains in dignity, and the value of its efforts is triumphantly affirmed. Thus the special appeal of

16. The importance of Lucretius and Epicurean skepticism to the portrayal of sacrifice in the *Aeneid* is emphasized by Bandera: "In Lucretius, the terrors of the mind are specifically associated with religion, they are religious terrors leading to such atrocities—in Lucretius' mind—as the ritual sacrifice of Iphigenia" (217). Hardie, *Epic Successors,* also discusses Virgil's use of Lucretius.

17. Freud, "Mourning and Melancholia." For further discussion of this essay and its implications for literary history, see chapter 6. In "Prospect of Tradition" and "Experience of Literary History," Budick argues that Virgilian negation exceeds the melancholy form I describe here, opening itself to a radically unforeseen future and evoking in its relation to Homer a potential experience of negativity (as death) which cannot be recuperated by self-consciousness.

18. *Vita Vergili,* also attributed to Donatus; in *Suetonius* 2.451–52.

epic, even for later ages that do not recognize the heroic ideal in anything like its Homeric form, is nevertheless linked to the ennobling force of sacrifice. . . .

It is Rome to whom in the last resort the glory of her sons belongs, and it is for her that they make their sacrifices not merely of life but of happiness and personal ambitions and all that the old heroic type took for granted as its right. Virgil abandons the scheme of life by which the hero lives and dies for his own glory, and replaces a personal by a social ideal. (60–61)

Bowra sees that the emotional appeal of epic relies on the pathos of sacrifice, and he understands that Virgil sees Roman heroes specifically as sons, sacrificed to a "social ideal" that empties them before they die.[19] What he does not quite see is that in Virgil's hands the theme of filial sacrifice also indicts the social ideal and even, obliquely, criticizes the poem itself for investing so extensively in the pathos of loss.

Virgil's distinctive innovation as an epic poet lies in the narrative structure of his historicism, which folds time into a complex knot by reimagining the Roman past as the future of a Trojan remnant. "If I am not mistaken," writes C. S. Lewis in "Virgil and the Subject of Secondary Epic," the *Aeneid* "is almost the first poem which carries a real sense of the 'abysm of time'" (64). Auden, in a poem mockingly titled "Secondary Epic," deflates this praise: "No, Virgil, no: / Not even the first of the Romans can learn / His Roman history in the future tense, / Not even to serve your political turn; / Hindsight as foresight makes no sense" (455).

But Virgil's political "turn" may be more labyrinthine than Auden wishes to allow. The figure of the *puer senex*, derived from the *Aeneid* and closely related to the sacrificial son, is a subtle emblem of this temporal knot, for within Virgil's layering of perspectives the Trojan boys always appear, explicitly or not, as Roman ancestors. Lewis's account is invaluable for my purposes because he sees so clearly this link between the narrative structure Virgil invents and the themes of masculinity and maturity. His comments echo the passage from T. S. Eliot quoted in chapter 1, which is perhaps not surprising; they were written at about the time that American New Criticism, equally under the sway of Eliot's sensibility, was promulgating "maturity" as its criterion of aesthetic merit:

19. Quint interprets the death of Palinurus as standing for the self-sacrifice of Aeneas (83–96). Suzuki notes that the resonant affirmation of 9.449, *accolet imperiumque pater Romanus habebit* ("And still the Roman Father governs all"), is immediately preceded by a reference to the Tarpeian rock, and hence to the sacrifice of victims: "Virgil understands that the Roman Empire was built on the sacrifice—decreed by the 'Father'—of those such as Nisus and Euryalus" (147–48).

In a sense [Aeneas] *is* a ghost of Troy until he becomes the father of Rome. All through the poem we are turning that corner. It is this which gives the reader of the *Aeneid* the sense of having lived through so much. No man who has once read it with full perception remains an adolescent. . . . I have read that [Virgil's] Aeneas, so guided by dreams and omens, is hardly the shadow of a man beside Homer's Achilles. But a man, an adult, is precisely what he is: Achilles had been little more than a passionate boy. . . . With Virgil European poetry grows up. For there are certain moods in which all that had gone before seems, as it were, boys' poetry, depending both for its charm and for its limitations on a certain naivety, seen alike in his heady ecstasies and in its heady despairs, which we certainly cannot, perhaps should not, recover. (65–66)

Lewis identifies completely with the masculinity and maturity he attributes to Aeneas, but he also sees that they are based on a pervasive and complex sense of loss, represented at once as boyhood, unself-conscious passion, and the Homeric poetry whose narrative structure Virgil has transformed.

In Lewis's account the braiding together of maturity, masculinity, loss, historicism, the sacrificial son, and the *puer senex* remains for the most part unanalyzed, but the poem itself develops a certain distance on this ethos. Consider the historical vision shown to Aeneas by *pater Anchises* (6.679) in book 6. At the midpoint of the procession comes Brutus, celebrated for his patriotism:

> "Do you care to see now, too, the Tarquin kings
> And the proud soul of the avenger Brutus,
> By whom the bundled *fasces* are regained?
> Consular power will at first be his, and his
> The pitiless axes. When his own two sons
> Plot war against the city, he will call
> For the death penalty in freedom's name—
> Unhappy man, no matter how posterity
> May see these matters. Love of the fatherland
> Will sway him—and unmeasured lust for fame."

> *"uis et Tarquinios reges animamamque superbam*
> *ultoris Bruti, facisque uidere receptos?*
> *consulis imperium hic primus saeuasque securis*
> *accipiet, natosque pater noua bella mouentis*
> *ad poenam pulchra pro libertate uocabit,*
> *infelix, utcumque ferent ea facta minores:*
> *uincet amor patriae laudumque immensa cupido."*
>                                          (6.817–23)

This passage, sixty-one lines from the start of the procession and sixty-two lines from the end, is balanced on an ax's edge: *minores*, translated "posterity," also means "younger people" (as opposed to *seniores*, elders); *ferent*, translated "they may see these matters," can also mean report them, praise them, or even endure them. This language carefully blurs the difference between the descendants who celebrate Brutus and the sons who suffer for his soul's pride. Meanwhile, Anchises, still balancing every word, takes exception to the praise, calling Brutus "unhappy," a man "conquered" by a deeply ambiguous mixture of love and lust, of *amor patriae* and *laudum immensa cupido*. The tragic dilemma that forces Brutus to choose between *pietas* toward his sons or toward the state is as unyielding as the will of God, and its price is the same: liberty, like deity, says, "Give me your sons."

This central and deeply equivocal sacrifice offers a critical perspective on the whole procession. Like fate, Anchises' review of the future is constituted by a historicist turn, a narrative pretense that lets the retrospective gaze of Augustan Rome cloak itself in a Trojan prospect.[20] This turn is announced early in the procession by an extended paean to Augustus: "This is the man, this one, / Of whom so often you have heard the promise, / Caesar Augustus, son of the deified" (*hic uir, hic est, tibi quem promitti saepius audis, / Augustus Caesar, diui genus*). Augustus *causes himself*, as it were, by inspiring the Trojan remnant whose duty it will be to create the historical possibility of Caesars (6.806–7). The same loop in time that lets Augustus enfold historical causality in this way also projects, as his ideological counterpart, the mirage of the *puer senex*. This "child of double form," the progeny-progenitor whose future is already past, is nearly as strange as the Minotaur (*mixtumque genus prolesque biformis*, 6.25). Set in the underworld, Anchises' ghostly parade of preexistent souls both makes this doubling manifest and takes it to the furthest extreme, for the *pueri senes* who come before him there are so old they are already dead and so young they are not yet born.

Like the central lines on Brutus, the first and last figures embody this fold in time, which provides the underlying structure of the procession. The first is Aeneas' "last-born" son Silvius (*tua postuma proles*, 6.763). Fitzgerald follows Aulus Gellius in reading *postuma* as "latest," but Servius (perhaps remembering that Aeneas will be killed before his city can be founded) read it as "posthumous" (Williams, 506). Whether literally posthumous or merely last in line, Silvius marks a distinctly belated point of departure for

20. See Feeney, "History and Revelation": "In formal terms, Anchises' eulogistic speech is genealogical protreptic, using historical *exempla* and the promise of glory to steer Aeneas towards virtuous rule" (1). Feeney also notes the recurrent, subtle ways in which these exempla are coded as less than exemplary.

the procession he initiates. The implications of this ambiguous beginning are realized fully in the younger Marcellus, the last to appear:

> "Never will any boy of Ilian race
> Exalt his Latin forefathers with promise
> Equal to his; never will Romulus' land
> Take pride like this in any of her sons."

> *"nec puer Iliaca quisquam de gente Latinos*
> *in tantum spe tollet auos, nec Romula quondam*
> *ullo se tantum tellus iactabit alumno."*
>                                                    (6.875–77)

Marcellus—Augustus Caesar's nephew and his son-in-law, designated heir to the scepter—died at age nineteen in 23 B.C.E., while Virgil was at work on the *Aeneid*. As the predestinate bearer of empire he is an Augustan Iulus, and like the Arcadian prince Pallas in book 10, he seems almost to have died in Iulus' behalf: the black shadow that whirls sad night around his head (6.866) is an exact counterpart to the flame that enlumines Ascanius in book 2, *tactu innoxia* (line 683, literally "doing no harm by touching").

Marked for death before he is born and celebrated for what he never achieved, Marcellus becomes "a symbol of all the Roman youth cut off in the flower of life" (Brenk 225). He is an especially striking version of the sacrificial son, combining the spectral and specular forms in a single figure whose darkened glory heightens the contradiction he embodies. This contradiction emerges as well in the way Virgil's syntax breaks down at the climax of the passage: "Child of our mourning, if only in some way / You could break through your bitter fate. For you / Will be Marcellus" (*heu, miserande puer, si qua fata aspera rumpas, / tu Marcellus eris,* 6.882–83). As Fairclough notes, the sentence is "mixed in form," shifting from subjunctive to simple future without completing the if-clause (569).[21] In other words, the temporal dislocation of the poem's historical perspective is concentrated in a syntactic "child of double form." Some Latin editions smooth the ruptured grammar, much as Fitzgerald does in translation by making *tu Marcellus eris* a separate sentence following an exclamation. But to do so loses the irony of the line's form. The grammar is broken just at the word *rumpas* (*rumpere*, to break or burst forth), and

---

21. Fairclough describes the *si* clause as conditional. Stephen Wheeler, citing the standard commentaries by Austin and (especially) Norden, advises me that it is better understood as an ambiguous mixture of optative and conditional; "the ambiguity of the syntax," he writes, "expresses the empathy for Marcellus not yet born but already dead" (personal communication).

in place of the missing then-clause comes, like an epitaph, the *name: tu Marcellus eris*. As Brenk notes in reviewing the conventions of Greek and Roman sepulchral epigram, this phrase arrives in exactly the place "where in the epigrams the subject would have finished his life" (224). In effect the name *Marcellus* is a retroactive death sentence, binding a future wistfully fantasized as *possibility* to the irreversible past it has already become for Augustan Rome.[22]

To witness this contradiction, to see objectified the *cost* of the imperial gaze that constitutes sons as ancestors, Aeneas has journeyed to stand—literally—in the place of death. We are told that the resulting vision fires his "love / Of glory in the years to come" (*incendit . . . animum famae uenientis amore*, 6.889). But what fires this love is a vision of the future as already completed, each spirit in the procession recognized as the hero of a story summed up in his name: "all his own [literally, his "beloved"] / Descendants, with their futures and their fates, / Their characters and acts" (*carosque nepotes / fataque fortunasque uirum moresque manusque*, 6.682–83). The glory Aeneas loves in them is a perfection conferred by death.

This love of death is distinctly if subtly implied in the lines that follow the eulogy for Marcellus:

> So raptly, everywhere, father and son
> Wandered the airy plain and viewed it all.
> After Anchises had conducted him
> To every region and had fired his love
> Of glory in the years to come, he spoke
> Of wars that he must fight.

> *sic tota passim regione uagantur*
> *aëris in campis latis atque omnia lustrant.*
> *quae postquam Anchises natum per singula duxit*
> *incenditque animum famae uenientis amore,*
> *exim bella uiro memorat quae deinde gerenda.*
> (6.886–90)

22. My sense of the syntactic break at *rumpas* as deliberate and significant gains a certain kind of corroboration from literary history, for Edmund Spenser appears to have read it in much the same way. Spenser "imitates" this line from the *Aeneid* in *The Faerie Queene* at 2.10.68, where Prince Arthur has been reading a chronicle history of England that corresponds to Virgil's procession of Roman worthies. This is not the place to comment at length on Spenser's transformation of the scene (from prospect to retrospect, from vision to reading, from the underworld to the human brain), but we may note that the chronicles break off at the word *succeeding*: "Succeeding There abruptly it did end, / Without full point or other cesure right" (68.1–2). "Cesure" puns on "Caesar"; I have discussed the broken syntax of Spenser's line, though without noting the specific imitation of Virgil, in "The Earl of Cork's Lute" 161. Perhaps it is also worth noting that many editors of both texts have felt it necessary to interpolate punctuation to rationalize the syntax.

The mood of the eulogy is carried over in the phrase *sic tota*, "wholly engrossed in this way," which describes Aeneas and Anchises as they finish surveying the Elysian fields. Yet their wandering ends in a rekindled love for glory: the two moods are balanced as ambiguously as Brutus' mixed motives. Anchises and Aeneas pass easily from mourning one set of losses to preparing for the next—hungry for glory and already contemplating the wars "that he must fight"—because what they admire in these unborn children *is* death: all posterity in their eyes is implicitly posthumous. Marcellus is the perfect emblem of this mortifying gaze because he reflects its contradictory desire so explicitly in the dark halo that marks his future as past, his glory as death, his name as an epitaph.

Virgil shows us here that the traumatic scene of filial sacrifice repeats itself so powerfully because it informs the very structure of fatherly desire. We see this conversion of trauma into desire with special clarity in book 5, where the games commemorating Anchises' funeral end with battle maneuvers performed by Ascanius and the boys' troop. In the movement and detail of the passage we can almost see Marcellus' cloud gathering over the young cavalry as they ride in "all shining before their parents' eyes" (*ante ora parentum . . . lucent*, 5.553–54).[23] The phrase that renders their shining entrance is the "leitmotif," as Lee calls it, of filial sacrifice, echoing the scene from book 2 in which Politës is cut down while Priam helplessly looks on. The same phrase returns in books 6 and 11 with all its dark connotations confirmed: Aeneas on the banks of Acheron sees a crowd of souls, among them "young sons laid on the pyre / Before their parents' eyes" (*impositi . . . rogis iuuenes ante ora parentum*, 6.308); and in the Latin wars, the rout of the Rutulians after Camilla's death concludes with a "wretched slaughter" (*miserrima caedes*, 11.885) of soldiers trapped when the city gates are closed, "kept out before the eyes of weeping parents" (*exclusi ante oculos lacrimantumque ora parentum*, 11.887).

Even the noun *parens* is deceptive: it can mean, as Fitzgerald translates, "parents"—it can even mean "mothers"—but we soon learn that the *parens* watching the boys' troop are all *patres*, for the women have gathered to weep "on a desolate beach apart" (*procul in sola secretae*, 5.613). The fatherly gaze is full of admiration (*Trinacriae mirata fremit Troiaeque iuuentus*, 6.555), but what exactly do the fathers admire?

> Number one squadron gloried in its leader,
> Little Priam, who bore his grandsire's name—
> Your noble son, Politës, and a destined
> Sire of Italians.

23. Compare the discussion of the *lusus Troiae* in Petrini 93–100.

> *una acies iuuenum, ducit quam paruus ouantem*
> *nomen aui referens Priamus, tua clara, Polite,*
> *progenies, auctura Italos.*

(5.563–65)

The reference here to Priam and Politës confirms the earlier echo of their
death scene, marking *paruus Priamus* as an heir to something more than
glory. Caught up in the destined movement from progeny to ancestry, the
little boy already is seen as *auctura Italos,* a sire of Italians.

So too the others: "Dardans with applause / Now greeted the shy boys
and loved their show, / Marking in each the features of his forebears" (*ex-
cipiunt plausu pauidos gaudentque tuentes / Dardaniae, ueterumque
agnoscunt ora parentum,* 5.575–76). The boys are *pauidus,* nervous or
timid, but as with Steele's little Jerry or Van Dyck's Filippo Cattaneo, this
is part of what makes the gazing fathers exult: their admiration is warmed
by the glow of confirmed superiority. Virgil makes this effect even
stronger, omitting the noun "boys" while naming the forebears emphatically (*ueterum . . . parentum*), enclosing the boys' fear—all that remains of
them in the language of the line—with their fathers' applause and exultant
gaze (*plausu . . . gaudentque tuentes*). Meanwhile, the phrase translated
"features of his forebears," *ueterum . . . ora parentum,* repeats what is elsewhere translated as "[before] the father's eyes," [*ante*] *ora parentum* or
*ora patris.* What the Dardanian fathers celebrate in their sons is, finally, the
very condition of existing *ante ora parentum,* of being constituted by the
father's gaze as a mirror of lineal descent, at once progeny and progenitor.

Having completed the circuit of the parental gaze (5.577–78), the boys
begin their elaborate maneuvers, wheeling and turning, skirmishing and
calling truce, "waking an armed mimicry of battle" (*cient simulacra sub
armis,* 5.585).[24] Virgil's detailed description ends with a striking double
simile:

> So intricate
> In ancient times on mountainous Crete they say
> The Labyrinth, between walls in the dark,
> Ran criss-cross a bewildering thousand ways
> Devised by guile, a maze insoluble,
> Breaking down every clue to the way out.
> So intricate the drill of Trojan boys
> Who wove the patterns of their pacing horses,
> Figured, in sport, retreats and skirmishes—
> Like dolphins in the drenching sea, Carpathian
> Or Libyan, that shear through waves in play.

---

24. For this phrase I have preferred the translation of Fairclough.

> *ut quondam Creta fertur Labyrinthus in alta*
> *parietibus textum caecis iter ancipitemque*
> *mille uiis habuisse dolum, qua signa sequendi*
> *frangeret indeprensus et inremeabilis error;*
> *haud alio Teucrum nati uestigia cursu*
> *impediunt texuntque fugas et proelia ludo,*
> *delphinum similes qui per maria umida nando*
> *Carpathium Libycumque secant.*
>
> (5.588–95)

As the passage continues, we withdraw even further from the scene, into a distance not just of visual perspective but of historical time as well:

> This mode of drill, this mimicry of war,
> Ascanius brought back in our first years
> When he walled Alba Longa; and he taught
> The ancient Latins to perform the drill
> As he had done with other Trojan boys.
> The Albans taught their children, and in turn
> Great Rome took up this glory of the founders.
> The boys are called Troy now, the whole troop Trojan.

> *hunc morem cursus atque haec certamina primus*
> *Ascanius, Longam muris cum cingeret Albam,*
> *rettulit et priscos docuit celebrare Latinos,*
> *quo puer ipse modo, secum quo Troia pubes;*
> *Albani docuere suos; hinc maxima porro*
> *accepit Roma et patrium seruauit honorem;*
> *Troiaque nunc pueri, Troianum dicitur.*
>
> (5.596–602)

With its slow dissolve into the long view, the passage recalls Priam's death scene, which closes in much the same way. There, it was Aeneas whose perspective faded to reveal behind it the gaze of history; here, it is the audience of Trojan and Sicilian fathers. This fading brings to the surface the imperial gaze that has constituted the boys as ancestors throughout the passage—for example, making "small Atys" the *dilectus* of Iulus, "cherished boy-to-boy" (*paruus Atys pueroque puer dilectus Iulo*, 5.569) because Augustus Caesar was born into the *gens Atia* and Julius Caesar into the *gens Julia*. This transformation of boys into ancestors is confirmed when they are handed over to the gaze of history with the awkward assertion "The boys are called Troy now, the whole troop Trojan" (5.602).[25] The sense of something forced in this phrasing answers to the broken syntax in

---

25. Williams comments on the awkwardness of the phrase (*The Aeneid of Virgil, Books 1–6* 438).

the address to Marcellus: both are caused by the retrospective gaze that
turns the boys into ancestors, gathering them into a collective self called
*Rome* or *Troy*.

Just for a moment—as we pass from one labyrinth to another, from the
"bewildering thousand ways" devised by Daedalus to the maze of Roman
history—the boys' exuberance flashes out in the image of dolphins cavort-
ing in the surf. This glimpse makes the shift into historical perspective all
the more poignant, especially if we catch its resonance. The boys' games
will be interrupted when the despairing Trojan women, stirred by Iris to
resist the uncompromising demands of imperial destiny, set fire to the
ships. In book 9, when Turnus tries to fire the Trojan ships a second time,
the mother-goddess Cybele releases the fleet from its imperial destiny. The
ships escape by turning into dolphins:

> Each broke her hawser instantly; their bows
> Went under like a school of dolphins diving
> Into the depths, then wondrously came up,
> So many virgin forms now seaward bound.

> *et sua quaeque*
> *continuo puppes abrumpunt uincula ripis*
> *delphinumque modo demersis aequora rostris*
> *ima petunt. hinc uirgineae (mirabile monstrum)*
> *reddunt se totidem facies pontoque feruntur.*
> (9.117–22)[26]

Cybele and the Trojan woman are excluded from the paternal gaze before
which the boys perform in book 5. Unlike the ships, released by a marvel
into the freedom of the sea, the boys in their sportive energy are bound to
*maxima Roma* even unto death.

When Trojan emissaries first approach the walled city of Latium in book
7, they see a mirror image of the Trojan boys (*Troia pubes*):

> In the fields outside
> Were boys and striplings practicing horsemanship,
> Breaking in chariot teams in clouds of dust,
> Pulling taut bows and throwing javelins,
> Challenging one another to race or box.

> *ante urbem pueri et primaeuo flore iuuentus*
> *exercentur equis domitantque in puluere currus,*

---

26. The lineation is correct; see *Opera* for the omission of line 121. I have corrected
*urgineae,* in line 120, to *uirgineae.*

> *aut acris tendunt arcus aut lenta lacertis*
> *spicula contorquent, cursuque ictuque lacessunt.*
> (7.162–65)

These are the Latin boys at *their* games, matched with their Trojan counterparts in fatal symmetry, on each side of the poem's central descent to the underworld. These *primaeuo flore iuuentus* ("youths in their first bloom," in Fairclough's more literal translation) are in turn reflected in the elegiac passages mourning Marcellus (*manibus date lilia plenis,* "Let me scatter lilies," 6.883), Euryalus (*purpureus ueluti cum flos succisus aratro,* "As a bright flower cut by a plow," 9.435), and Pallas (*qualem uirgineo demessum pollice florem,* "Most like a flower a girl's fingers plucked," 11.68). Death makes these young men as delicate and voluptuous as brides.

The image of the boys as dolphins flashes forth against the shadowy outlines of the Cretan Labyrinth with its *inextricabilis error* ("maze no one could untangle," 6.27). The intricate pattern evolves before us, as voluntary and virtuosic as if the boys were governed by a single mind. But the enthusiastic precision of the military drill gives way in the simile to inextricable error: the pattern becomes a trap, a maze no one can untangle. The logic of this metamorphosis identifies the Trojan boys with their Athenian counterparts, sacrificed to the Minotaur:

> In the entrance way
> Androgeos' death appeared, then Cecrops' children
> Ordered to pay in recompense each year
> The living flesh of seven sons. The urn
> From which the lots were drawn stood modeled there.
>
> *in foribus letum Androgeo; tum pendere poenas*
> *Cecropidae iussi (miserum!) septena quotannis*
> *corpora natorum; stat ductis sortibus urna.*
> (6.20–22)

In the poem's architecture, this passage describing the temple of the Cumaean sibyl stands in the entryway to the underworld, suggesting that the Trojan boys, drilled as soldiers and admired as ancestral progeny, are also sacrificial victims led into the subterranean labyrinth of death—from the *inextricabilis error* of the Cretan Labyrinth to the *inremeabilis undae* ("irretraceable wave," 6.425) of the river Styx—as the accumulated mass of dead sons pulls the living into its orbit.

## The Structure of Imperial Desire

Virgil's description reveals how the sacrificial scene inheres in the structure of the imperial gaze, "historicizing" its objects by turning them into avatars of death, and it shows how the power of this scene is expressed in the affects it elicits, the father's pride or the son's eagerness for glory. The trauma repeats itself *as desire* on many levels of experience.

Virgil's portrait of Andromachë illustrates this point. The whole episode reveals clearly how the primal scene persists unspoken within the Trojan remnant. The settlement at Buthrotum is generally recognized as a diminished repetition of its prototype. After relating her own story, Andromachë asks Aeneas about his son:

> "What of your child, Ascanius?
> Alive still, nourished still by the world's air?
> Even at Troy, one thought . . .
>                    But does the boy
> Remember her, the mother who was lost?
> And do his father and his uncle Hector
> Stir him to old-time valor and manliness?"

> *"quid puer Ascanius? superatne et uescitur aura?*
> *quem tibi iam Troia—*
> *ecqua tamen puero est amissae cura parentis?*
> *ecquid in antiquam uirtutem animosque uirilis*
> *et pater Aeneas et auunculus excitat Hector?"*
>                                                    (3.339–43)

The half-line that Fitzgerald renders "Even at Troy, one thought . . ." is in a special way untranslatable. (Fairclough hazards a present tense construction: "Whom now, lo, when Troy . . .") As R. D. Williams notes, it is "the only half-line in the *Aeneid* where the sense is incomplete." He continues, "It is very difficult to see what was in Virgil's mind when he wrote these four words; all we can say is that he began some thought which he could not bring into the form in which he wanted it, and he left it there and went on" (297).[27] *Bis patriae cecidere manus:* twice the hands of the father fell. Williams here turns Virgil into Daedalus, unable to execute the definitive scene of his temple statuary (6.33). Classicists seem unanimous in the conviction that Virgil could not have intended to leave a broken line, but I suspect it is no accident that the *Aeneid* reg-

---

27. The observation that "nearly all the half-lines in Virgil are complete in sense and meaning, the sole exception being 'quem tibi iam Troia'" comes from *Vita Vergili* (*Suetonius* 2.456–57).

ularly shatters its own glassy surface at moments when the historical perspective puts special pressure on its language, or that these tend to be moments associated with sacrificial sons: Marcellus, the Trojan boys, or Astyanax.

Since Andromachë when she speaks these lines has just mistaken Aeneas for Hector, it is not hard to guess that she (like Daedalus) is remembering a lost son, the unspoken reference of her first question: "Alive still?" In her farewell to Ascanius she makes this thought explicit: "You that alone remind me of Astyanax. / His eyes, his hands, his look—all were like yours. / He would be your age, growing up like you" (*o mihi sola mei super Astyanactis imago. / sic oculos, sic ille manus, sic ora ferebat; / et nunc aequali tecum pubesceret aeuo,* 3.489–91). Line 340 breaks off like Astyanax himself, though the recognition is inarticulate: Andromachë is asking about Ascanius while thinking about Astyanax. Carried back momentarily to a time before the fall of Troy when both boys, and both futures, were still alive, she breaks off as Anchises does in book 6 when he catches himself wishing that Marcellus might somehow "break through [his] bitter fate" (*si qua fata aspera rumpas,* 6.882). In her unfinished thought, the future that *might have been* for Astyanax and the one that *may still be* for Ascanius meet in an unconstruable crossing.[28] In a sense, Andromachë's lapse anticipates Octavia's collapse, precipitated, we are told, by the line *tu Marcellus eris,* "you will be Marcellus" (6.883). In this line the clash of tenses is unstated but no less powerful, for Anchises' *you will be* is wrenched by a shift in perspective into the *you have been* that Octavia must hear. In book 3, as Andromachë loses her syntactic way, her thought is similarly reversed—for the question with which she emerges on the far side of her aporia is not whether *she* remembers Astyanax, but its opposite: does Ascanius remember Creusa, "the mother who was lost"? In this question we may hear her lingering attachment to a son and a future that no longer exist, and with it her sense that, in their destruction, she herself was lost *as a mother*.[29]

In Andromachë's speech, then, we encounter the inexpressible scene

---

28. Unconstruable because, in the line's unfinished state, we cannot determine the temporal reference of the adverb *iam. Quem* is a straightforward accusative singular, meaning "whom"; *tibi,* a dative (of reference?), meaning something like "to you" or "for you"; *Troia* a nominative. *Iam* is an adverb without a verb, a temporal marker that, according to Greenough et al., can mean "now, already, at length, [or] presently," and that "includes a reference to previous time through which the state of things described has been or will be reached. It may be used of *any* time" (197). I am grateful to Stephen Wheeler and Patricia Harris Stäblein for assistance with this enigmatic fragment.

29. Wiltshire remarks that "the final two questions are really questions about herself and her own situation. The *cura* of a child for a lost parent is the mirror image of a mother's own grief for a lost child" (44–45).

that keeps bleeding through into the present for the Trojan remnant. The fall of Troy appears again as a filial sacrifice so traumatic that it invades the future, preempting all efforts at a new beginning because, in its melancholy intensity, it has become the very template of desire. And yet curiously, the scene that insinuates itself with such persistence was in an important sense never *there:* Homer does not describe the sack of Troy. In a poem made up almost entirely of allusions to Homeric epic, this central and traumatic scene of origin is imagined, not remembered.[30]

W. R. Johnson remarks perceptively that Virgil "discovered . . . the heart of his poem" in Priam's abject plea to Achilles for the body of Hector (*Darkness Visible* 74). Priam begins by asking, "Remember your own father, great godlike Achilles," and ends by proclaiming, "I have endured what no one on earth has ever done before—/ I put to my lips the hands of the man who killed my son" (24.570, 590–91). An irresistible moment of shared grief follows as filial piety is traced to its origin in passionate mourning. Robert Fagles translates the passage with force and clarity:

> Those words stirred within Achilles a deep desire
> to grieve for his own father. Taking the old man's hand
> he gently moved him back. And overpowered by memory
> both men gave way to grief. Priam wept freely
> for man-killing Hector, throbbing, crouching
> before Achilles' feet as Achilles wept himself,
> now for his father, now for Patroclus once again,
> and their sobbing rose and fell throughout the house.
>
>                                    (24:592–99)

The knot is tied as Priam stirs Achilles to imagine his own father dying and defenseless, rejoicing in the hope—which Achilles already knows to be deluded—that he may yet see his son alive. Priam dresses himself in the emotions summoned by this thought, soliciting pity in the name of grief.

The power of his appeal is that it arouses not just grief but also "a *deep desire / to grieve*" (emphasis added), even for a father who remains alive.

---

30. Heinze affirms that "there was no single earlier version of the *Sack of Troy* which was regarded as canonical to the extent that any deviation would meet with disapproval" (5); of Priam's death in particular he comments, "[Neoptolemus] himself drags the old man in the most brutal manner to the altar . . . as if to butcher him for a sacrifice. Here Virgil goes further than any of our other accounts" (26). Williams notes that "the tradition of the murder of Priam by Pyrrhus," though not in Homer, "was in cyclic epic, and occurs in Euripides," as well as being depicted on vases (*The Aeneid of Virgil, Books 1–6* 250). It is always possible that Virgil had a non-Homeric source for the scene, if such material from the epic cycle of Troy stories survived late enough among the Alexandrian school; but it remains unrepresented in Homer, and Virgil would have followed the Alexandrians in regarding material from the epic cycle as non-Homeric. (My thanks to Lillian Dougherty for advice on this point.)

Achilles' sorrow looks back to Patroclus and forward to himself, the object of his father's still imaginary grief. Through this roundabout path, Achilles finds his way to an unacknowledged desire, the urge to grieve for his own fate. This fusion of sadness and longing leads to the delicate gesture with which Achilles loosens the suppliant's embrace of his knees. Against the tender dignity of Achilles' touch, Priam convulsed at his feet seems even more nakedly abandoned to emotion. This emotion is at once strikingly masculine—circling through imaginary identifications between father and son, father and father, father and lover—and strikingly fluid. It joins the two men to each other, momentarily breaking down barriers too great to be removed, and it does so by joining them to the dead through a series of displacements, winding loss upon loss. In this way Achilles, who could not pity Hector, can feel Priam's grief. The fluency of this emotion is captured in the mingling of the two men's voices, a shared sobbing that rises and falls rhythmically "throughout the house."

Since Virgil has no corresponding scene, Johnson's description of the *Aeneid* makes it a poem whose heart, paradoxically, lies elsewhere. This seems intuitively right; the Homeric episode resonates throughout Virgil's poem. Priam's plea "remember your own father!" springs to the lips of many dying warriors in books 10–12, including Turnus; but their pleas for mercy, unlike Priam's, fall on deaf ears, for Aeneas is reliving the wrath of Achilles after the death of Patroclus, not his divinely willed reconciliation with Priam. Instead, the meeting and embrace between bitter enemies is displaced, dismantled, and distributed into repeated missed encounters.

Ironically, the episode most closely modeled on Priam's embassy to Achilles is that of Aeneas' journey to Arcadia seeking alliance with Evander. This scene duplicates the structure of displaced and circling identifications that join Priam and Achilles in a single emotion, but it disguises what Homer's scene makes so clear—the origin of these emotions in mourning and the wish to mourn. Evander sees in Aeneas a memory of his youthful infatuation with Anchises, and this reawakening of *iuuenali amore* (8.163) in an old man becomes the emotional basis for the pact between Trojans and Arcadians. Aeneas approaches his diplomatic objective circumspectly, reviewing legends of their common descent from Atlas and declaring that this is why he has come in person rather than sending delegates. In response, Evander personalizes the meeting quite passionately, recalling how as a boy he burned to accost Anchises and clasp his hand. He approached (*accessi*, line 165), and led Anchises eagerly (*cupidus*), but also with a sense of longing, into the city. Pallas, who has inherited one of the parting gifts Anchises left, is meanwhile conceiving the same kind of longing admiration for Aeneas.

This pattern has each figure ardently seeking *something else* in and through the masculine other to whom his desire is addressed. Evander seeks Anchises in Aeneas, loving the father in the son. Pallas, too, admires in Aeneas what Evander once admired in Anchises—beauty, strength, and command. But these qualities take added luster from fame, for what *both* see in the warriors they admire is the glorified image of legendary heroism to which they themselves aspire: *o lux Dardaniae, spes o fidissima Teucrum, / quae tantae tenuere morae?* This repetition of filial desire, wrapped around a central absence by memory and fantasy, knots the bond between the two clans as surely as it bound Achilles and Priam in a moment of common sorrow.

Virgil portrays the meeting of Aeneas with the Arcadians as a texture of missed encounters, but he suppresses the deeper loss around which these circles of admiration revolve—disguising his recourse to book 24 of the *Iliad* much as Cacus conceals his theft of Hercules' cattle by holding their tails and pulling them backward, "traces of passage thus reversed" (*uersisque uiarum / indiciis raptor,* 8.210–11). But Evander's pact with Aeneas, like Achilles' reconciliation with Priam, is woven through with the sorrow of an imagined filial sacrifice. Evander's parting words to Pallas nod toward this fantasy by anticipating his death: "Fortune, if you threaten some black day, / Now, now, let me break off my bitter life / While all's in doubt, while hope of what's to come / Remains uncertain, while I hold you here, / Dear boy, my late delight, my only one" (*sin aliquem infandum casum, Fortuna, minaris, / nunc, nunc o liceat crudelem abrumpere uitam, / dum curae ambiguae, dum spes incerta futuri, / dum te, care puer, me sola et sera uoluptas, / complexu teneo,* 8.578–82). This passionate embrace, so clearly poised against Aeneas' futile attempt in book 6 to clasp the ghost of Anchises, draws the father's wish for death from the fantasy of his son's destruction. Enfolding the beloved son in the shadow of this mutual death, the embrace draws the meeting with Evander toward the epic's primal scene. By giving Pallas to Aeneas, Evander is, in effect, sacrificing him to the god of war.[31]

The *Aeneid*'s primal scene inhabits book 8 as the unconscious structure of its profoundly masculine passions. In a sense, the Homeric episode of Priam's visit to Achilles is divided between these two moments in Virgil, for the loss veiled in the meeting with Evander is isolated and intensified in the unspeakable ritual of Priam's courtyard. There the child of Achilles reenacts his father's victory, once again killing Priam's son before the king's horrified gaze, but now the killing has moved *inside* the walls of the

---

31. Evander's address to Pallas as "beloved boy, my late and only pleasure" (*cara puer, mea sera et sola uoluptas,* 8.581) matches the *aqedah*'s threefold formula, "Your son, your only son Isaac, whom you love." Cf. Levenson 127.

city, inside the royal palace—indeed, to the very altar—and it is followed immediately by the death of the father, his strength pathetically unequal to his mythic status. The repressed Homeric memory that Virgil "recovers" in this scene delineates the inner logic of empire as a destruction of the father in the son and of the kingdom in the father. The episode is unspeakable, *infandum,* in a special sense, then, because it renders visible this unresolvable contradiction, which persists in the emotional knots that bind men to each other in passionate mourning. Virgil treats Priam's embassy to Achilles for the body of Hector as a kind of "screen memory" for this traumatic scene, but he also reconstructs the repressed memory directly—taking care to link the two scenes when Priam tries to shame Pyrrhus by invoking his father's mercy.

The difference—and the link—between these two scenes is that between a living horror and the sorrow which follows, a sorrow expressed not only in grief but also in "the deep / desire to grieve." By withholding the embassy to Achilles, keeping it always half present to his narrative but never fully there, Virgil manages to sustain the ambiguous passage from sorrow to desire throughout much of the *Aeneid*. Often, too, he reverses it, foreshadowing unrealized sorrows in the quickenings of desire, as he does in Evander's last embrace of Pallas.

This particular foreshadowing begins when Pallas first encounters Aeneas and is "struck by that far away great name" (*obstipuit tanto percussus nomine,* 8.121). *Obstipiscere,* astounded or struck with amazement, carries also the sense of receiving a blow, reinforced by *percussus,* a beating or striking. Fitzgerald's translation imports a magnifying haze around the name; he nicely captures the sense of something at once distant, almost insubstantial, yet potent enough to strike a blow. Virgil's diction lends more force to the impact, anticipating the wound that will come to Pallas in battle. The implications of this line reach into book 9, where Apollo congratulates Ascanius on his first kill in battle with the words "Blessed be / Your new-found manhood, child" (*macte noua uirtute, puer,* 9.641). The deliberate paradox of the line is stressed, as commentators have often noticed, by its juxtaposition of the terms at stake: *uirtute, puer.*[32] Numanus Remulus has been taunting the Trojans by calling them women, and Ascanius, whose manhood is explicitly in question throughout books 9 and 10, "could not abide the man" (*non tulit Ascanius,* 9.622).

Apollo stresses that by killing Numanus, Ascanius *becomes* a man. But his language implies more: the vocative *macte* is a form of the adjective *mactus,* glorified or honored, and both are linked to the verb *mactare,*

32. See, for example, O'Hara, *True Names* 221.

which has homonymous forms that are almost antithetical in meaning: to
magnify, honor, glorify—or to slay, smite, afflict, or punish.[33] Ascanius,
who gains manhood by smiting Numanus, is himself smitten with honor,
infatuated with the heroic ideal, just as Pallas was struck by the greatness
of Aeneas' name. In this mirroring system, the blow that magnifies the
boy returns upon him. Men and gods conspire to protect Ascanius from
this blow—Apollo's next words order him withdrawn from battle—but
the blow returns upon his delegate, for the withdrawal of Ascanius clears
the way for Pallas to thrust in.[34]

This system of analogies is extended when Aeneas confronts an excruci-
ating image of himself in the death of Lausus:

> But seeing the look
> On the young man's face in death, a face so pale
> As to be awesome, then Anchises' son
> Groaned in profound pity. He held out
> His hand as filial piety, mirrored here,
> Wrung his own heart.

> *At uero ut uultum uidit morientis et ora,*
> *ora modis Anchisiades pallentia miris,*
> *ingemuit miserans grauiter dextramque tetendit,*
> *et mentem patriae subiit pietatis imago.*
> (10.821–24)

Lausus is a mirror for Aeneas, as the anadiplosis of *ora, / ora* suggests, because both are images of filial piety (Aeneas, tellingly, is designated as *An-
chisiades,* "Anchises' son"). Anchises' son offers the dying Lausus his hand
in a more poignant version of the missed encounter glimpsed so often in
the poem.

This moment sums up and comments on a series of linked passages: Aeneas' first words, envying those who died at Troy *before their fathers' eyes;*
his response to the murals at Carthage; his witnessing of the scene in
Priam's palace, of the war games practiced by the Trojan boys, and of the
carvings in Apollo's temple; his own subordination to death, which makes
him *tantae pietatis imago;* the images of filial sacrifice he beholds in Elysium; and the emotional resonance of his encounter with Evander and

33. As mentioned previously, *mactare* is the verb used to describe Laocoön's sacrifice of a
bull at Neptune's altar in book 2.

34. Numanus Remulus is another of the poem's bridegroom warriors, having just married
Turnus' sister; when Turnus kills Pallas and takes the baldric ornamented with slain bride-
grooms, one of the many implications of this moment is that he is taking revenge for the
death of his brother-in-law.

Pallas in Arcadia. One thing these scenes share is their power to "wring the heart."

Even as he exploits this power, Virgil subjects it to unsparing analysis, tracing the pleasures of his own narrative back through sorrow and pathos to their origins in trauma. We have seen the deliberate ambiguity of Aeneas' and Anchises' response to the procession of Roman worthies. Dido responds to Aeneas' tale of horrors at the banquet in Carthage with a similar mixture of pleasure and pain:

> When the day waned she wanted to repeat
> The banquet as before, to hear once more
> In her wild need the throes of Ilium,
> And once more hung on the narrator's words.

> *nunc eadem labente die conuiuia quaerit,*
> *Iliacosque iterum demens audire labores*
> *exposcit pendetque iterum narrantis ab ore.*
> (4.77–79)

Dido's hunger for the narrative repetition of Troy's suffering must be attributed partly to the aura of melancholy intensity the tale imparts to its teller, Aeneas, and partly to the intervention of Cupid (who comes, not accidentally, in filial disguise). Dido falls in love with the same mingled figure we encounter everywhere in the poem, "the image of so much piety," concentrated in Aeneas as both father and son. Here as elsewhere, Virgil is representing and commenting on the pathos of this figure: *Si te nulla mouet tantae pietatis imago,* says the Sibyl to Charon, "If the image of so much piety moves you not at all" (6.405). At such moments the poet acknowledges his own narrative as yet another repetition of the pleasure and horror bound up together in the primal scene. What we admire, he seems to say, what we love and long to repeat, is an image of terrible suffering.

Love therefore comes to Dido the way glory comes to Pallas, as a wound. The simile comparing her to a doe struck by a hunter's arrow is among the most celebrated passages of the poem; in book 10, as Aeneas avenges the death of Pallas, we read of a very different wound that is, nevertheless, strangely similar. Having slain Tarquinus while he pleads vainly for mercy, Aeneas speaks "from his pitiless heart" (*inimico pectore,* 10.556):

> "Lie there now, fearsome as you are. No gentle
> Mother will ever hide you in the earth
> Or weight your body with a family tomb.

> Either you stay here for the carrion birds
> Or the sea takes you under, hungry fishes
> Nibble your wounds."

> *"istic nunc, metuende, iace. non te optima mater*
> *condet humi patrioque onerabit membra sepulcro:*
> *altibus linquere feris, aut gurgite mersum*
> *unda feret piscesque impasti uulnera lambent."*
> (10.557–60)

The hunger of these fish, nibbling the wounds, offers a disturbing analogy for Dido's "wild need" to be wounded again and again, for the pleasure with which Aeneas feeds on the murals in Juno's temple (*pictura pascit inani,* 1.464), and for the love of glory ignited in him by the procession of the unborn dead in Elysium. But it is also, more immediately, a terribly evocative image for the pleasure Aeneas takes in his cruelty, feeding his pitiless heart on the wounds of others, repeating in them the wound Pallas suffered. *Cur haec vulnera cerno?* Virgil's analysis shows how the desire for glory and the hunger for revenge mirror each other like Aeneas and Lausus, the boy he must disembowel before "filial piety, mirrored here" can wring his own heart.

### Inextricabilis Error

If the *Aeneid,* like its hero, feeds endlessly on pathos in the wake of horror, does this mean that Virgil's answer to the question of Rome's being-in-history is negative? The poem delineates a sacrificial imaginary within whose *inextricabilis error* we see Roman history trapped. But does the delineation itself remain similarly trapped? Is the *Aeneid* lost in its own labyrinth? Virgil's consistent attention to the function of *witnessing* and to the structure of the gaze suggests that the answer to this question cannot come from the poem itself but only from its readers.[35] So long as we regard it from within the imperial gaze, the poem will continue to be at once Virgil's child and our progenitor, begetting critical offspring that, like Bowra and Lewis, uncritically repeat the language of sacrifice, whether dressed out as a social ideal, as the more personal virtue of "maturity," or as an unanalyzed "historicism" with a retrospective gaze constructing the

---

35. Barchiesi asserts, "More than any other ancient poet Virgil stresses the importance of the viewing subject in the construction of visual meaning" (275). The analogy basic to ekphrasis would extend this point to the reading or listening subject, as well.

past as a story of how the modern came to be.[36] That this historicism considers itself anti-imperialist is an irony worthy of Virgil. Nietzsche's meditation on history (also *intempestus*) focuses its closing exhortation on the Virgilian topos of the *puer senex,* recast now as the "greybeard child" of modern historical education.[37] The proximate target of this polemic is Hegel's philosophy of history, but its more distant target is Virgil, who invented the form of historical narration taken over by Hegel's dialectic. Virgil also, however, provides the language of Nietzsche's critique; at the origin of imperial historicism he has already measured its cost, already created terms Nietzsche can employ more than two thousand years later to resume Virgil's unfinished deconstruction of its narrative form.

Virgil's achievement, then, is not to have escaped the labyrinth but to have objectified it from within, "questioning the Augustan regime and its party line," as Quint puts it, "*from the inside* and in its own terms" (53). There are different ways of repeating a primal scene. Virgil does not simply show it and repeat it: he expresses the forms and motives of its repetition. To do this is to locate a viewpoint neither inside nor outside the spectacle itself, but somehow at its edge or border. In this way Virgil's text affords it readers a position like that of Aeneas on the rooftop: we may turn away, shuddering, only to repeat what we have just seen, but because Aeneas on the rooftop, turning

---

36. The point is widely attested. Kennedy puts it well: "This Virgilian meditation on 'utterance' raises the possibility that any attempt to order the past in relation to the present, to say 'this is how it was,' by virtue of its narrative structure incorporates, albeit at a level that may escape our attention, the claim 'this is how it was-to-be'" (149). A further example of the poem's capacity to prefigure criticism and historical argument may be found in Griffin's introduction to *The Oxford History of the Roman World:*

> The "way of the ancestors" (*mos maiorum*) possessed a great moral force, and within the family, at least in the upper class, the father enjoyed a degree of power over his sons, even when they were grown men, which astonished the Greeks, and which is reflected in many stories of fathers who put their own sons to death and were admired for doing so. It is not difficult to imagine the stress produced in Rome by such pressures, and it is tempting to connect it with the double Roman obsession, on the one hand with parricide, and on the other with *pietas,* dutiful behavior to parents, the archetype of which was the figure of Aeneas, founder of Rome, carrying his old father on his shoulders out of burning Troy. The anxiety engendered by such conflicts within the psyche, issuing in restless energy, might be part of the explanation for that astonishing fact, which seemed to the Romans themselves to be explicable only by constant divine favour: that this city, not particularly well sited or obviously well endowed, conquered the world. (4–5)

Note that in this passage the modern historian first recognizes filial sacrifice as the logical expression of extreme patriarchy, then moves by way of a broadly psychoanalytic model of group dynamics to a deep ambivalence toward the figure of the patriarch, which emerges in a "double . . . obsession" with parricide and *pietas,* the temptation to kill the father or to submit to him so thoroughly that filial obedience becomes an aspect of religious veneration. Finally, the psychoanalytic model concludes by retracing the path marked out by Virgil: linking filial sacrifice *causally* to the advent of world empire.

37. I return to this point in chapter 6.

away shuddering only to repeat what he has just seen, *is itself part of what we have seen,* we may be able to imagine an alternative response.

In reaching toward this threshold of representation, Virgil's poem goes beyond celebrating triumph, or even mourning loss, to record the limits of its own commemorative effort. Even when losses are remembered, something about them may escape commemoration; as Freud famously puts it in his definition of melancholy, the patient "knows *whom* he has lost but not *what* he has lost in him" ("Mourning and Melancholia" 245). The *Aeneid* does not always know what it has lost, but it does reserve traces of its neglect for recognition by future witnesses.

Virgil's account of Daedalus in book 6 makes explicit the contrast between losses that are represented, remembered, and mourned, and those so deeply buried that they remain unexpressed. Just before the passage describing the carvings in Apollo's temple, we read of the artist's escape from Crete:

> They say
> That Daedalus, when he fled the realm of Minos,
> Dared to entrust himself to stroking wings
> And to the air of heaven—unheard-of path—
> On which he swam away to the cold North.

> *Daedalus, ut fama est, fugiens Minoia regna*
> *praepetibus pennis ausus se credere caelo*
> *insuetum per iter gelidas enauit ad Arctos.*
>                                        (6.14–16)

Daedalus escapes the realm of Minos, but not his destiny as a sacrificer of sons. Putnam remarks that "by steering a course toward the chill Bears, Daedalus saved himself from the fate of Icarus whose wings melted as he drew too near the sun's heat" ("Daedalus" 177). Icarus, however, is not mentioned: "both Daedalus within this initial segment of the narrative and the narrator expounding his tale, seem in different senses careless— and leave the reader thus far unaware—that more than one person was involved in this strange itinerary." The passage thus tempts a reader to cross the *inremeabilis unda* (the irretraceable wave) with Daedalus, repeating his neglect of Icarus, yet all the while Virgil's language is *marking* the boy's absence in its description of Daedalus.[38]

---

38. In the word *praepetibus,* for example, Putnam discerns multiple ironies: "The reader, wondering why the narrator does not have Daedalus here include Icarus in his daring, sees *praepes* as 'well-omened' (at least for Daedalus!), as 'flying directly ahead' (without a concern for the tragic events occurring behind?), and as 'lofty' (unlike Icarus who, after rising too high, fell into the sea?)" (177). Significantly, when Putnam reprints this essay in *Virgil's*

Putnam sees the reference to Androgeos and the annual sacrifice of Athenian youths as continuing a theme covertly introduced with the conspicuous forgetting of Icarus, "the theme of sons killed or sacrificed" (178). Since it was the sun that destroyed Icarus and it is Apollo, the sun god, whom Daedalus honors—first by dedicating his wings, then by erecting the temple—the death of Icarus looks in retrospect like an unintended sacrifice to the god. Is not this the thought, lurking unarticulated in the details of the narrative, that Daedalus cannot bear to confirm by including his son among the temple carvings?

When Icarus is apostrophized at the end of the passage, the reader who *has* neglected him will be caught short:

> In that high sculpture you, too, would have had
> Your great part, Icarus, had grief allowed.
> Twice your father had tried to shape your fall
> In gold, but twice his hands dropped.

> *tu quoque magnam*
> *partem opere in tanto, sineret dolor, Icare, haberes.*
> *bis conatus erat casus effingere in auro,*
> *bis patriae cecidere manus.*
>
> (6.30–33)

The passage reenacts the father's belated recognition, but more than that, it links his forgetting to the failure of representation: the hands of the grieving father fall *like Icarus*, forced to relive the fate they cannot fashion. (Compare Virgil's own failure to complete line 340 of book 3 by providing an explicit reference to Astyanax.) Lines 32 and 33 insist that Daedalus' failure as an artist repeats his failure as a father: not only does *cecidere* repeat *casus* (both are forms of *cadere*, to fall), but also, the fall of the artist's hands itself happens twice—and we are told twice, the word *bis* repeated emphatically in the initial position of each line.

None of this can appear to Aeneas: the lines on Daedalus' flight come before the description of the temple and are addressed directly to the reader, while the lines addressed to Icarus are cast as contrary to fact because they name what is not there for Aeneas to see. In Juno's temple at Carthage—the poem's first ekphrastic set piece, paralleled here—Aeneas, gazing on "empty images" (1.645), was able to *see himself* while remaining invisible. Here the reverse happens: his own reflection in Icarus remains invisible to Aeneas—but that is revealed to us. Icarus, then, by

---

*Aeneid*, he comments, "I would now stress still more how its details help clarify the problematical relationships between fathers and sons that run through the epic" (6).

virtue of not being there, is not only an image of Aeneas himself as already dead; he is also an image of this loss as itself lost on Aeneas. But if Aeneas refuses to know his own emptiness, Virgil never does; the *Aeneid* does not lose track of its hero's losses. Their record is present in the spectacle of the boys' troop, where the simile of the Cretan Labyrinth defines not only what Aeneas and the other onlooking fathers see, but also what they do *not* see. The loss they repeat but do not recognize inheres in the labyrinth of their own gaze, which constitutes them no less than their sons. Virgil's simile objectifies this structure brilliantly in the maneuvers of the boy warriors lost in the maze of their fathers' admiration.

The logic of the passage on Daedalus should force us, though, to ask again what losses escape Virgil's poem. A definitive answer is out of the question (there is no omniscient gaze), but attention to gender lets us discern one set of traces that is carried forward by the text without being represented in it. I have argued that filial sacrifice sustains the peculiarly displaced and misrecognized homoeroticism of patriarchal masculinity. It seems to me that the *Aeneid* does this as well: it remains erotically attached not just to death but to the imaginary figures of the dead father and the dying son.

Aeneas takes up the gaze of imperial history not only in the place of death but also in the company of his dead father, who has presided *in absentia* over the poem's first half. Anchises dies just before the storm at sea that opens book 1, but books 2 and 3 recount his wanderings with Aeneas, from the fall of Troy to his death on the island of Sicily. Book 4, the Dido episode, is framed by recollections of this death, which closes the inset narrative at the end of book 3 and is commemorated in the games that take up book 5. Near the end of book 4 and again near the end of book 5, Anchises visits Aeneas in dreams, calling him forward on his quest and summoning him to the underworld. When Aeneas then descends to Avernus in book 6, he is responding to a desire imparted by his dead father. The dreams that have drawn him there suggest that he may in some sense be descending into his dream *of* the dead father; the underground setting hints that he has descended into the grave. There he beholds the patriarchal body in its historical extension, identified with a future already past and with the already-dead sons in whom it appears. Anchises fades from his son's embrace, "fugitive as a dream" (6.702), thus repeating the dream that had ended with Aeneas crying, "Who can forbid you to be held by me?" (*aut quis te nostris complexibus arcet?* 5.742). The repetition of this missed embrace suggests in yet another way that the underworld vision in book 6 is a dream—it suggests, indeed, that whatever Aeneas yearns for is as insubstantial as the dead, *tenuis sine corpore uitas* (literally, "faint lives without bodies," 6.292).

It is tempting to identify this lost object of desire with the phantasmic body of patriarchy, whose funeral pyre devours Troy in book 2. But Virgil complicates these equations, for the motif of the missed encounter begins in book 1 with the disappearance of Venus, who fades from her son's sight just as he recognizes her, and continues in book 2 with Creusa, even more deeply lost than Anchises. When Aeneas tries three times to embrace his father's shade in Elysium, he is reenacting his effort to clasp the shade of Creusa: lines 701–2 of book 6 repeat verbatim lines 793–94 of book 2. Then, too, his desire seemed responsive only to death: Aeneas had few enough thoughts for Creusa *until* she was lost, but then he wanted to plunge back into the flames of Troy to find her, like Orpheus in search of Euridice. This whole scene, however, is subsequently lost to the poem, for when Aeneas does visit the underworld Creusa is not there. Ascanius still remembers her in book 9, but the narrative centered on Aeneas has forgotten her already in book 4: we hear a great deal about Dido's devotion to her dead husband, Sychaeus, but nothing about Creusa, there or in book 6, despite the repetition of two complete lines. The woman Aeneas encounters in the underworld is Dido; the shade that slides from his arms is Anchises.

Book 6 of the *Aeneid* looks back to book 11 of the *Odyssey*, but Odysseus summons the shades of Teiresias *and* of his mother, Antikleía. Teiresias gives the prophecy on which Anchises' vision of posterity is modeled, but the ghost Odysseus seeks vainly to embrace is that of his mother. Virgil has substituted the father loved in loss for the ghosts of wife and mother, leaving Creusa, and behind her Antikleía, as the objects whose loss slips away from the poem in its preoccupation with dying fathers and sons. Virgil also omits the pageant of women's souls witnessed by Odysseus. He masculinizes the episode strikingly; at the same time, he makes the souls even less substantial than they were in Homer. Homer's shades, though shadowy and dreamlike, want to drink blood; Odysseus holds them at bay with a sword, letting one at a time drink and then speak. Virgil's shades have no such appetite, and the moments when they threaten or are threatened with the sword turn out to be mockery. Through the device of retroactive prophecy, Virgil historicizes the scene; through the highly selective way he remembers Homer, he renders it at once masculine and insubstantial. It is as if these transformations were all aspects of a single process, one that traces imperial history back to a melancholy, profoundly masculine desire for the historical father.

Aeneas has often been described as passionless, but what looks like a simple absence or blocking of the emotions we expected to see may express the force of a passion we are slower to recognize, an intensely militaristic homoeroticism, bound always to a masculine object apprehended in death.[39] Lyne, noting Aeneas' failure in book 2 to be moved by his wife's appeal, remarks that he is moved instead by "his father's response to a dynastic Iulus, Iulus designated by an omen as a king" (185). This moment foreshadows the men's responses to Marcellus and the vision of Roman history in book 6. In a sense the crown of light bathing Ascanius differs little from its apparent opposite, the cloud that darkens Marcellus' brow. It may not signify that Ascanius is destined for premature death, but it does signal that he is already loved *as* the dead ancestor he will become, illuminated by a glow cast backward from the future—specifically, from the comet that appeared just after the death of Julius Caesar, "commonly supposed to be Caesar's deified soul."[40] Virgil's poem, obsessed with the pathetic loveliness of its dying boys, seems unable to detach itself from this structure of emotion. Yet it manages to objectify and even to critique the structure, and in this way builds into itself a distance which *might* become the first step toward realizing an alternative.

Between Aeneas' failed attempt to embrace his father's shade and the procession of Roman worthies in book 6, there is a passage modeled on Plato that has sometimes been mistaken for Virgil's metaphysic. In it Anchises describes how the souls of the unborn "wish re-entry into bodies" (*in corpora uelle reuerti,* 751). They do so, apparently, only because the waters of Lethe have left them *immemores,* "unmemoried" (750)—otherwise they would remember what embodiment entails, the likelihood that they will be "poisoned or clogged / By mortal bodies, their free essence dimmed / By earthliness and deathliness of flesh" (*noxia corpora tardant / terrenique hebetant artus moribundaque membra,* 731–32). Even after the body's death the soul retains the "inveterate" imprint of worldly distresses, purged away slowly in the afterlife. In this sardonic vision, immortal souls are mirror images of living beings, yearning to embrace their own death because they cannot retain the memory that would free them from the desire for such an object.

More specifically, these souls mirror the poem's most degraded image of filial sacrifice. Mezentius is the quintessential "bad father," the unworthy figure for whom Lausus, blinded by filial piety, rushes to his death (10.811–12). Mezentius is also a tyrant so vicious that his own people have driven him out and now seek his death, allying themselves with Aeneas. His crimes are perhaps the most hideous detail in the poem:

39. Putnam discusses the eroticism of the relation between Pallas and Aeneas in chapter 2 of *Virgil's Aeneid.*

40. Fairclough, note to 8.680–81, where Virgil alludes to the comet again in his description of Octavius at Actium. This is the pattern of imagery alluded to by Statius in his reference to "starbright Ascanius," discussed in the introduction.

> He would even couple carcasses
> With living bodies as a form of torture.
> Hand to hand and face to face, he made them
> Suffer corruption, oozing gore and slime
> In that wretched embrace, and a slow death.

> *mortua quin etiam iungebat corpora uiuis,*
> *componens manibusque manus atque oribus ora,*
> *tormenti genus, et sanie taboque fluentis*
> *complexu in misero longa sic morte necabat.*
> (8.485–88)

Yet even more striking than the nauseating detail of this passage is the precision with which it echoes and parodies both Aeneas' desire to embrace his father's shade and the immortal souls' eagerness to take on bodies. The rotting corpse poisons the living body just as the living body poisons the immortal soul, and this vividly rendered torment shows what it means—literally—to "embrace" death. When Mezentius himself dies, we glimpse the darkest secrets of filial sacrifice as an erotic disposition. On learning of his son's death, he indicts himself with a rhetorical question that reverberates through the entire poem: "Am I, your father, / Saved by your wounds, by your death do I live?" (*tuane haec genitor per uulnera seruor / morte tua uiuens?* 10.848–49). His last request to Aeneas, as he faces the sword's edge with open eyes (*haud inscius,* literally "not at all ignorant," 10.907), offers an unforgettable image of the filial bond. For him it will be an embrace in which father and son are joined together only as each embodies the other's death: *me consortem nati concede sepulcro,* "allow me room / In the same grave with my son" (906).[41]

Virgil has looked with the eyes of Mezentius, *haud inscius.* He knows the losses Roman masculinity can embrace, and writes their poem of mourning. He knows too, and records his awareness, that something else he cannot name slips beyond his grasp.

---

41. S. J. Harrison notes that "the desire for burial together with a loved one was a commonplace as old as Homer" (*Aeneid 10* 283); my reading assumes that in context, this commonplace takes on added significance.

... through the ghost of the unquiet father
the image of the unliving son looks forth.
—James Joyce, *Ulysses* 9.380–81

## A Thing of Nothing

Sometime around 1610, just thirteen years before Anthony Van Dyck painted his portrait of Filippo Cattaneo, we find the familiar topic of the *puer senex* invoked in Shakespeare's *The Winter's Tale*. King Leontes of Sicilia has been playing host for nine months to his boyhood friend Polixenes, the king of Bohemia. In the play's second scene, Polixenes has just announced his intention to depart. By a fateful coincidence, Leontes' queen, Hermione, is about to give birth to their second child, meaning that the term of her pregnancy has coincided with that of Polixenes' visit. When Polixenes resists the king's entreaty to stay on but then yields to Hermione, Leontes' suspicions are aroused. Watching the queen entertain his friend with a familiarity he finds unbearable, Leontes turns aside, seething with jealousy. In the passage that follows he talks partly to himself and partly to his son, Mamillius; shifting awkwardly between dialogue and asides, he draws the asides out into broken soliloquies. This uncertainty of address acts out the instability, for Leontes, of the boundary between father and son. Questions about this boundary are also the explicit content of the passage, for the king's suspicion of his queen registers immediately as doubt about his son's legitimacy: "Mamillius," he asks, "Art thou my boy?" (1.2.119–20).

This could be any father's question, a routine invitation to affirm the bond of affection. Leontes goes on in just such solicitous tones: "I'fecks, / Why, that's my bawcock. What? Has smutched thy nose?" (1.2.120–22). But his dark underthought surfaces repeatedly: "They say [the nose] is a copy out of mine"; "they say we are / Almost as alike as eggs. Women say so, / That will say anything" (1.2.122, 129–31). Leontes generates a whole series of jocose nicknames that magnify the child beyond his years ("bawcock," "captain," "mine honest friend") or reduce him to the status of a morsel ("you wanton calf," "Most dear'st, my collop" [bit of flesh], "this kernel"). Sometimes he condenses both impulses into the same phrase ("sir page," "sweet villain," "This squash, this gentleman"). The king's friend Polixenes, speaking of his own young prince, echoes the faintly belligerent undertone of this patronizing address:

> If at home, sir,
> He's all my exercise, my mirth, my matter,
> Now my sworn friend, and then mine enemy;
> My parasite, my soldier, statesman, all.
> He makes a July's day short as December,
> And with his varying childness cures in me
> Thoughts that would thick my blood.
> (1.2.165–71)

Shakespeare unsettles the overfamiliar rhetoric of such fatherly affection by embedding it in several transactions. The mock rivalry between father and son plays against a latent rivalry between the two kings, while both relationships turn on the question of proximity to the queen: paddling palms, pinching fingers, whispering. Once Hermione comes under suspicion, both relationships break down because the dimension of proximity has turned sinister: when Polixenes (the friend so close he might be oneself) turns into a deadly rival for the queen, then Mamillius (the son who should be his father's copy) must be snatched from her presence. The "varying childness" that makes the little boy "now my sworn friend, and then mine enemy" may seem to offer only a token challenge, flattering the indulgent father. Yet by invoking this language just as the relations that sustain it are turning murderous, Shakespeare suggests how volatile the underlying tensions may be. All the elements so innocently present in Polixenes' speech—the hint of darkness in "thoughts that would thick my blood," the alternations from friend to enemy, July to December, child to statesman—have specific counterparts in Leontes' distracted inspection of Mamillius. But the thoughts that thicken Leontes' blood keep breaking in on the rhetoric of indulgent fatherhood like a subtext that will not stay hidden.

At such moments in the plays, Shakespeare sets forth vividly the system of relations in which an image like Van Dyck's *Filippo* is suspended. The points of view from which the portrait is painted and to which it is addressed are not only shown along with the boy; they are also thrown into crisis. In the present scene, Queen Hermione's pregnant body—charged and imposing, tense with imminent birth—silently dominates the stage, conditioning all that is said, heavy with meaning as well as with child. In representations like the portrait of Filippo or the *Tatler* passage about "little Jerry," the maternal body is twice removed, serving only as the unacknowledged ground of a perspective that is tacitly paternal. Shakespeare, by contrast, first pulls the father into the scene, and then—against the background of the mother's enlarged abdomen—stages the father's fraught and anxious demand to be copied.

In doing so the playwright lets us see yet another rivalry, that between himself and Hermione. Only the mother, whose art is nature and whose body is a competing "globe," can answer in the flesh the father's desire to be copied. But the playwright also lets us see how the mother's superiority can devastate the fatherhood it makes possible. All the while, as Leontes gazes on his son, Hermione's body mutely displays the connection to children that a father can never have. His connection is always nominal, legal, testimonial, and therefore speculative—in short, fatherhood is language. In a resonant *non sequitur*, Leontes redraws this distinction as a contrast between "signs" and "blood" when he forbids Hermione to come near Mamillius because "though he bears some signs of me, yet you have too much blood in him" (2.1.57–58). Words like *chastity* and *adultery* may *formulate* the difference on which fatherhood depends, but they cannot point it out. Even when the evidence includes physical resemblance, it remains a matter of conjecture, a difference that can only be witnessed, never seen.

In this system the queen's virtue, the prince's legitimacy, and the king's fatherhood are all one thing—or they are all nothing.[1] When Camillo, the king's loyal counselor, reproaches him for slandering the queen, Leontes harps on this word as if it could annihilate the world:

> Is this nothing?
> Why then the world and all that's in't is nothing,
> The covering sky is nothing, Bohemia nothing,
> My wife is nothing, nor nothing have these nothings,
> If this be nothing.
>
> (1.2.292–6)

What would this ultimate "thing," on which the world depends, look like if we could see it? Can we even imagine the *body of paternity*? Within the

---

1. My argument in this chapter is indebted to Lacan's discussion of the scopic drive in *Four Fundamental Concepts* and his discussion of the phallus in "Desire"; see also Lacan, "Introduction."

culture of patrilineal patriarchy the answer must be no: fatherhood, to adapt a line from Iago, "is an essence that's not seen."[2] In a deeply ironic twist, this makes fatherhood equivalent to the female genitals, at least in the reductive terms that define sexual difference by the presence or absence of the penis. And there is ample evidence that in Elizabethan England, the female genitals were regarded (to echo Hamlet now) as "no thing." This logic supposedly reinforces the privilege of the phallus in male-dominant cultures, but it also returns to haunt this privilege in the contrast between the visible tumescence of motherhood and the irremediably verbal or symbolic status of fatherhood. As Hamlet also memorably remarks, " 'The king is a thing . . . Of nothing' " (4.3.26–28).

In *The Winter's Tale* Shakespeare demonstrates the reality of this "nothing," which takes on traumatic force as the missing cause of Leontes' madness precisely *because* it can neither exist nor be represented. In the words of Polixenes, "The King hath on him such a countenance / As he had lost some province, and a region / Lov'd as he loves himself" (1.2.368–70). Shakespeare's dramaturgical coup, which baffles most readers and has never quite been understood, is to have staged the paternal body's absence so precisely while lending it such devastating power. Like God, and according to a similarly inscrutable logic, Leontes seems to require his own son's death in order to substantiate his fatherhood, both in the sense of proving it beyond doubt and in the sense of providing it with a body. His much-debated madness, which short-circuits the canons of dramatic realism, comes into focus readily as a transposition of sacrificial logic into the dimension of psychology. "Apollo's angry," says Leontes on learning of his son's death, "and the heavens themselves / Do strike at my injustice" (3.2.146–47). But Apollo strikes at the father's injustice in the person of the son, and the father's remorse, as Stanley Cavell has shown, carries overtones of relief—as if what Leontes really meant were, "The heavens themselves do strike at my injustice—at last!"[3] It is only when the heavens finally strike that he can *see*, in the dead bodies of his wife and child, divine assurance that he really was a father after all.[4]

To pursue this knowledge in so relentlessly negative a form seems un-

2. For a brilliant reading of the play that reverses my emphasis on the visible by tracing the textual and historical relations of adultery and idolatry, see Lupton 175–218. Her discussion of "Christological and sacramental resonances" in the statue scene is especially apposite, although she places more emphasis than I am willing to do on "the play's rationalizing deflation of its carefully staged mystery" (216).

3. My argument is much indebted to Cavell's seminal analysis of the filial dynamic in this play.

4. Hermione is presumably not, in fact, dead when Leontes views what he takes to be her corpse, but this moment happens offstage, and the play equivocates as to whether Hermione is dead or in hiding during the years of her absence.

thinkable, much as the historical reality of child sacrifice has seemed un-
thinkable to archaeologists faced with its evidence. But what are the foun-
dational stories of Isaac and Christ about, if not the terrible necessity of
this knowledge for the system of patrilineal patriarchy? In Shakespeare this
logic begins to appear not as sacrificial ritual or narrative but as the subjective basis of masculine identity. Debora Shuger suggests how such a
translation may have occurred historically; she argues in *The Renaissance
Bible* that the Calvinist polemic which broke apart the early modern economy of sacrificial witnessing also worked hard to install this ruptured
economy as the internal dynamic of reformed selfhood. Such a conflicted
process should yield just what we find in Leontes—an *inherently traumatized* subject, whose fantasies translate the logic of ritual into the form of
pathology. When Janet Adelman, for example, explains Leontes' madness
as a defensive fantasy that negates birth, she is attributing to his madness
the same function, in the economy of the psyche, that Nancy Jay attributes to sacrifice in the economy of kinship relations.[5] Both stand in formal
opposition to childbirth.

But this analogy between sacrifice and psychosis is *only* formal. The relationship I propose in this chapter is also genealogical. How is a social
practice like ritual *transformed into* a subjective structure? Once again the
answer lies in the notion of an economy of witnessing, for in both early
modern *and* postmodern understandings of subjectivity, selfhood is
shaped by internalized versions of this economy. Lacan calls this internalized witness "the Gaze"; in this respect as in others, his thought echoes a
Christian (specifically, Augustinian) understanding of the human subject
as a creature whose innermost thoughts and feelings are the objects of
God's witness. Katharine Maus puts the traditional notion succinctly: for
Shakespeare and his contemporaries, she observes, "the structure of internal experience is thought necessarily to imply observation by a deity."[6]
The problem for Elizabethan England is that the ritual economy which
guarantees this witness has been shattered; all that remains to be internalized is its crisis. And so in *Hamlet,* for example, we find "observation by a
deity," which seems necessarily implied by the structure of internal experience, inescapably thrown into doubt by the theatricality of social experi-

5. Adelman 220–38; for Jay, see the introduction and chapter 1.

6. Maus, *Inwardness and Theater* 10–11 n. 33. While Protestantism arguably intensifies
this sense, it can be traced at least to Augustine. Nicholas of Cusa, in *De visione Dei* (1453),
pursues an Augustinian meditation on the invisibility of a God whose creatures exist only insofar as He beholds them. Beginning with the image of a painting with eyes that follow the
viewer around the room, Cusanus develops the thought that all creatures "exist by means of
Your [God's] seeing"; qtd. in Hopkins, *Dialectical Mysticism* 165.

ence. What was once ritual is now split between conscience and theater, and Hamlet struggles in vain to bring them together.

Shakespeare's plays look with fear and loathing (and some very dark laughter) at the historical destruction visited upon the sacrament of fatherhood. As drama, they submit this destruction to what we might call theatrical analysis. Not just in the content of his plays but above all in their dramaturgy, Shakespeare recognizes the central importance of performance, in all its senses, for the creation of selves and social roles. He grasps the historical novelty of the commercial theater as a scene of public witnessing made possible by the dismantling of ritually based social technologies. Finally, in the drama that embodies these recognitions he discovers how profoundly fatherhood depends on the modes his drama comes to displace. In the romances, and especially in *The Winter's Tale*, he extends Hamlet's quest for a theater of conscience in which father and son might encounter one another. He seeks in theatrical practice new ways of bearing witness to that ancient but newly vulnerable artifact called fatherhood.

The miraculous close of *The Winter's Tale* most fully enacts this desire for a theater of redemptive witnessing. Recent criticism has tended to stress the limitations of this vision, noting, for example, that the specifically *maternal* body, which triggers Leontes' madness, is absent when Hermione's statue comes to life.[7] In this miracle, pregnancy has been sublimated into the playwright's immaculate power of conception, leaving the female body split between a mother past childbearing and a prenuptial daughter. Such a transformation recovers fatherhood as symbolic *form* in the political body of the dynastic marriage, and as symbolic *function* in the regenerative potency of theatrical illusion.[8] Yet this reassertion of the paternal body as a dynastic and aesthetic symbol masks, even as it reenacts, its loss *as body*. Corporeally the father remains a thing of nothing.

In keeping with the logic of filial sacrifice, the play names this loss "Mamillius." "At the end of *The Winter's Tale*," writes Cavell, "a dead five- or six-year-old boy remains unaccounted for" (193). I cannot imagine accounting for such a thing, but it seems important to recognize that

7. Similarly, the play's seasonal rhythm jumps from winter to late summer, skipping over spring; see Lupton 199–202. My reading of the play has benefited considerably from Erickson 148–72; Adelman works hard to recuperate the maternal body's absence in the final scene but is not, finally, persuasive. See also Paster 278–79; Orgel, "Introduction" 77–79; and Traub 25–49.

8. The scene is aesthetically self-reflexive to a degree unusual even for Shakespeare; as Barkan has shown, it stages a rivalry in which sculpture is surpassed by theater. Enterline, in a strong reading of the play's revisionary engagement with Ovid, balances critical emphasis on Hermione's pregnancy by attending to the importance of women's speech (and silence); see *Rhetoric of the Body* 196–228.

the death of the royal heir is required not only by the king's madness but also by the dynastic plot, which merges the kingdoms *instead* of the kings. The plot opens a path to this merger by substituting Florizel, through marriage with Perdita, for the "little lost one" who will not be found. Mamillius, as the flesh-and-blood sign of Leontes' fatherhood, must die so that the patriarchal body can be reconstituted in the *corpus mysticum* of the dynastic union. The play's romance ending thus depends on a sacrificial economy, although this dependency is disguised by the masterful sleight of dramaturgy through which Shakespeare replaces the fatherly body's loss with the restoration of Hermione, purged of natural fertility and reborn through the triumph of theatrical illusion.

Shakespeare's concern with this sacrificial economy is apparent throughout his work, from the emphasis on father-son conflict and the killing of children in his earliest history plays to the carnival of infanticide in *Macbeth*. Virgil's *Aeneid* is specifically linked to this motif as early as *Titus Andronicus,* where (as Heather James observes) the Andronici "virtually claim the *Aeneid* as family history": "Titus," she notes, "has buried twenty-one of his 'five and twenty valiant sons, / Half of the number that King Priam had,' suggesting that he begets sons according to epic precedent and sacrifices them to the state."[9] The play opens with an act of human sacrifice cast as ancestral piety, and the increasingly baroque violence that follows spins out a cycle of revenge initiated by that ritual cruelty. In keeping with the deliberately outrageous decorum of the play, this proliferation of violence ends only after the ostensible villain, Aaron, has inverted Roman, Hebrew, and Christian piety by trading his own life to save his son.

The importance of Virgilian sacrifice to Shakespeare's dramaturgy is apparent once again in *Hamlet,* where the ghost of the dead king seems more than willing to sacrifice his living son in the name of revenge. The father's paternity is demonstrated by the son's performance of this familiar role—a point that may be obscured, at times, in Hamlet's ruminations, but one that is clear enough to Laertes, who bursts into the royal presence after Polonius is killed, declaring, "That drop of blood that's calm proclaims me bastard, / Cries cuckold to my father, brands the harlot / Even here between the chaste unsmirched brow / Of my true mother" (4.5.118–21). Laertes is the more Pyrrhus-like avenger; when Claudius asks, "What would you undertake / To show yourself indeed your father's son / More than in words?" (4.7.124–26), he answers without hesitation, "To cut his [Hamlet's] throat i' th' church."

---

9. See Heather James 49–55; I quote from 51 and 52, adjusting the citation from *Titus Andronicus,* for consistency's sake, to the Riverside text (1.1.79–80) from which I quote elsewhere.

For Hamlet, things are not so simple. To understand what is finally at issue for him (and for Shakespeare) in the performance of revenge, we must be prepared to see how, for Elizabethan England, the dilemmas of filial piety and revenge in classical epic are transvalued by the aftershocks of the Reformation. To establish a context for this discussion, I propose to glance not only at the debate over the Eucharist, but also at its discursive twin, the religious polemic against blasphemy, and at one of its historical consequences, the immolation of Protestant martyrs during the reign of Mary Tudor. My purpose is to frame the Reformation as an epochal disturbance in the history of witnessing, both as a social practice and as a symbolic economy. In this crisis, I argue, the late medieval economy of witnessing breaks down because the social practices that sustain it are dispersed by new technologies into different imaginary and material settings—among them, the commercial theater. The result is a crisis of sacrificial witnessing that is structurally parallel to the breakdown of *pietas* explored by Virgil in the *Aeneid*. This parallel, I suggest, complicates and intensifies the already powerful resonance of Priam's death scene for an Elizabethan audience. The notorious ambiguity of that scene in act 2 of *Hamlet* replicates the ambiguity of the religious martyrdoms that polarized the community of witness in Tudor England. Hamlet seems to apprehend this polarization of values as a problem of dramaturgy: how can he stage his own sacrifice so as to make its meaning unmistakable? It is the same problem Leontes confronts, but seen from the other side: how can the son display his filial truth in visible form? In their search for a common ground on which father and son might encounter and recognize one another, *Hamlet* and *The Winter's Tale* together enact a powerful and distinctive response to the early modern crisis of sacrificial witnessing—not only as an exemplary instance of these developments, but more crucially, as an extraordinary reflection upon them.

## Show Me the Body

In Shakespeare, the fatherly gaze that we find embodied in Steele's little Jerry or Van Dyck's Filippo—an essentially modern and secular formation—appears suspended against the background of an archaic sacrificial economy, one that seems forever to be rupturing in the wake of some great, unspecified historical trauma. Among the names by which we know this rupture is "the Reformation," the most familiar definition of which takes doctrinal disputes over the Communion ritual to be its central feature. In medieval and early modern culture the Mass is the preeminent instance of a symbolic transaction in which the body of a boy is presented to

a third party to substantiate the reality of fatherhood. Like the gospel narratives, the Eucharist is necessary because the transcendent Father of the New Testament has no body of his own. He achieves immanence only in, and as, the Son.

By the twelfth century in Europe, the consecration of the Host during Mass was beginning to emerge as a "second sacrament" distinct from Communion; the elevation of the host dates from this period. "By the thirteenth century," Carolyn Walker Bynum reports, "we find stories of people attending Mass only for the moment of elevation, racing from church to church to see as many consecrations as possible, and shouting at the priest to hold the host up higher" (*Holy Feast* 55). Theologians describe the Son's descent into the wafer as reenacting the Incarnation; "insistently," writes Bynum, "the host forced itself onto the senses of believers as flesh with firm boundaries" (62, 63).

However firm, of course, these boundaries were also subject to extraordinary metamorphoses, and in many of these Jesus takes female form. Bynum and other historians have explored the range of symbolic identifications his body sustains in the writings of female mystics, who used the cultural association of women with flesh to envision the suffering Jesus as female, and often maternal. Bynum goes so far as to speak of "the startling reversal at the heart of the Mass" in which God and priest, as food and preparer of food, become symbolically female (278–79). Such reversal of attributes is typical of religious symbolism and may lend itself to the critique of dominant practices. Yet as Bynum also observes, "Women's images [are] informed and made possible by the symbolic oppositions of the dominant theological tradition" (292–93). Such imagery does not always sustain the tradition from which it arises, but it does pad out the disembodied father with the values and capacities of women's bodies. If the priest can be seen as symbolically female in the pivotal moments of the Mass, then women may also represent themselves as symbolically priestlike—and they have done so, as Bynum has shown. But this asymmetrical reversal makes it easier as well to accept women's literal exclusion from the priesthood. In this respect such imagery may be compared to the *Vierges ouvrantes*, those "late medieval devotional objects in which the statue of Mary nursing her baby opens to show God inside" ("Body of Christ" 101). Their message might be paraphrased, "Our Bodies, Himself."

The action of the Mass in making God visible is mirrored with curious precision in the rhetoric of a very different cultural practice—that of blasphemy. References to the Eucharistic body and its members are the most common profanities in early modern English, and the polemic against them offers an explicit parallel to disputes over the nature of the Communion. Blasphemers routinely swear by God's blood, wounds, nails, and bones. These oaths belong to a class formed by adding nouns (with or without adjectives) to a version of the possessive "God's."[10] Many are simple, yeomanly expletives that pay their respects to the deity by taking the work of transgression seriously; such are earnest references to God's blood, death, dignity, heart, mercy, mother, passion, or wounds. Others, by contracting or distorting their terms, find offbeat ways to compound the offense of profanely invoking God's body. The *Oxford English Dictionary* (new ed.) lists eleven "minced forms" of the divine possessive, some of which dice it into a slang term for the penis (*Cods, Cocks*). Among the fifty-six nouns and adjectives the *OED* finds in such oaths are a number that seem similarly impertinent. Such would include references to God's foot, his eyelids, his guts, his hat, his lady, his malt, and perhaps (depending on how it is construed) his nails. There is even a group of "corrupt or fabricated" nouns that occur in no other contexts—words like *bodykin, pittikins,* and *sonties* (s.v. "God" II.14). A quaint oath like "Odd's bodykin," for example, first minces God's name into the common term for peculiarity, and then yokes it incongruously to his "little body."[11] Such expressions have something in common with the rhetoric of fatherly affection: a jocular mingling of the impulses to magnify, to diminish, and to take calculated liberties with the subject's dignity. Perhaps such oaths might be thought of as a displaced counterblast—a rhetoric of filial impertinence.

In a ritual economy such oaths are not just overly familiar, however—they are violent and genuinely obscene. Geoffrey Chaucer's Pardoner, describing the profanity of the rioters in his tale, echoes one of the popular commonplaces of fourteenth-century sermons:

> Hir othes been so grete and so dampnable
> That it is grisly for to heere hem swere,
> Oure blissed Lordes body they totere—
> Hem thoughte that Jewes rente hym noght ynough—
> And ech of hem at otheres synne lough.
> ("The Pardoner's Tale" 472–76)

Before the Reformation, this theology of oaths was by no means merely a trope used for vividness. This point is illustrated by a tale from Robert

---

10. For an extended catalogue of examples, see Swain; on the rhetorical motives of blasphemy, see Benveniste.

11. The etymology of *bodkin* and *bodykins* (or *bodikins*) is uncertain. *OED*, s.v. "God," cites Hamlet's oath "God's bodykins, man" (2.2.529), but does not define the word. Swain glosses it as a diminutive of *body* (33, 41), as do most modern editors of Shakespeare. In the Riverside edition, Evans follows typical practice by modernizing the spelling to *bodkin*. *OED*, s.v. "bodkin," does not record this usage.

Mannyng's *Handlyng Synne* (1303). A rich man given to swearing great oaths is lying alone in his sickbed when a woman comes before him weeping and carrying a bloody child:

> Of þe chyld þat she bare yn here armys
> Al to drawe were þe þarmys.
> Of handys, of fete, þe flesh of drawyn,
> Mouþ, eʒyn, & nose were al tognawyn,
> Bak and sydys were al blody.
> (lines 701–5)

Rising up in pity and alarm, the rich man asks who she is and who has mauled her child:

> "Þou," she seyd, "has hym so shent,
> And wyþ þyn oþys al to rent.
> Þus hast þou drawyn my dere chyld
> Wyþ þyn oþys, wykkyd & wyld.
> And þou makst me sore to grete
> Þat þou þyn oþys wylt nat lete.
> Hys manhede þat he toke for þe,
> Þou pynyst hyt, as þou mayst se.
> Þyn oþys doun hym more greuusnesse
> Þan al þe Iewys wykkydnesse.
> Þey pynyde hym onys & passyd away,
> But þou pynyst hym euery day."[12]
> (lines 711–22)

Superficially Mannyng's strategy in these passages resembles that of the Purdy photomontage discussed in chapter 1; the montage mocks the rhetoric of fatherly affection by embodying its trope with disconcerting literalness. Yet Mannyng fleshes his trope to different effect, for he conceives of the strategy not as literalizing a figure of speech but as portraying realistically the effects of a language of sacramental potency. His blasphemer's vision bears a stronger resemblance to the "proliferating Eucharistic miracles of the twelfth and thirteenth centuries—in which the host . . . turned visibly into Christ" (Bynum, *Holy Feast* 51).

In *The Anatomy of Swearing* Ashley Montagu cites instances of this motif as late as the 1540s in England. A verse pamphlet by Stephen Hawes titled *The Conversion of Swearers,* prefaced by an illustration of the bleeding Christ, revives the tale of the bloody child: "With awful realism," says Montagu, "Hawes . . . describes how the hands and feet of Christ

---

12. I cite the edition of Idelle Sullens, omitting superscript glosses that Sullens reproduces from the manuscripts. For the passages quoted, "þarmys," in line 702, carries the gloss "guttys" (from Bodley MS 415 and Harley MS 1701), and "grete," in line 715, carries the gloss "wepe" (from Bodley MS 415 only).

were being literally pierced anew and every member and portion of his body torn and lacerated by the imprecations of unheeding Christians" (128). A related and equally durable trope represents the material effects of swearing as butchery. The *Ayenbite of Inwit* (1340) says that swearers "break" the Lord's body "smaller than one doth swine in butchery"; nearly two centuries later Sir Thomas Elyot in *A Boke Named the Governour* (1531) disparages oaths that call on God's "glorious heart, as it were numbles chopped in pieces" (qtd. in Montagu 123, 128). *Numbles* is a butcher's term of art for innards chopped in preparation to be eaten.

This polemic sees oaths as a travesty of the Eucharist, a diabolical counterpart to the sacred reenactment of Christ's Crucifixion. Such a polemic had to change, however, once the shock value of confounding mystical and material bodies had been co-opted by Reformation apologists and turned back against the Eucharist itself. By 1560, Roger Hutchinson's *Image of God* offered a very different description of oaths as speech acts:

> You swearers and blasphemers which use to swear by God's heart, arms, nails, bowels, legs and hands, learn what these things signify, and leave your abominable oaths. For when thou swearest by God's heart, thou swearest by God's wisdom; when thou swearest by God's arms, thou swearest by Christ; when thou swearest by his hands or legs, thou swearest by his humanity; when thou swearest by his tongue and finger, thou swearest by the Holy Ghost; and swearing by his head thou swearest by his divine and blessed nature; and swearing by his hairs, thou abusest his creatures, by which thou art forbidden to swear. (qtd. in Montagu 135)

Theological conceptions of blasphemy thus mirror the central dispute over the Eucharist: a theory insisting on the real presence of Christ's body in oaths yields to a theory of "what these things signify."

As I suggested earlier, the transcendence of God the Father in the Gospels means that he has no material form other than the "little body" of his son. This body is little—not just a body, but a bodykin—in part because Jesus is imagined as a child, but also because his body, even in its fully grown and crucified form, stands in for the Father's "big" body, a mystical entity whose reality is otherwise unimaginable. This line of reasoning suggests that the medieval theology of blasphemy may contain its own ironic double, a symmetrical reversal that is distinct from the Reformation polemic. This double is made explicit in the ordinary denunciation of blasphemy from Chaucer's Pardoner ("Hem thought that Jewes rente hum nought ynough") to Thomas Becon's 1543 *Invective against Swearing*: "The Jews crucified Him but once, and then their fury ceased; but these wicked caitiffs crucify him daily with their unlawful oaths" (qtd. in Montagu 129). In this view the real function of blasphemy would be the same as that of the Eucharist: to transform the Crucifixion from a unique into an endlessly repeated event.[13]

Such a transformation is necessary because the historical duration of Christianity depends on the repeatability of its founding sacrifice, the cultural work of which is never finished. This is the work, as Elaine Scarry has argued, of lending substance to a God who cannot persist historically as an object of worship if he doesn't assume material form (181–243). The Crucifixion not only provides Him a body, it does so over and over again, for the Pardoner's drunkards are right: once was not enough. From this perspective, "The Tale of the Bloody Child" only appears to rebuke the blaspheming rich man. In fact it satisfies his implicit demand, which is the same as that of the crowds at Mass "shouting at the priest to hold the host up higher," and might be paraphrased "Show me the body!" In other words, the chastisement provoked by the rich man's oaths is an extra-ritual occasion for the presentation of God's little body. This performs a cultural function that seems, in Shakespeare's plays, to be in crisis—the function Leontes *wants* his inspection of Mamillius to perform: it uses the son's body to display the reality of a fatherhood that remains unknowable.

## Dismembering the Ritual Economy

Comparing patriarchal anxieties about legitimacy with Reformation disputes over the Eucharist may seem to be a stretch. But suppose that sacrifice does serve, in Scarry's phrase, to "confer the force and power of the material world on the noumenal and unselfsubstantiating" (205). Is it merely a coincidence, then, that the God who cannot be seen is also the one who deifies paternity? In an obvious way, fatherhood too is invisible and "unselfsubstantiating"; this would explain why its historical fortunes have been tied to technologies of representation. Nancy Jay's work on rituals of blood sacrifice makes precisely this connection, for Jay demonstrates, across a historically and geographically diverse range of social systems, that *the function of blood sacrifice is to create patrilineal descent by substantiating fatherhood*. Offering the flesh and blood of the victim as a spectacular counterpart to the flesh and blood of pregnancy and birth,

13. This description of the Eucharist is of course quite conventional. Compare Haller's characterization, published in 1963: "The life of faith had centred in the preceding ages on the great dramatic rite in which the body and blood of the Lord, once sacrificed on the Cross for the sins of men, were offered up again in the guise of the bread and wine of the sacrament of the altar. For the performance over and over again of that act of propitiation, the Church was believed to have been instituted. . . . The be-all and end-all of the Church was the continuous administration of the sacrament by an apostolic priesthood, and the high point of individual religious experience was participation in the Mass" (20).

sacrifice compensates for the invisibility that godhead and fatherhood share.

On the basis of this reasoning, the link between the real presence of Christ in the wafer and the real presence of fathers in their children would seem to lie in ritual's gift of substance to entities that otherwise remain inapprehensible. But sacrifice can accomplish this only in the right circumstances: the ritual *works* only for a social group capable of drawing itself together into a community of witness. As an epochal disturbance in the Christian version of such community, the Reformation confirms this model by demonstrating the consequences of its failure.

The culture wars that shaped the Protestant state in Tudor England led to a splintering of the community of witness that gave the Eucharist meaning. The prosecution of Protestant churchmen under Mary began in 1554 with a series of disputations staged at Oxford, where interpretation of the Eucharist was the first point of doctrine addressed. Subsequent efforts to hold a religious community together in the Elizabethan Settlement show what a stress point the Eucharist was. The Articles of Religion (1563, 1571) explicitly reject the doctrine of transubstantiation (XXVIII, "Of the Lordes Supper"), but also seek to exclude Anabaptist and Zwinglian views of the ritual as merely festive or memorial. They speak ambiguously of "a parttakyng of the body of Christe" (*communicatio corporis Christi*) while repudiating the elevation and adoration of the consecrated host (Hardwick 328–31; Bicknell 382–83). The 1559 liturgy is equivocal in a similar way: "The body of our Lord Jesus Christ, which was given for thee, preserve thy body and soul into everlasting life: and take and eat *this* [body? wafer?] in remembrance that Christ died for thee, and *feed on him in thine heart by faith,* with thanksgiving" (Clay 195, emphasis added).

Not only did the Tudor culture wars place interpretation of the Eucharist at the center of doctrinal dispute, they also *dis*placed the scene of this ritual's symbolic enactment from the altar to the public square, associating it in a violent and compelling way with the horrors of public immolation. Protestant martyrs saw themselves as reenacting in the flesh the sacrifice commemorated in the Mass: in the words of Janel Mueller, the martyr's body "as it burned for failing to believe in the miracle of transubstantiation . . . experienced just such a miracle" (171).[14] The martyrs, then, were sacrificed by their heavenly father as Christ himself was, witnesses to divine paternity. But such proof is efficacious only for those already prepared to see it in these terms. The martyrs who celebrated their "marriage"

---

14. Earlier, Mueller observes that "many of Foxe's Protestant martyrs prepare for their burnings by figuring this mode of dying as an entry into bodily relation with divinity" (169).

to Christ by way of fire bore witness to a contested construction of the mystical body, and the *meaning* of their sacrifice was precisely the point in dispute. Polemicists on both sides turned to the new technology of print to widen the scope of the debate that followed, publishing rival re-figurations of the sacrament in their rhetorical struggle to shape the meanings of events. Such published accounts displaced the symbolic reenactment of the ritual yet again, from the public square to the dispersed and partly imaginary scene of reading. Religious polemic thus widens the scope of debate and (so to speak) raises the stakes as it transforms and extends the notion of witnessing through the medium of print.[15]

John Foxe's *Acts and Monuments* gathers a vast archive of stories modeled on the Passion and set forth in a rhetoric of pious horror. Among the unforgettable episodes recounted by Foxe, one in particular features the image that seems to haunt the tradition of filial sacrifice (figure 7). Steven Mullaney calls this passage "one of the most well-known and fiercely debated . . . in the sixteenth century" ("Reforming Resistance" 237); Eirwen Nicholson describes the accompanying woodcut as "perhaps the most notorious image from the *Acts and Monuments*" (163–64):

> The tyme then beyng come, when these three good servauntes and holy Saintes of GOD, the Innocent mother with her twoo daughters shoulde suffer, in the place where they should consumate their Martyrdome, were three stakes set up. At the midle post was the mother, the eldest daughter on the right hand; the yongest [Perotine Massey] on the other. They were firste strangled, but the Rope brake before they were deade, and so the poor women fell in the fire. Perotine, who was then great with child, did fall on her side, where happened a ruefull sight, not onely to the eyes of all that there stode, but also to the eares of all true hearted Christians, that shall read this history: for as the bely of the woman brast a sonder by the vehemencie of the flame, the Infant being a faire man child, fell into the fire, and eftsones beyng taken out of the fire by one W. House, was layd upon the grasse.
>
> Then was the child had to the Provost, and from him to the Bailife, who gave censure, that it should be caried backe again and cast into the fire. And so the infant Baptized in his owne bloud, to fill up the number of Gods innocent Saincts, was both borne, and died a Martyr, leavyng behind to the worlde, whiche it never sawe, a spectacle wherein the whole worlde maie see the Herodian crueltie of this gracelesse generation of Catholicke tormentours, *Ad perpetuam rei infamiam.*[16]

15. On the role of the printed book in the Reformation, see Greenblatt, "The Word of God in the Age of Mechanical Reproduction," in *Renaissance Self-Fashioning.*

16. I quote from the edition of 1576 (STC 11224), 1851. For the only readily available modern edition, see Pratt 8.229–30. The text of this description varies considerably among the early editions. Mullaney's effort to historicize the intersection between affect and ideol-

Many of the martyrdoms in Foxe are horrifyingly vivid in their details. If the execution of Perotine Massey stands out even in such grim company, the reason is surely what Foxe refers to as the "horrible strangeness of the fact": when the mother's body breaks open, the spectacle of execution is itself ruptured by an event as powerful as it is shocking. This moment transforms the scene's essential character, collapsing into a single stunning image the polarity of birth and sacrifice that underlies the whole symbolic economy.[17]

Foxe doesn't simply depict a community of scandalized witnesses responding to this unprecedented horror; he seeks explicitly to replicate the scandal on a much larger scale—to carry the "ruefull sight" of the martyrdom (as he puts it) "not only to the eyes of all that there stode, but also to the eares of all true hearted Christians, that shall read this history."[18] As a written account, the *Book of Martyrs* (as *Acts and Monuments* came to be known) trades not in ritual but in rhetorical sacrifice. The description closes with a flourish, first refiguring the blood that covers the child as a baptism, then collapsing the antithesis of birth and death, which it translates (through the figure of inheritance) into a more elaborate antithesis that turns on the child's inability to see the world for which it becomes a spectacle. In this way, through the spectacle of its own rhetoric, Foxe's text forcefully transvalues the events it depicts. Like the crucifixion of Jesus, the immolation of heretics under Mary was *meant* as a ritual of humiliation.[19] Foxe, like Paulina in *The Winter's Tale*, boldly reverses the

---

ogy in Foxe, and to link Foxe's narrative with the emergence of the Elizabethan theater, is of considerable interest. Nicholson, studying the later history of the book's illustrations, finds the woodcut depicting this incident echoed in prints as late as 1829.

17. No father is literally present in this scene, a point that Catholic polemicists were quick to use against Perotine Massey's character. Foxe re-legitimated the martyrdom by producing a legal father, but the value of that maneuver is to preserve the innocence that makes Perotine and her child such appealing victims. The symbolic potency of this mother-son pair is no more diminished by the literal absence of the sacrificing father than is that of the *Pietà*, discussed in chapter 1. At the same time, the very openness of the martyrdoms to disputes about their meaning is itself equivalent to the Father's absence, and constitutes a breakdown of the paternal function in Tudor religious culture. The absence of this more rarefied paternal presence is my whole point.

18. Mullaney notes the synesthesia in this clause, which marks the shift in economies of witnessing (236). Foxe, who worked in a print shop during his exile, was explicit about his providential view of the new technology: "The Lord began to work for His Church not with sword and target to subdue His exalted adversary, but with printing, writing, and reading. . . . Either the pope must abolish knowledge and printing or printing at length will root him out" (III.718–22; qtd. in Haller 110). Kastan, " 'noyse of the new Bible,' " describes Henrician fears that "the nation offering unrestricted access to and uncontrolled interpretation of its sacred book seemingly threatened to disintegrate into sectarian fragments," or, in the words of a seventeenth-century pamphleteer, to be "Amsterdamnified by several opinions" (47, 63).

19. Mullaney 239–40; see also Breitenberg, "The Flesh Made Word" 402. Marotti discusses the parallel reversibility of Catholic martyrdom under Elizabeth in "Southwell's Re-

**Figure 7.** Detail of woodcut from John Foxe, *Actes and Monuments* (1576). By permission of the Folger Shakespeare Library, Washington, D.C.

terms: "It is an heretic that makes the fire, / Not she who burns in't" (2.3.115–16).

Inevitably, Foxe's martyrology reached Catholic polemicists who challenged its version of events, competing for rhetorical mastery of the pathos stirred by his tales; these accounts reassert a sense of the event as

---

mains." Helgerson attributes Foxe's opposition to the execution of heretics, during the reigns of both Edward VI and Elizabeth I, less to a spirit of religious toleration than to an awareness of just this reversibility: "To ward off the effect of such a reversal, Foxe had to keep Elizabeth and her bishops from imitating Mary and hers . . ." (*Forms of Nationhood* 259). Needless to say, the reversal of significance began with the behavior of the heretics themselves, who were clearly conscious of their sufferings as performances. "In these burnings," writes Mueller, "Catholic enactment of authority serves protestant truth—to the extent that the condemned maintain, during their torture, the integrity of self-possession that signifies the truth of their being" (165). Mueller employs the concept of "torture" because she is extending and revising Scarry's thesis; on the executions as "social drama" in the anthropological sense defined by Victor Turner, see Knott 13. I do not greatly emphasize the signifying power of the events themselves as opposed to Foxe's rendition of them, for the simple reason that Foxe provides our only access to them; analyses that read through the accounts to the reality of the events place themselves in the awkward position of presuming the descriptive reliability of eyewitness reports gathered in Foxe's martyrology.

lawful execution. Foxe answered his challengers, incorporating further attacks and counterattacks in new editions of the *Acts*, which grew apace as
warring partisans vied for interpretive possession of the martyrdoms. As
the two sides repeatedly summoned their readers to bear imaginary witness in diametrically opposed ways to the same charged scenes of human
suffering, each effort to secure closure prompted further debate. Under
such conditions of ideological warfare, the community of witness sustained by ritual practice is shattered by the very contest for consensus.

Sacrificial narrative and imagery are crucial to this struggle because they
ignite passions strong enough to consolidate a religious community, but
the horror and pathos they arouse are as fluid as they are irresistible. Modern assessments of Foxe's martyrology have understandably stressed its
constructive force: in *Acts and Monuments,* accounts of the Marian martyrs are incorporated into an encyclopedic history of the true Church and
its persecuted defenders, a prophetic and typological narrative that culminates in the regime of Elizabeth Tudor. They are embedded as well in an
extended, steadily proliferating network of documentation—an archive of
royal proclamations, transcripts of examinations by Catholic authorities,
letters from accused heretics to family and friends, eyewitness accounts of
trials, disputations, and executions, and much more. "The effect of such
an 'open' text," writes Mark Breitenberg, "is to fashion a Protestant community by including a vast number of texts, authors, events and individu-
als while at the same time discrediting those who are not part of the community" ("The Flesh Made Word" 388). Published and republished, cited
and circulated, augmented over the years by many hands, Foxe's book is
justly celebrated as a powerful instrument of community.[20] But its narrative and rhetorical powers depend on an accumulation of horrors with a
shock value that lingers, never fully absorbed by the ideological ends they
serve. What happens when religious controversy obsessively repeats its
sacrificial stories while submitting them to endless transvaluations, creating a steady supply of new martyrs in its effort to settle the meaning of old
martyrdoms? If conflicting ideological discourses generate powerful cur-
rents of feeling they can only imperfectly control, what becomes of the
surplus?

---

20. The precise nature of this community has been disputed. The view of Foxe as nation-
building was advanced by Haller but challenged by historians who emphasize that Foxe embraces a universal and international Church. Haller's view resurfaces, however, in modified
form in Mullaney, "Reforming Resistance"; Breitenberg; Helgerson, "Apocalyptics and
Apologetics" (chapter 6 of his influential *Forms of Nationhood*), which offers an especially
balanced and compelling account of the issues under dispute; Collinson; and Lander. For my
purposes, the most important point is one stated clearly by Lander, who writes that at the
end of the sixteenth century, *Acts and Monuments* had become "a ubiquitous presence, differently marked but accepted as authoritative by a broad range of protestant opinion" (69).

One result of this volatile surplus of fantasy and affect is, in a word, the-ater. Stephen Greenblatt offers a model of the way theater can produce "social energy" by drawing on the culture's symbolic capital, subjecting its social practices to theatrical transformation. Steven Mullaney suggests that as it did so, the Elizabethan popular theater had a transformative effect on its audience, "demanding and producing new powers of identification, projection, and apprehension [that altered] the threshold not only of dra-matic representation but of self-representation, not only of the fictional construction of character but also of the social construction of the self."[21] Debora Shuger describes a similar process in exploring what she calls "the rupture between archaic and modern culture" in the religious discourse of the Reformation (81). Shuger's concern is not with Marian martyrdoms so much as their biblical prototype, Christ's Passion, although she does suggest that "the endless ugly violence recorded in the passion narratives can be read as a projection of the religious strife tearing apart the social fabric of the sixteenth century" (120). Calvinist models of the self, she ar-gues, are based on narrative accounts of Christ's inner struggle. In the Calvinist retellings, this episode takes on a lurid sadomasochistic intensity; at the same time, it is conveyed through a "rhetoric of identification" which demands that the reader occupy by turn all the narrative's subject positions, including those of torturer and victim (112–13). This model, argues Shuger, "having detached itself (as it were) from its biblical locus, becomes the exemplary subtext for Calvinist representations of Christian selfhood," which generalize and promulgate its structure while suppress-ing its "appalling sacrificial subtext" (89–90). The result is a crisis in the conception of masculine selfhood that "leaves its traces throughout the characteristic discourses of the period" (116), among them Shakespearean tragedy.

The suppression is necessary because "the modern individual," as Shuger puts it, "is defined in terms of alienation from sacrifice" (73). To be constructed through alienation in this way requires, on the one hand, that the subject respond to sacrificial spectacle with the kind of horror Foxe so clearly solicits from his readers; and, on the other hand, that this same subject *internalize* the horrific spectacle, as the Calvinist passions ask their readers to do. Shuger describes the biblical discourses that col-lectively enjoin this twofold process as the site of a "rupture between ar-chaic and modern culture, between sacrificial victims and ethical sub-jects" (81). Foxe's rhetoric, courting this rupture in order to provoke the pity and horror that emerge on its modern edge, suggests the *intimacy* of the subject's alienation from sacrifice in a culture that continues to stage ritual killings and to rehearse sacrificial imagery in a wide range of texts and events. Under such historical conditions, sacrifice becomes a profoundly disturbing and volatile fantasy lodged at the heart of the social imaginary.

In Shakespearean tragedy, Reformation discourses of filial sacrifice converge with a range of classical texts, including Seneca, Plutarch, and Virgil. The conjunction is fateful because the Calvinist and classical traditions mirror each other's sacrificial patterns in mutually reinforcing ways. *Hamlet* explores this conjunction by reaching back to recall the key scene in Virgil's *Aeneid:* " 'twas Aeneas' tale to Dido, and thereabout of it especially when he speaks of Priam's slaughter" (2.2.446–48).[22] This allusion locates the play in an epic patriline reaching back to Homer and Virgil, for the death of Priam marks the intersection between the *Iliad* and the *Aeneid,* the juncture at which Troy ceases to exist and the prehistory of Rome begins.

A review of this literary genealogy takes us to a series of linked scenes, centering in Homer on Priam's visit to Achilles to beg for Hector's body, and in Virgil on Priam's slaughter at the hands of Achilles' son Pyrrhus. These scenes turn on endlessly reversible images of real or imagined filial grief—the son's grief at the father's death, the father's grief at the son's death, the son's grief at the thought of the father's grief. Both Homer and Virgil explore the powerful ambivalence at the heart of this fantasy, which may become an irresistible motive either for reconciliation (as when Achilles takes pity on Priam) or for revenge (as when Pyrrhus slays Priam). Virgil's exploration in particular shows how this spiraling logic, like the cross-identifications Shuger finds in the Passion narratives, suspends the masculine subject between the poles of a sacrificial scenario. In the celebrated close of Virgil's poem, Aeneas pauses before killing Turnus, arrested for a moment between these alternatives. When he then kills Turnus in the name of the slain Pallas, Aeneas not only contravenes the great Roman principle announced by Anchises' shade—*parcere subiectis,* or "spare the conquered"—he also combines the language of sacrifice and revenge in a deeply symptomatic way. "This wound will come from Pallas," he cries; "Pallas makes this offering, / And from your criminal blood exacts his

---

22. If Shakespeare had a specific model for the Player's speech, it has not been identified, despite much speculation. He would have known the scene from a school edition of Virgil based on the Aldine text of 1558, according to Baldwin, who concludes that "in some way Shakespeare had acquired a firm and lasting knowledge of at least the first two, the fourth, and the sixth books of the *Aeneid*" (2:456, 495). On Shakespeare's use of the scene from Virgil, see especially Brower 89–95, 291–92; Miola, "Virgil in Shakespeare" 241–58 and *Classical Tragedy* 44–48; and Loewenstein, "Plays Agonistic" 74–77.

due" (12.1292–94; *Pallas te hoc uulnere, Pallas / immolat et poenam scelerato ex sanguine sumit*, 12.948–49). In calling the death of Turnus an "offering," Aeneas is sanctifying his murderous wrath as sacrificial piety. He turns himself into an avatar of the vengeful Pyrrhus in this way precisely *because* he yields to a total identification with the slain Pallas. This identification momentarily revives the dead boy, transporting him from the position of victim to that of avenger, just as Christ, in the Calvinist Passions, turns from abject victim to triumphant avenger in the destruction of Jerusalem.

Aeneas' moment of hesitation becomes, in Shakespeare's play, the duration of Hamlet's much-discussed delay, just as the ethical question it suspends—when is revenge murder and when is it piety?—defines the central issue that he, unlike Laertes, must confront. But Shakespeare also reads the moment of delay back from the end of the poem into the scene on which the ending is modeled, the death of Priam. This twist leads us back from the son to the sacrificial father-king (the same path followed in the biographical tour de force spun out by Stephen Daedalus in James Joyce's *Ulysses*).[23] When Shakespeare brings Aeneas onstage in the second act of *Hamlet*, then, he is summoning many ghosts. Behind the image of Priam, cut down on the steps of his ancestral altar, we may glimpse Aeneas himself, sanctifying his killing rage as sacrificial piety. And behind them both, haunting the scene with an undisclosed burden of cultural memory, are the religious martyrs of the sixteenth century— actors who often recorded their own dialogues for the sake of posterity, and who played out the social drama of their martyrdom with an eye to the crowd.

### Theater as Witness of the Subject in *Hamlet*

*Hamlet* represents the commercial theater as both supplementing and displacing the inner theater of divine witness. The play is almost entirely taken up with mortal schemes to approximate, through some combination of spying, eavesdropping, and guesswork, the divine privilege of *seeing* human motives. The Elizabethan Settlement had renounced this ambition: as Francis Bacon would put it, looking back in 1589, "Her

---

23. In his biographical speculations about Shakespeare (the source for my chapter epigraph), Stephen Daedalus grasps the play's deep reversal of the specular logic governing sacrificial masculinity. The facts are tantalizing: Hamnet Shakespeare died in 1596; in 1597, William Shakespeare revived and carried through his father's long-lapsed effort to gentrify the family with a coat of arms. What path, if any, leads from the loss of an only son to the repair of a father's declining name and reputation? See *Ulysses*, episode 9, "Scylla and Charybdis," and Loewenstein's subtle extension of the Joycean reading ("Plays Agonistic" 78–79).

Majesty, not liking to make windows into men's hearts and secret thoughts except the abundance of them did overflow into overt and express acts or affirmations, tempered her law . . ." (8.98).[24] Hamlet himself vigilantly defends the heart of his own mystery, all the while laying traps for the king's conscience. When Claudius refers complacently to "purposes" he imagines concealed in his thoughts, Hamlet responds (as if he has been reading Cusanus), "I see a cherub that sees them" (4.3.47–48). His own depth "passes show," but he seems to feel that this inaccessibility to outward demonstration paradoxically makes it more authentic than "actions that a man might play" (1.2.84–85). Play, however, is what carries Hamlet from contempt for suits and trappings, in act 1, to his confident knowledge of Claudius in act 4. Even before he sets his mousetrap for the king, his own conscience is caught by the Player's speech in act 2; not coincidentally, the inspiration for *The Murder of Gonzago* comes to him in the wake of his own turbulent response to the death of Priam.

The problem of using theatrical means to open the self for public display confronts both Shakespeare and his protagonist: Hamlet studies Claudius as we do him, testing the screen of appearances to discover what lies within. Far less obvious is the way this concern with theatrical witnessing emerges as a cultural trope for the Reformation crisis of sacrificial witnessing. On the most general level, the mystery Hamlet harbors within himself is that of his relation to his father; sacrificial ritual is a cultural solution to the structural embarrassment that the father-son relation *always* "passes show." *Hamlet* thus confronts the dilemma of representing a crisis that is doubly invisible, first because this crisis breaks down the conventions that enable a community to witness what it cannot see, and second because it involves the internal, subjective dimension of this breakdown. If the purpose of playing is to hold the mirror up to nature, how do you hold up a mirror to the hidden disappearance of something invisible? How do you stage what only God can see?

Not only Hamlet but also the play itself worries covertly, insistently, whether God is even watching. The question is never asked (in so many words) about the murders of Claudius, Polonius, or King Hamlet, but the Player's speech in act 2 asks it about their mirror image, the murder of Priam:

> But if the Gods themselves did see her then,
> When she saw Pyrrhus make malicious sport
> In mincing with his sword her husband's limbs,
> The instant burst of clamor that she made,

---

24. The text is a letter to Sir Francis Walsingham written in 1589 or early 1590; the remarks on Elizabeth would be repeated in "Observations on a Libel" (1592).

> Unless things mortal move them not at all,
> Would have made milch the burning eyes of heaven,
> And passion in the Gods.
>
> (2.2.512–18)

The Player emphatically hedges his affirmation: Hecuba's grief *would have* impassioned the gods *if* they had seen her then, and *if* mortal things can move them at all. These conditional clauses give voice to a question already there in the scene from Virgil, in which Pyrrhus carries his brutal revenge for Achilles all the way to the ancestral altars in the central palace courtyard. How *do* the gods receive such terrible offerings? Christopher Marlowe and Thomas Nashe answer in one way, adding a statue of Jove that frowns "as loathing Pyrrhus for this wicked act" (*Dido Queen of Carthage* 2.1.258). No question there about God's attitude. Thomas Sackville, by contrast, thinks Pyrrhus was acting with divine approval: the destruction of Troy "by the wrathful will of Gods was come: / And Jove's unmoved sentence and foredoom / On Priam king . . ." (438–40).[25] No question here, either—just the opposite answer.

Shakespeare does not answer this question; he transforms it. The special horror of the scene in the *Aeneid* is concentrated as much on the death of the king's son Politës as on Priam's own death. Or rather, it is concentrated on the father's *witnessing* of his son's destruction. Pyrrhus enters chasing the boy and kills him "before his father's eyes" (*ante ora parentum*). Priam denounces Pyrrhus for this in particular: "You forced me to look on / At the destruction of my son: defiled / A father's eyes with death." Later Aeneas, as if echoing a formula, warns his own father that Pyrrhus "kills the son before his father's eyes, / The father at the altars."[26] Clearly the sacrilege for Virgil lies in defiling not just the altars but also the father's gaze—almost as if the two could be equated. In adapting the scene, however, Shakespeare reverses this gaze. Unlike Marlowe and Sackville, he simply *omits* Politës. Instead, he stages the father's destruction *ante os fili*, bringing forward in place of the dying son his mother, Hecuba (whose response is never mentioned in Virgil), as the figure on whom pathos and sympathy fasten.[27]

---

25. I have modernized spellings. Sackville may seem a bit confused about Jove's motives—is he wrathful, or unmoved? I take it he is unmoved by pity because of his wrath, but the relation for Zeus between implacable fate (the "unmoved sentence and foredoom") and personal feeling (wrath or, for Sarpedon, sorrow) is a problem even in Homer.

26. In Fitzgerald, 2.699–701 and 2.865–66. In *Opera*, 2.538–39, *qui nati coram me cernere letum / fecisti et patrios foedasti funere uultus*, and 2.663, *natum ante ora patris, patrem qui obtruncat ad aras*. These lines and the scene in which they occur are discussed in chapter 2.

27. Most commentators stress how problematic it would be for Hamlet to identify with Pyrrhus; the disappearance of Politës is less often noted. But even if Shakespeare had not consulted or remembered Virgil's text, he would have found Politës mentioned prominently not only in sixteenth-century English translations but also in the looser "imitations" already

Harry Levin's classic analysis of the Player's speech emphasizes the displacement of "passion" from Priam into a chain of empathy, concentrated metonymically in Hecuba, that reaches from the gods at one extreme to the theater audience at the other (159–61 and 168, fig. 3). In Virgil the scene of Priam's death is witnessed by Aeneas, whose response, anticipating Shakespeare's reversal of the scene, may in fact be Hamlet's "cue for passion": "I stood unmanned, / And my dear father's image came to mind / As our king, just his age, mortally wounded, / Gasped his life away before my eyes."[28] But if Priam is the slain father and Hecuba a grieving Gertrude, then Hamlet's point of entry into the scene, according to his father's dread command, is to identify not with the passive Aeneas but with the hypersanguinary Pyrrhus. As commentators have often noticed, this transforms the analogy, which now anticipates Gertrude's horrified response to the murder of Claudius. In other words, as soon as Hamlet projects himself into the scene, the pathos concentrated on Priam attaches itself to the wrong king. Here indeed is a mousetrap for the conscience.

This feature of the Player's speech is understood as crystallizing the terms of Hamlet's impasse, but Shakespeare is also putting theatricality onstage, asking what it shows us and why it moves us. "What's Hecuba to him, or he to Hecuba, / That he should weep for her?" (2.2.559–60): this is a question about theater as an economy of witnessing. We find it inscribed not only in Hamlet's second soliloquy, but also in the structure Shakespeare creates by doubling both the represented scene (the space we imagine as "Denmark" is transformed before our eyes into "Troy") and the scene of representation (an English player plays the Danish Player playing Aeneas). At the center of this reduplicative structure Shakespeare locates a spectacle of harrowing moral and emotional ambiguity—one in which filial revenge turns sacrilegious, even hideous, but also one that the horrified Aeneas reenacts *from the other side* when he avenges the death of Pallas in the epic's closing lines. Shakespeare, recognizing the affinity between these matched and weighted moments in the *Aeneid,* carries the image of Aeneas' fateful pause, sword stroke suspended, from the later passage back to the earlier—from the son's death back to the father's—as if tracing Virgil's path in reverse.

In this way Shakespeare brings together at the focal point of his scene a double exploration, unfolding the ambiguous pathos of sacrificial spectacle on the one hand, and the ambiguous dynamics of theatrical empathy on

---

cited: Sackville's "Induction" (1563), 466–69, and Marlowe's *Dido* (published 1594), in which Pyrrhus appears for the first time bearing "on his spear / The mangled head of Priam's youngest son" (2.1.214–15).

28. Fizgerald 2.731–34; *Opera* 2.560–62: *subiit cari genitoris imago, / ut regem aequaeuum crudeli uulnere uidi / uitam exhalantem.*

the other. Out of pagan sources, this strategy synthesizes, in the scene of Priam's death, a theatrical analogy to the traumatic breakup of Christian sacrificial witness. In doing so, it suggests the *emergence* of the theatrical analogy *from* the shattering of ritual. Shakespeare's staging of the Player's speech thus models, in its dramaturgy, a dynamic in which the shattering of the ritual economy yields two new cultural forms—theater and "modern" subjectivity—bound together in an economy of spectatorship.

## From *Hamlet* to *The Winter's Tale*

Christianity has its equivalent to the question of the gods' response: how does the Father regard the Crucifixion? As I pointed out in chapter 1, God enjoys a strategic invisibility in the gospel accounts, as our horror at the victimization of Christ is drawn off onto human agents in the narrative. The dominant tendencies of medieval and early Renaissance art follow this strategy: there are many images of God elevating the crucified Christ to his seat of glory, but none of God triumphing cruelly over Christ in his agony. This, however, is exactly the scenario so vividly rehearsed in the Calvinist Passion narratives Shuger has studied. She notes that before the Reformation, medieval culture had used the figure of the grieving virgin to stabilize the sacrificial spectacle. Mary offers precisely what the Calvinist and Virgilian scenarios exclude: a mode of witness that stands outside the cycle of victimization and vengeance and stabilizes the distribution of identities within it.[29] This is the power of Michelangelo's first *Pietà*, as it mutes and transforms the horror of filial sacrifice.

The *Pietà* gives its viewer what Hamlet seeks in the figure of Hecuba, an idealized maternal presence that can compensate for the father's absence and ensure the benevolence of his demand. In draping the recumbent body of Christ across the lap of a strangely youthful Madonna, Michelangelo seems to be mirroring the Son's timelessness in her. In Hamlet's relations with Gertrude, this mirroring exchange has gone terribly wrong. The ambiguous age of the grieving son, an adolescent who turns out to be thirty years old, is reversed in his assessment of Gertrude as a matron with youthful lust rebelling in her bones; the grotesquely juvenile sexuality he sees in her might almost be a travesty of the eroticism so quietly evoked by Michelangelo's Madonna. For Hamlet, the *crisis of*

---

29. Shuger writes, "By remaining outside this dialectic [of victim and torturer], the Virgin grounds the distinction between sacred and demonic, between the faithful who mourn their dying Lord and the barbaric soldiers who kill him" (100).

sacrificial witnessing is concentrated in his mother's failure as witness and guarantee of the father's identity.[30]

Both Gertrude's reformation and the felt presence of God's providential witness are therefore essential to Hamlet's "readiness" for death in act 5. But the play's nearest approach to the sublime acquiescence of the *Pietà* comes in Horatio's loving farewell, which tempers horror with its wishful flights of angels (5.2.359–60). To appreciate the quality of this moment we should recognize that Horatio has won his place in Hamlet's heart of hearts because he is the play's one consistently reliable witness. The palace guards call on him to verify the appearance of the ghost, and the play itself entrusts him (at some expense of plausibility) with a first-hand report of King Hamlet's victory over Fortinbras thirty years earlier. Hamlet recruits him as a reliable second in observing the king ("even with the very comment of thy soul" [2.2.79]) during *The Murder of Gonzago*, at the same time sealing the bond between them in an awkwardly passionate speech about Horatio's indifference to passion. In context it seems inescapable that this rush of feeling for Horatio expresses the urgency of Hamlet's need to anchor the sacrificial witness in just such an unmoved point of reference. The intimacy established in this speech seals the play's election of Horatio as its personification of reliable witnessing, and this in turn authorizes him not only to report Hamlet's cause aright in the play's imagined aftermath, but also to reconcile the audience to the hero's death. It is Horatio, finally, who will shape the Prince's rough-hewn end, supplying its proper meaning: "all this can I / Truly deliver" (5.2.385–86). The delivery is strategically deferred—no actual report could make good on such a promise—but in the meantime, Horatio's loving witness graces Hamlet's death amid the butcheries of the final scene.

In repudiating the cult of the Virgin, Reformation culture dismantled a powerful strategy for containing the volatile emotions aroused by the spectacle of sacrifice. My purpose in locating the *Pietà* alongside Roman and biblical narratives as a point of reference for reading Shakespeare is initially to emphasize the consequences of this loss, for Calvinist and classical models are mutually reinforcing: both construct an unstable masculinity that turns on revolving identifications between father and son. But Michelangelo's sculpture also anticipates Shakespeare's strategy for redeeming sacrificial masculinity: *The Winter's Tale* is celebrated above all for its statue scene, featuring the resurrection of the mother in a theatrical "miracle."[31] This scene makes Hermione's recovery depend on the re-

30. Hence the quest to reform Gertrude takes precedence over the task of revenge. See Adelman, chapter 2.

31. Compare Barber and Wheeler: "One can place the spiritual process involved in such sanctification of a particular individual by imagining, for contrast, a medieval Leontes who,

demption of the patriarch, which depends in turn on a transformation in the economy of witnessing, from paranoia to wonder. If *Hamlet* is deeply marked by the son's need to reform his mother, as Adelman argues, *The Winter's Tale* is just as deeply marked by the wish to redeem its murderous patriarch.

To move from the earlier to the later play, then, is to follow Shakespeare's search for a resolution to the dilemmas of sacrificial manhood. Much as the second half of *The Winter's Tale* repeats the events of the first three acts with a redemptive difference, the play as a whole repeats key elements of Hamlet's deranged sexuality in an effort to imagine their redemption. Hamlet's disgust with his mother becomes Leontes' revulsion toward the mother of his children, a conversion already mapped in the way Hamlet condenses Gertrude with Ophelia: if Leontes is another Hamlet, Hermione is his breeder of sinners. The persistent doubling that keeps linking Hamlet with Claudius becomes in *The Winter's Tale* a repeated, symptomatic confusion between Polixenes and Mamillius. And while the pathos of filial sacrifice in *Hamlet* is drawn off onto Ophelia, *The Winter's Tale* turns it back onto Mamillius: Leontes threatens Perdita, Paulina, and Hermione with burning at the stake, but only Mamillius and Antigonus perish.

This last reversal brings to the surface the sacrificial paradigm that remains half-buried in *Hamlet*. Mamillius and Antigonus both die on Leontes' behalf—Antigonus, as his name suggests, to indicate the purging of infanticide, Mamillius so that his father may be spared for redemption (the gods strike at the father's injustice in the person of the son). In this way, *The Winter's Tale* first excavates filial sacrifice as a traumatic fantasy underlying masculine subjectivity, and then seeks to regenerate the masculine self by re-creating its mode of witness. Finally, though, the play looks beyond its fairy-tale conclusion. In the ambiguity of a divided ending, it begins to open the space for a critique of the cultural work performed by sacrificial symbolism in a post-sacrificial social order.

### *Hamlet* in *The Winter's Tale*

For clarity's sake, I shall restrict my attention somewhat artificially to three moments in which *The Winter's Tale* appears to resume and transform *Hamlet*. No doubt readers will detect other echoes of *Hamlet* in the play; readers have certainly heard echoes of other plays—of Lear's madness, for

---

after similar aberration, might recover his relation to his wife through the intercession of the Holy Mother. The Shakespearean situation requires the discovery of the Holy Mother in the wife" (333).

example, and the storm that overtakes him, or Othello's jealous rage—in many passages. Indeed, there is something a bit overwhelming about *The Winter's Tale* as a retrospect on the canon: capacious and extreme, it seems to gather up the whole range of Shakespeare's characteristic modes and themes in a tour de force that defies analysis.

The play's revision of *Hamlet* may be described, a bit schematically, as a series of three transformations. The first, a reversal, enacts on a purely formal level the mirroring that binds fathers and sons. On this level *The Winter's Tale* presents itself literally as an inversion, or chiasmus, of *Hamlet*. The second transformation turns on the substitution of the daughter for the son. *The Winter's Tale* brings filial sacrifice to the surface in the threat to Perdita and carries it out in the death of Mamillius. But more than this, it takes the sacrificial economy itself as an object of transformation, breaking outside the closed circle of masculinity to seek a redemptive mode of witnessing. For all its theatrical bravura, however, this redemption is still a limited, and in some ways retrograde, achievement.[32] Like the rejuvenation of the Madonna in Michelangelo's *Pietà*, the recovery of the daughter and restoration of the mother tend to repair the dynamics of patriarchy, masking their dependence on the logic of sacrifice. But in a third transformation, *The Winter's Tale* reworks its predecessor play more radically. Hermione's symbolic death and resurrection carry out an extreme version of Hamlet's desire to sequester Ophelia and reform Gertrude. But this action is set in a context that implicitly critiques the purifying impulse, celebrating instead an aesthetic of mongrelization (tragicomedy as "Nature's bastard"), and situating the patriarchal family somewhat precariously in an economy of improvised and transgressive circulation—Autolycus and his traffic in sheets. Not only, then, does *The Winter's Tale* resume, clarify, and seek to redeem the sexual paranoia of *Hamlet;* implicitly, it also critiques the impulse governing this fable of redemption. In this self-critique, the play registers a contradiction it cannot resolve—the contradiction of a Jacobean social order that clings to fantasies of patriarchal redemption in the face of irreversible systemic change.

These analogies between *Hamlet* and *The Winter's Tale* crystallize around three striking moments. The first comes just after the Leontes' explosion in act 1. When Polixenes and Hermione notice that something is wrong, the king explains that he has been lost in thought:

> Looking on the lines
> Of my boy's face, methoughts I did recoil

---

32. Orgel, "Introduction" 77–79. My sense of the play is indebted to Orgel's thoughtful account. As he notes, Valerie Traub offers a strong statement of this view (25–49).

Twenty-three years, and saw myself unbreech'd
In my green velvet coat, my dagger muzzled,
Lest it should bite its master, and so prove
(As ornament oft does) too dangerous.
How like (methought) I then was to this kernel,
This squash, this gentleman.

                                            (1.2.153–60)

The care with which Leontes dates his recollection harks back to a graveyard in Denmark: "Here's a skull now hath lien you i' th' earth three and
twenty years" (5.1.173–74).[33] The gravedigger has already mentioned
that he started digging the day young Hamlet was born and has been
"sexton here, man and boy, thirty years" (143–48, 161–62). These details
tell us that Yorick died when Hamlet was seven—the "breeching age" to
which Leontes alludes—and they suggest that Hamlet (the son) and
Leontes (the father) are both about thirty.

Each of these scenes shows us one face staring into another, searching
for traces. The texts also mirror each other: in one, the son seeks himself
in a lost father figure, while in the other, a lost father seeks himself in the
son before him. The link has to be dug up like Yorick's skull, but once it is
recognized, the effect is both mordant and prophetic: from behind the
living features of Mamillius, a death's head grins back at the uncompre-
hending Leontes. Hamlet's recognition of Yorick is often singled out as a
turning point in his progress toward revenge, although just what the
recognition involves is harder to decide.[34] The corresponding moment for
Leontes is not one of clarification but of deepening illusion. He has been
imagining the child as a piece of his body ("my collop!") and worrying
that the physical link between them must pass through the language of
women "that will say anything" (1.2.122–37). But his account of these
thoughts a moment later turns them around: rather than seeking his fatherhood in Mamillius, he claims to have been finding the "boy eternal"
in himself. This mythic childhood, when he and Polixenes frisked together
like "twinn'd lambs" (63–75), is the play's equivalent to Yorick's kisses
and piggyback rides. But whereas Hamlet, holding the skull at arm's
length, repositions himself at a distance from the memory as he repos-

33. On the link between these passages, see Mullaney, "Mourning and Misogyny"
154–57.
34. Mullaney understands the moment as evidence of a successful work of mourning in
which Hamlet assumes the jester's persona in order to mock the skull, and in which a mo-
mentary regression to a cultural and political pre-oedipal stage triggers a resolution of the
misogyny that has troubled Hamlet's unfinished mourning for his father ("Mourning and
Misogyny"). Kerrigan sees Hamlet's disgust with death subsuming his disgust with sexuality
and resolving the contradiction between Christianity and revenge (133–38).

sesses it, Leontes is only drawn deeper into a fantasy that clearly possesses him. He is reversing Hamlet's progress, working his way backward into madness and misogyny.

The next reminiscence of *Hamlet* is unmistakable. Act 5 opens with Paulina's insistence that the king must not think of remarrying. Chastened, Leontes imagines the queen's ghost returning "soul-vexed" by a second marriage, and Paulina chimes in:

> Were I the ghost that walk'd, I'ld bid you mark
> Her eye, and tell me for what dull part in't
> You chose her; then I'ld shriek, that even your ears
> Should rift to hear me, and the words that follow'd
> Should be "Remember mine."
>
> (5.1.59, 63–67)

This time the play is recoiling sixteen years rather than twenty-three, but once again the "wide gap of time, since first / We were dissever'd" (5.3.154–55) refigures the ten-year gap separating *Hamlet* and *The Winter's Tale*.[35] The dead king's ghost had cried, "Remember me," to which Hamlet replied, "Remember thee! / Ay, thou poor ghost, while memory holds a seat / In this distracted globe. Remember thee!" (1.5.91, 95–97). Paulina's echo of these lines evokes a kind of intra-theatrical memory, fulfilling Hamlet's pledge in its own way by demonstrating that memory does hold a seat in the Globe. Once again, however, the repetition turns crucially on a reversal, as the words of the betrayed father are given to the slandered mother-wife (King Hamlet's ghost replaced by Gertrude's, as it were). The earlier play's indecorous mixture of "mirth in funeral, and . . . dirge in marriage" (*Hamlet* 1.2.12) has been corrected in *The Winter's Tale* by sixteen years of resolute mourning. This pattern of reversal is carried out with formal precision on a textual level as well: the recollection of Yorick transposes a moment from act 5 of *Hamlet* into act 1 of *The Winter's Tale,* while the echo of King Hamlet's ghost transposes a moment from act 1 of *Hamlet* into act 5 of *The Winter's Tale.* This is a hopeful sign: if the first reversal showed Leontes slipping into the sexual paranoia that consumes Hamlet, the second, by substituting Hermione's ghost for Old Hamlet's, shows him climbing painfully back out of it.

The final echo of *Hamlet* comes at the end of the play, where it associ-

---

35. In a nuanced discussion of the statue's reanimation, Gross connects this fantasy of Hermione's ghostly return, along with the dream recounted by Antigonus, to the ghost in *Hamlet:* "Such images," he writes, "are indeed like ghosts that Shakespeare must both conjure and exorcize before any further enchantment or disenchantment of the statue is possible; they are, for one thing, intimations of a tragic economy that the play is eager to renounce" (103).

ates the redemption of witnessing in the statue scene with Hamlet's intuition of providence in the fall of a sparrow. "Let be," says Hamlet to Horatio, and the royal court sweeps on stage with cushions, foils, and daggers as if the climax had been poised to descend on cue, waiting only for the hero to resign his puzzled will (5.2.224 and scene direction). In *The Winter's Tale* these words are repeated by Leontes when Paulina threatens to withdraw the statue from his gaze: "Let be, let be. / Would I were dead but that methinks already—" (5.2.61–62). Leontes breaks off, but clearly the unfinished thought is both proleptic (even before the statue moves, he already thinks it does) and reflexive (he would rather be dead himself than find it immobile). In this way the allusion marks an elevation of mood, recasting Hamlet's readiness for death as Leontes' readiness for rebirth.

In leaping ahead to anticipate the statue's animation, Leontes shows that he is prepared to witness what he cannot see. The theater audience is in a similar position: all that they or Leontes can *see* in the final scene is a woman holding very still who finally moves and speaks. The miraculous animation of a statue can only be witnessed. In this respect it is like sacrificial ritual; it is, in fact, what the play offers instead of sacrifice: dramatic illusion as the witness of a collective desire. Ritual, like drama, is more than spectacle; it includes as well the presence of the spectacle to an audience whose participation determines its meaning. In the play's first half, the covenant binding spectacle to witness has broken down for Leontes, opening an abyss between the visible and the meaningful. In his inspection of Mamillius, what he wants to *see* is fatherhood, written in "the lines / Of my boy's face" (1.2.153–54). But fatherhood is language, and language is unstable. This is why Leontes inevitably proves as obsessed with words as he is with adultery. Repeatedly he recruits others to his mad witness by trying to *show* them something he has only heard, or overheard, in the pregnancy of words, in the maddening *whisper* of their semantic excess. His speech, meanwhile, is notorious for its incoherence. This may well reflect a Jacobean taste for bombast, as Stephen Orgel proposes—but it may also reinforce the pervasive sense in these early scenes that language is as "slippery" as an unfaithful wife (1.2.273).[36]

*The Winter's Tale* explores these issues in theatrical terms, associating the derangement of witnessing with the orthodox perception of theater itself as a corrupting influence. Katharine Maus, noticing that drama in the Renaissance is far more preoccupied than narrative forms are with the ex-

---

36. Orgel, "Poetics," observes that modern editorial practice "assumes that behind the obscurity and confusion of the text is a clear meaning, and that the obscurity, moreover, is not part of the meaning" (433). I am arguing that the obscurity is part of the meaning in a very specific way.

perience of the jealous husband, reflects on the theater's peculiar complicity with his demand for "ocular proof." Antitheatrical polemic, she notes, relies "upon a time-honored association between female promiscuity and theatrical display" to characterize "the dramatic spectacle, whatever its apparent content, as essentially a sexual act performed before an audience." Hence "for the antitheatricalists, all theater is pornographic . . . the performers enact precisely the scene the jealous husband sees, or thinks he sees" ("Horns of a Dilemma" 567–68). But at the same time, this is also the scene the jealous husband, like the audience, *never* sees. When Leontes arraigns Hermione before his attendant lords, he seems less obsessed with her guilt than with this discrepancy between the essence and the apparent content of her spectacle—or, as he puts it, between what can be seen and what can be said:

> You, my lords,
> Look on her, mark her well; be but about
> To say she is a goodly lady, and
> The justice of your hearts will thereto add
> 'Tis pity she's not honest—honorable.
> Praise her but for this her without-door form
> (Which on my faith deserves high speech) and straight
> The shrug, the hum or ha (these petty brands
> That calumny doth use—O, I am out—
> That mercy does, for calumny will sear
> Virtue itself), these shrugs, these hums and ha's,
> When you have said she's goodly, come between
> Ere you can say she's honest. . . .
>                                             (2.1.64–76)

Leontes has earlier insisted on the queen's guilt as "a vision so apparent" that Camillo must have seen it, "or your eye-glass / Is thicker than a cuckold's horn" (1.2.270, 268–69), words that make sense only if we take them as referring to Hermione's pregnancy. And yet this same guilt stubbornly remains a fact "that lack'd sight only, nought for approbation / But only seeing" (2.1.177–78). This invisible, unspeakable something arises in the gap between the voice and the eye. It is at once a blemish that taints the visible object without being seen and a verbal stumbling, a *hum* or a *ha*—some barely articulate noise brought forth from the confusion of calumny and mercy. It acts upon speech from within to disrupt what rhetoricians call the deictic function, the ability of language to *point* at a thing.

Leontes and the antitheatricalists share a dementia in which spectacle as such, "whatever its apparent content," provokes a crisis of witnessing.

This crisis centers on what we might call the primal spectacle, the act of sex, which not only can be seen but, in a sense, is *always* seen: Hamlet, Othello, Leontes, and William Prynne cannot help seeing it, even though it is never *there* before them. Its opposite, a wife's "honesty," can never be seen: there is no "ocular proof" of sex not happening. This is one reason Paulina's first attempt to cure Leontes through a revised scene of witness only drives him deeper into his frenzy: he cannot *see* that Perdita is his, and all Paulina's appeals to visible evidence, to eye, nose, lip and the very trick of his frown, simply confirm what he has already imagined—namely that his status as a father exists only in, only *as* language. And language is like women: it will say anything. The spectacle that confirms paternity is not resemblance but sacrifice—to "*see* it instantly consum'd with fire" (2.3.134, emphasis added). Leontes resorts to this fantasy as an alternative to the scene Paulina offers him because unlike words and resemblances, immolation offers a moment decisively "available to the senses"—an unforgettable image that will, like the *aqedah,* protect the father's status by denying it.

## The Obscure Object of Patriarchal Desire

The second part of *The Winter's Tale* sets out to redeem Leontes according to the terms of Apollo's oracle: "the King shall live without an heir, if that which is lost be not found" (3.2.134–36). Oracles are not known for their perspicuity, but this one is quite explicit ("Hermione is chaste, Polixenes blameless . . ."), reserving a touch of enigma only for its closing prophecy. "That which is lost" refers to Perdita, as her name indicates, but *The Winter's Tale* is a play of many losses, some of which—Antigonus, Mamillius, the wide gap of time—are not to be recovered by any art. Perdita's name itself may refer beyond her to the "little lost one" she replaces, the son whose death Leontes embraces when he opens his arms to the dynastic couple in act 5. Yet the play's named and known losses cover a deeper hunger for the body of fatherhood—the loss of which goes unrecognized, though its traces remain for us to read.

Only with reference to this loss can we fully grasp the dramatic value of Hermione's extremely visible pregnancy in the play's early scenes or her spectacular metamorphosis in the last. The female body at the full term of pregnancy is, so to speak, a loaded image, as Foxe had already discovered. As an object of persecution, it evokes singular intensities of both pathos and horror. The speech in which Leontes first arraigns Hermione before his lords, scanning her "without-door form" for traces of the blemish to her honor, is peculiar enough in itself. But the bizarre contrast between the invisible trace he seeks and the conspicuous swelling of her body— "Look on her, mark her well"—pushes the moment to so perilous an extreme that only the king's lethal malice keeps it from sliding into dark hilarity.

Invariably, the statue scene draws the gaze of criticism into its marvelous witness. Yet *The Winter's Tale* does bear traces of its missed encounter with another body, too deeply lost for recovery. Camillo (the Horatio of *The Winter's Tale*) is regularly associated with this fantasy object: invested with an intense, yet strangely mobile intimacy, he migrates from Leontes to Polixenes and from Polixenes to Florizel, playing second self to each. Along the way he bears witness to the fantasy informing these relations: first he describes the two kings embracing "as over a vast" (1.1.24–31); later he imagines Leontes "opening his free arms, and weeping / His welcomes forth" as he "asks thee there, son, forgiveness, / As 'twere i' th' father's person" (4.4.547–50). Both passages evoke an imaginary embrace that, if it could take on flesh, would realize the fantasy of pre-sexual twinning recollected by Polixenes. And like the twinned speeches in which the kings independently recall their shared boyhood, Camillo's lines carry this fantasy over from friendship into the filial relation: the first passage, like Polixenes' memory, dwells on the affection of the kings, while the second, like Leontes' memory, rediscovers this lost union in the relation between father and son.

The lines from act 4 are especially poignant because, although addressed to Florizel, they can scarcely help evoking other reconciliations. This is partly a matter of syntax, since the modifying clause "as 'twere i' th' father's person" may refer to either party. But the ambiguity does no more than extend Camillo's point, for if Florizel can substitute for Polixenes in the embrace Camillo envisions, then other substitutions may equally be imagined: Florizel may stand for Mamillius, or Camillo himself; and Leontes too may stand for Polixenes. The image of the king spreading his arms "as 'twere i' th' father's person," weeping and begging forgiveness *of the son*—his own son—is the most deeply buried of these scenarios, yet insofar as this deepest scenario replaces Florizel with Mamillius, it simply mirrors in reverse the requirements of the dynastic plot. This plot in turn answers to Camillo's earlier lines describing the kings' paradoxical embrace in absence, for it rejoins them while preserving their separation, finding in the gap between them a space for the "loving embassies" of their children.

The play's repeated embrace of absence culminates not in the statue scene but in its shadow—the play's *other* reconciliation scene, realized only through description. In act 5, scene 2, the kings are restored to one another "as it were from the ends of oppos'd winds" (cf. 1.1.21–32), and with this reunion come all the other reconciliations that circulate through Camillo's anticipatory fantasy, with the exception already noted: Leontes embraces Perdita, not Mamillius. The spectacle as described could never be seen—presenting it would be like trying to stage the alternative embraces that hover in the language of Camillo's fantasy. Only a rhetorical and imaginary embrace can gather so many figures at once into its free arms. The scene must therefore remain a spectacle "even then lost when it was found" (5.2.72), cast out of the play's action to be recovered in its language. Returning *as* language, these restorations enact yet again the paradoxical embrace of absence: "Our king, being ready to leap out of himself for joy of his found daughter, as if that joy were now become loss, cries, 'O, thy mother, thy mother!'" (49–52). In this scene, the play rediscovers the initial separation of its two kings as an aspect of dramaturgy—as the difference between telling and showing. In doing so it prepares for the closing sleight of hand in which a spectacular *coup de théâtre* replaces the "body fantastic" that was never there.

This magic, however, depends on a willing suspension of dislike for Leontes. As Orgel observes, "The fact that so many audiences and critics since the eighteenth century have seen this ending as profoundly satisfactory says much for the tenacity of patriarchal assumptions as the subtext to aesthetic judgments" ("Introduction" 79). In Greene's *Pandosto,* the narrative source for the story, the jealous patriarch kills himself; reforming him is Shakespeare's idea. The final scene wagers the play and its art on this desire; if we are unable share it, the statue's animation is apt to feel more like an inspired gimmick than a miracle.

The redemption of Leontes depends on the shift from Mamillius to Perdita. The father-daughter relation brings in a different dynamic, centered not on rivalry and identity but on the conflict between retention and separation. The daughter who must be given in marriage embodies the dispossession of fathers by the demands of kinship, but as a daughter preemptively cast out at birth Perdita masks this loss, presented dramatically as a subordinate aspect of her recovery.[37] The play does record some resistance to the incest taboo when Leontes begins to act like a sexual rival to

---

37. The daughter, as Boose observes, is the distinctively "exchangeable figure" presumed by anthropological models, and as such is the one to whom the incest taboo, in prescribing exogamy, especially applies. While the son is "structurally homologous" with the father, the daughter is "a temporary sojourner within her family, destined to seek legitimation and name outside its boundaries" (19, 21). She is thus a liminal figure in whom the tensions of this boundary are made manifest: sons defend it, daughters cross it.

Florizel, but this moment, which might have revived the king's paranoid jealousy (or prompted his suicide, as in *Pandosto*), instead signals a reawakening of sexual desire leading to the revival of Hermione. From the sheep-shearing festival on, Perdita serves not as an object of rivalry but as a figure in whom all the threats that attend upon hospitality—exchanges, separations, boundary crossings—are repeatedly defused.

The dangers of trespass and exchange are deflected onto Autolycus, who surfaces in act 4 as the character most likely to sluice his neighbor's pond. Slipping from role to role, picking pockets while selling his wares, Autolycus personifies the wandering and transgressive principle associated in one of his songs with money itself: "Come to the pedlar, / Money's a medlar, / That doth utter all men's ware-a" (4.321–23). As the currency of exchange, money goes everywhere, surpassing even Camillo's ability to insinuate himself into the business of others. It is to commerce what daughters are to kinship, but where the daughter circulates within a restricted economy, money crosses every boundary: Autolycus trades not in daughters but in doxies. Money, as Jean-Christophe Agnew reminds us in *Worlds Apart,* has less in common with the daughter than with the player, who mimics every man's business because he has none of his own: the player, too, is a meddler who utters all men's ware.

In act 4 these figures of unregulated exchange cluster around Autolycus, making him in obvious ways a figure for the theater itself. If Leontes sounds at moments like the author of an antitheatrical tract, Autolycus seems to have stepped off the pages of one. Through him *The Winter's Tale* identifies itself with the rogue economy embodied in the theater. Such an image of the playwright's art may seem antithetical to the marvelous witness of the statue's animation, but the play is at pains to remind us that its concluding miracle is a fiction straight out of Autolycus' pack. It is after all "the wolf himself" who inadvertently sets up the recognitions of act 5 by steering the Shepherd and Clown, with their tokens of Perdita's birth, onto Florizel's ship. Leontes' redemption comes to him, then, not just at the hands of a domineering woman and not just at the price of awakening the faith he lacked in act 1; it comes to him from an economy of roguery that embodies his worst fears because it routinely subverts the imaginary foundations of patriarchy.

The references that tie the play's closing miracle to Autolycus and his traffic in sheets (pilfered linens, ballad news, and prostitutes) associate it with a very different image of Shakespeare's theater. Among the entertainments at the sheep-shearing festival is "a dance which the wenches say is a gallimaufry of gambols," performed by "four threes of herdsmen" that have "made themselves all men of hair" (4.4.326–36). The herdsmen "call themselves Saltiers," a name whose hybrid reference to both leapers and satyrs reflects the uncouth hodgepodge of the dance.[38] *The Winter's Tale,* a gallimaufry of genres that grafts comedy onto tragedy and tumbles hairy swineherds into the midst of its flowery pastoral, identifies itself just as much with the leaping satyrs' dance as it does with Hermione's resurrection. Vividly and with pleasure, it summons a world beyond the repentant Leontes' transformed gaze, defined not by the intuitive nobility of the royal foundling but by the aesthetic of impurity she rejects. Implicitly, the play acknowledges itself as Perdita's opposite—Nature's bastard, Shakespeare's gillyvor.[39]

In its divided resolution, the play lets us glimpse something beyond its craving for the body of fatherhood: a recognition that the patriarch, the ideological figure to whom this craving binds us, may be moribund, a social deity who survives only as an object of wishful attachment, required by the subject's inward sense of himself as the object of the father's witness. Autolycus, who has left the court, seems drawn in spite of himself to support the romance ending of the royal drama—an uncharacteristic piece of charity that he keeps trying to pass off as opportunism. This is an ambiguous conversion: it may mean, as Burt and Orgel suggest, that Autolycus is neutralized as a figure of subversion, but it may also insinuate a more skeptical, disenchanted response to the fairy-tale ending.[40] In its portrait of a rogue economy that remains sentimentally attached to the order of the patriarchal family, *The Winter's Tale* does two things at once.

---

38. The word *gallimaufry* has a similar effect, reinforcing the suggestion of odds-and-ends assortment through its own associations with the idea of English as a verbal ragbag: thus E. K. (the perhaps fictional glossator of Spenser's poem) had defended Spenser's use of archaic English terms in *The Shepheardes Calender* by complaining that authors who borrow from French, Italian, and Latin "have made our English tongue, a gallimaufray or hodgepodge of al other speches" (*Yale Edition* 16).

39. This view of Elizabethan theater in general is well expressed by Kastan and Stallybrass: "On stage and in the audience, the playhouse thus registered and rehearsed a variety of social and linguistic conventions; diverse accents and dialects, styles and values, sounded, intermingled, and clashed; the polyphony challenging the homogenizing and unifying pressure of the theater of state. In presenting the spectacle of power, the commercial theater with its multiple and often contradictory voices revealed the fantasy of univocality *as* a fantasy, while it simultaneously exposed the heterogeneity that it would anxiously deny" ("Introduction" 7–8).

40. See the discussion of Autolycus in Orgel, "Introduction" 50–53, and in Burt, *Licensed by Authority* 92–100. Burt argues that "the structural comparison between Shakespeare and Autolycus serves to differentiate between forms of cozening. Shakespeare attempts to guarantee the legitimacy of his theater by contrasting professional forms of autotelic deception to criminal, mercenary forms" (94); like Orgel, he sees in Autolycus's aid to Florizel a closing-down of "critical potential" (97). I do not find the differentiations between theater, cozenage, and commercial exchange nearly so firmly drawn; here, as with the question of the statue's animation, I resist the tendency to read in sharp distinctions where the play seems to me thoroughly equivocal.

It exemplifies the ideological work of sacrificial fictions in a post-sacrificial culture; and it splits off an image of what patriarchy has cast out and grafts its happy ending onto this wild stock. In this way it points toward a growing discrepancy in the early modern period between social reality and its symbolization, which clings to archaic structures and draws on their residual charisma.[41]

Both the discrepancy and the charisma persist in contemporary culture. The retrograde appeal of the patriarchal imaginary is at once our point of attachment and of rupture, the dimension of our intimate alienation from the archaic. Donald Barthelme's fable of postmodern parricide, *The Dead Father*, projects an absurd totemic giant who reminisces wistfully about his ancient godhead while being dragged unceremoniously across the landscape toward a large hole in the ground. Barthelme's gross deity has not fallen from the skies but has been excavated from the urban landscape, and he now sustains a twilight existence: "Great to be alive, said the Dead Father," who is, as Thomas explains to the children, "dead only in a sense."[42] Barthelme seeks to finish off his not quite mortal blusterer through sheer force of travesty. In an early episode the Dead Father, denied the favors of the daughter-wife Julie, pitches a murderous tantrum, slaying a whole grove of musicians. Barthelme renders the scene as a mock-epic catalogue, turning the slaughter into a quaint game of style: how long can the writer sustain an a capella rendition of musical archaisms? ("Whanging his sword this way and that the Dead Father slew a cittern plucker and five lyresmiters and various mandolinists," etc. [11].) Julie's dry comment on this orchestral massacre re-sounds its emptying strain: "Impressive," she says; adding, "had they not been pure cardboard" (12). Barthelme is impressive, too, at improvising strategies for finishing off a dead father who is not dead enough. He offers us travesty as a way of letting go.

41. Mullaney articulates the ideological function I am associating with Autolycus in his description of Shakespeare's "royal plays" as "critical histories of the contemporary moment, anamorphic genealogies of power" characterized by a "two-eyedness (in A. P. Rossiter's phrase) that opens up a critical perspective on [the playwright's] own day and age" (*Place of the Stage* 129). I take Autolycus to be a metonymic figure for the marginal and contradictory "places" of the stage in the cultural and topographical senses Mullaney describes. Construing the popular theater's various metaphoric, ideological, and economic relations to the emergent early modern marketplace is proving a rich vein for criticism. It is Loewenstein's central concern in "Plays Agonistic" and a number of other articles in recent years; in addition to which, see Agnew, Engle, and Leinwand.

42. Barthelme 13, 14. As the anonymous voice of the prologue explains, the Dead Father is "*Dead, but still with us, still with us, but dead*" (3, emphasis in original).

# Charles Dickens:       **4**
# A Dead Hand at a Baby

Dickens is a dead hand at a baby.
  —*Atlas,* 23 December 1848

Dickens is often compared to Shakespeare.[1] Each arrived at a decisive moment in the social and economic history of his chosen medium—Shakespeare during the early years of the commercial theater in London, Dickens during the early years of the double-cylinder steam press, the mass production of paper, and the success of the Sunday school movement in spreading literacy among the working class.[2] In a lifetime of struggle with his publishers, Dickens achieved unprecedented control over the production and circulation of his work; he also promoted the respectability of writing as a public profession. Shakespeare never decreed the specifics of cover design, pricing, or serial run for a quarto, but he was a shareholder and a performer in the King's Men, and the commercial success of his work undoubtedly added to his clout, especially in artistic negotiations over how to stage plays he had written. It is conceivable that he thought of himself as poet and businessman in roughly equal parts, but in either role he probably wanted his speeches spoken trippingly on the tongue. There is little evidence that Shakespeare cultivated any special authorial status, though he did, like Dickens, seek through commercial success as an artist to gentrify an aspiring family line. And like Dickens he did come to embody the popular concept of literary authorship. Shakespeare remains unrivaled in the history of the drama as a formal innovator of techniques for representing human experience as essentially dynamic. Dickens,

1. Alfred Harbage and Valerie L. Gager have devoted books to the topic, but incidental comparison is a hardy perennial.
2. On the steam press and mass production of paper, see Patten 56; on the Sunday school movement, see Pickering, chap. 1.

the most popular and influential novelist who ever wrote, was also a formal innovator. His most striking experiments include the use of a child
protagonist in a novel for adults and the creation in little Paul Dombey of
the child's *point of view*—Paul being the first child in a major English
novel to offer his consciousness directly as an angle on the world.[3]

Like Shakespeare, Dickens refashioned for his own historical moment
an inherited cultural machinery, the symbolic economy of filial sacrifice.
He took up at a later stage in its history the same evangelical culture that
Shakespeare encountered in Foxe. Starting in the late eighteenth century,
an ambitious program to produce and circulate pious works like the
*Cheap Repository Tracts,* capitalizing on the success of the Sunday school
movement, had built up a broad readership for the narrative and rhetorical conventions of didactic sentimentalism. Seizing on the conventions
together with the audience, Dickens incorporated both into the main-
stream of English fiction, meanwhile gleefully satirizing the religious
movement whose tool bag he was ransacking.[4] As a reformer he sought to
redirect the evangelical impulse into a secular, post-Enlightenment community of witness based on the sacredness of the child. To do this, he was
of course required to sacrifice children, a task he executed with such flam-
boyance that England responded to the death of little Paul Dombey with
"a national period of mourning." Critics wept, rivals grew pale, and sales
without precedent in the history of the novel gave Dickens lasting finan-
cial security.


## Evangelical Piety and the "Sacrifice to Feeling"

Modern critics disagree about religious elements in *Dombey and Son* and
in Dickens's fiction generally; so did their Victorian predecessors. The dis-
parity between recent assessments by Dennis Walder and Janet Larsen (for
example) reflects a similar division in the responses of the nineteenth-century readers, ministers, and "sages" they so frequently quote. Larsen sees
Dombey at the novel's close as a "soggy cardboard regenerate" whose author is "yielding up his characters to the fatal embrace of conventions
unimaginatively employed and perhaps no longer found deeply credi-
ble . . ." (116–17). She describes "the witness of Word and deed in the
Midshipman group, in Paul's life and death, and in the characterization of

---

3. Dickens's specific innovation was not, as Tillotson states, to have "put a child at the
centre of a novel for adults" (50), but to have narrated parts of the story *from the child's
point of view.*

4. Pope describes Dickens's hostility toward the evangelical movement, and his recurrent
tendency to satirize it, in the first chapter of *Dickens and Charity.*

Florence" as "Dickens's alternative gospel—one that largely fails" (100). Larsen understands this failure to be at once aesthetic and moral:

> The Bible and the Prayer Book become repositories of clichés from which to draw to evoke automatic reactions for certain kinds of novelistic occasions, such as the child's deathbed or the exaltation of the heroine's virtues. Such bids for Victorian solidarity, when Dickens bribed his readers' uncritical assent with the small change of conventional religious language, have become prime exhibits of the least attractive side to us of "that particular relation (personally affectionate and like no other man's)" which he savored with his public. (6–7)[5]

Larsen is not denying that Dickens created solidarity across class lines and attained a special intimacy with his readers. On the contrary, she is quick to recognize that "with the death of little Paul, Dickens not only dramatized in fiction but created in fact that 'sad community of love and grief' [315] so lacking in the Dombey world" (103). She deplores the way he did it, however, objecting that his use of the sacred represents the author at his "least inventive and most pandering" (7) and hence "can foster the worst sort of complacency" in readers.

Larsen's distaste for the conventions of popular culture strongly colors her account of Dickens's "alternative gospel." This lack of sympathy was shared by Victorian religious writers who assailed what they saw as Dickens's "miserable pantheism": "poetry and sentiment are not religion," wrote the *North British Review* in a scathing indictment of Florence Dombey's prayers for little Paul, "and most miserable substitutes for it" (qtd. in Larsen 114). The more prevalent view was reflected in funeral sermons that celebrated "the sacredness of fictitious narrative" in Dickens, asserting that his "'parables of wisdom, truth, and love' . . . had done more than those of 'any other man to humanize society'" (qtd. in Larsen 4, 76). These, for Larsen, are the voices of "Victorian solidarity" and "uncritical assent."

What Larsen repudiates in Dickens is the cultural model of reading as a conversion experience rather than an exercise of critical intelligence—or, for that matter, a coherent vision of economic reform. There is no question that Dickens borrowed this model from the evangelical movement, redirecting it toward secular reformation. Dennis Walder quotes John Forster, Dickens's lifelong friend and chosen biographer, who reported that, during the 1840s, "'the hopelessness of any true solution by the ordinary Downing-street methods' was 'startlingly impressed' upon [Dick-

---

5. The phrase in quotation marks is Dickens's, from a letter to John Forster (30 March 1858) on the question of paid public readings; see *Letters* 8:539.

ens] by Carlyle's writings, as well as by his own observations, with the result that he began to try to 'convert Society' by showing that its happiness
rested 'on the same foundations as those of the individual, which are
mercy and charity not less than justice'" (113).[6] Walder notes that Dickens, "like Carlyle . . . believed in a conception of conversion which did
not primarily involve an acceptance of Christ, or the innate sinfulness of
man, but which *did* involve a spiritual transformation affirming a new
consciousness of oneself and one's place in the universe" (114). "In a
sense," he goes on to suggest, "this aligns [Dickens] with the evangelicals,
who considered the sacrament of baptism less important in itself than the
idea of regeneration or conversion; and in stressing the need for conversion, Dickens was participating in the evangelical tradition" (130).
George Orwell neatly summed up the political implications of this model
when he described Dickens as "essentially a 'change of heart' man: 'he is
always pointing to a change of spirit rather than a change of structure'"
(qtd. in Walder 113).

In the late eighteenth century, gathering forces of evangelical Christianity brought forth the Sunday school movement, which sought to reduce
class division by reforming the working poor.[7] The success of this movement in teaching workers and their families to read opened the way to a
popular religious literature exemplified by Hannah More and the *Cheap
Repository Tracts*. In *The Moral Tradition in English Fiction*, Samuel Pickering suggests that this literature played a significant role in making the
novel "morally respectable in the nineteenth century" (89). He argues
that Dickens was significantly indebted to it for both the shape of his early
narratives and the breadth of his reading public (107).[8] Pickering examines a serious rift *within* the evangelical movement over the value of fiction, showing how the didactic sentimentalism of More and others gradually won acceptance. Meanwhile, as he notes, evangelical writers relied

6. For the quoted phrase see Forster 347.
7. On the importance of Dickens to working-class readers, see Rose, "Reading," esp. 56,
60–61, and 64. In discussing the tendency of many working-class readers to read "the flood
of goody-goody literature which was poured in upon us" (67, quoting George Acorn) by
scanning for plot, Rose may also suggest one reason that Dickens's appropriation of evangelical conventions was such a commercial success: it gave readers what they wanted without
the "pill of religious teaching." See also Rose, *The Intellectual Life of the Working Class,* esp.
111–15.
8. Qualls seconds Pickering's emphasis, noting that "to put a child at the center of a novel
was not a Dickens innovation . . . dying youngsters like Little Nell simply repeated a pattern
which evangelical magazines had been using for decades" (88; cf. n.3). Qualls offers an excellent discussion of Dickens's affinities for popular religious narrative and iconography,
though I think he tends to read the canon retrospectively, as destined for the *telos* of *Our
Mutual Friend,* and therefore overemphasizes the elements of religious skepticism and disenchantment.

heavily on the very qualities they denounced in fiction: "While condemn-
ing novels as the food of vitiated and sickly imaginations, religious jour-
nals published, under the guise of biography, the most sensational stories
that appeared during the age" (67). It would be 1806 before *The Christian Observer* "measured a collection of tracts by a literary standard for the
first time" (76), but fictional techniques had been central to its journalism
all along: "The people in the *Observer's* biographies and obituaries were
regularly fictionalized to fit a didactic pattern. Leaning heavily on tearful
but apocalyptic death scenes, the biographies teetered on the abyss of sensibility" (70–71).

Dickens reversed this strategy. As *The Christian Observer* had appropriated novelistic techniques while denouncing the novel, Dickens adapted
the conventions of the tracts while satirizing evangelicalism. In the process, he did more than simply pander to morally complacent readers while
registering the disintegration of religion as a basis for social life. Larsen asserts that "Dickens's mature fictional reconstructions . . . never achieve
the 'new Mythus' Carlyle had called for" (14), but what this means is that
she finds the synthesis of popular religion and progressive politics in this
"Mythus" unsatisfactory. It was, however, spectacularly successful: if John
Stuart Mill articulated the political theory underlying modern democratic
liberalism, Dickens synthesized its ideology, its imaginary form.[9]

This engagement with popular culture is central to Dickens's work and
to his faith in the writer as a public figure. Walder suggests that "for Dickens and his readers the details of Tract XC, for example, or of Bishop
Samuel Wilberforce's clash with T. H. Huxley over evolution, were of far
less interest and concern than, say, the fate of *The Dairyman's Daughter*
(Richmond, n.d.), a young girl whose premature death was piously recounted by the chaplain to Queen Victoria's father [Legh Richmond] in
what became probably the most successful tract ever published" (2–3).
*The Dairyman's Daughter* was republished along with two other tracts by
Richmond as *The Annals of the Poor, or Narratives of The Dairyman's
Daughter, the Negro Servant, and the Young Cottager.* In this volume from
the 1840s we can see what is bound up in the tension between truth
claims and fictional techniques. The disavowal of fiction, it is clear, arises
from the fantasy of reading as religious conversion.

*Annals of the Poor* is dedicated to William Wilberforce as "This Little
Work, Designed to Bear a Testimony, Drawn from Real Facts and Occurrences, to the Infinite Value of Christian Truth When Received in the

9. Rose cites "a 1906 survey of the first large cohort of Labour Members of Parliament.
The 51 MPs were asked to name the books and authors that had influenced them most."
Dickens, cited by 16 of the 51, finished a close second to Ruskin, with 17 citations—and just
ahead of the Bible, with 14 ("Reading" 56).

Heart and Exemplified in the Conduct." Clearly the *reality* of its incidents is crucial in linking the "little work" to the "infinite value." Even so, these same "facts and occurrences" are crudely fictionalized. Little Jane, the "young cottager" of the third narrative, dies of consumption after a long and pious decline. With a fine sense of melodrama, she sits up and throws her arms around the minister before surrendering to death. "At this affecting moment," reports Richmond,

> the rays of the morning sun darted into the room, and filled my imagination with the significant emblem of the tender mercy of our God; whereby the dayspring from on high hath visited us, to give light to them that sit in darkness and in the shadow of death, to guide our feet into the way of peace.
>
> It was a beam of light, that seemed at once to describe the glorious change which her soul had now already experienced; and at the same time, to shed the promised consolations of hope over the minds of those who witnessed her departure.
>
> This was an incident obviously arising from a natural cause; but one which irresistibly connected itself with the spiritual circumstances of the case. (300–301)

Richmond is working in a typological vein for which nature has always been a divine symbol. But his need to *rationalize* the coincidence of natural cause and spiritual circumstance suggests that he can no longer take the conventions of biblical typology for granted. To reassert them is his constant labor, and as a result long stretches of the tracts are devoted to crudely moralized landscapes—a sort of evangelical picturesque.

Editions of the *Annals* published after 1830 include an account by James Milnor, chairman of the Executive Committee of the American Tract Society, of his party's pilgrimage to the locations described in Richmond's tracts. They visit the house of the "dairyman's daughter," look at her room, meet her brother, and sign the register. Milnor supplies repeated assurances along the way that all the scenery really is just as Richmond had described it. Visits to particular locations are accompanied by readings aloud from corresponding sections of the text, always of course confirming its perfect accuracy: "In full view of this elevated spot we read his extended description, and turned southward, and southeastward, and northward, and westward, and admired, as he had done, the unequalled beauty of the scene" (315). Adding his testimony to that of the author, Milnor shares in the labor of spiritualizing natural facts while holding the subversive force of fiction at bay.

This labor is crucial because emblematic sunbeams can do *their* ideological work only if we accept them as at once natural and divine. They dart in with exquisite timing, linking the deathbed scene to the sacrifice of

Christ ("the dayspring from on high") and so to the resurrection, consoling the witnesses of Little Jane's death by signaling "the glorious change which her soul had now already experienced." Bridging all potential gaps in the perfection of the moment, they "irresistibly" join the event itself to a proper witnessing response (filling the author's imagination with an emblem of God's mercy, shedding "promised consolations of hope" on the others). In this way they transform the surrounding group into a community of witness, a community that sees death but beholds rebirth.

All this is a tall order for a sunbeam. Richmond works hard to deny the labor of his text and to disavow his role in fashioning the "incident obviously arising from a natural cause." When he does imagine the force of his "simple memorial," though, Richmond hopes it will do on a broader scale just what the sunbeam does:

> The last day will, if I err not, disclose further fruits, resulting from the love of God to this little child; and through her, to others that saw her. And may not hope indulge the prospect, that this simple memorial of her history shall be as one arrow drawn from the quiver of the Almighty to reach the hearts of the young and the thoughtless? Direct its course, O my God. May the eye that reads, and the ear that hears the record of little Jane, through the power of the Spirit of the Most High, each become the witness for the truth as it is in Jesus. (277–78)

Richmond wants the text to be as artless as the facts of nature, each of which "proclaims in glowing language, 'God made me'" (59), and to become in this way a work not of the minister but of his God. At once natural and divine—anything but human, anything but mere fiction and rhetoric—the text will extend the conversion effects of its emblematic sunbeam.

Another of the supplemental texts added to later editions of the *Annals* demonstrates clearly how this fantasy models reading as a conversion experience:

> The Rev. Mr. Grimshaw, in his memoir of Mr. Richmond, 1828, estimates that of *The Dairyman's Daughter* no less than four million copies had then been circulated, in nineteen languages. Many testimonies that it had been blessed in the conversion of sinners to God, were transmitted to the author, the last of which, received but twenty-four hours before his death, was that of a clergyman whose antipathy against Tract Societies had induced him to select *The Dairyman's Daughter* for the purpose of criticising and exposing its defects. In the perusal of it he was so penetrated by the truths it contained, that the pen of criticism fell from his hand, and he was himself added as another trophy of divine grace. (319)

Here the opposition between criticism and conversion could not be more striking: when truth penetrates the heart, the pen of criticism falls from the hand. No wonder, then, if critics have little patience for didactic sentimentalism: conversion and critical analysis are competing fantasies, imagined scenes of reading, each of which triumphs at the other's expense.

The imaginary effects of the religious tracts depend, like the sunbeam itself, on the commanding pathos of a child's death. The questions that such deaths always raise—why does God permit them, and how does the author profit from them?—run through Richmond's tracts like a bad conscience. In one particularly egregious fit of complacency, the author extols the spiritual benefits of tuberculosis: "What a field for usefulness and affectionate attention on the part of ministers and Christian friends, is opened by the frequent attacks and lingering process of *consumptive* illness" (108). Describing the lingering process of Little Jane's consumption, he observes that the fever "produced a flush on her otherwise pallid countenance, which in no small degree added to her interesting appearance" (288). At such moments Richmond starts to sound like a Dickensian parody, rank with pious humbug and impervious to the suffering in front of him.

Such awkward rhetorical gestures betray the self-consciousness of a contrived spectacle. In his too-eager solicitation of the reader, Richmond blurts out his own conflicts of interest "when it is the Lord's pleasure to remove any of his faithful followers out of this life at an early period of their course" (96). As a minister, he has routinely made the spectacle of death central to his teaching. On Saturday afternoons he would meet with a group of children. In summer they would gather under a shade tree near a fence, beyond which lay a graveyard—"a scene," he blandly observes, "which rendered my occupation more interesting" (212). He would point to the graves and tell the children that "young as they were, none of them were too young to die; and that probably more than half of the bodies which were buried there, were those of little children." He would also "call to their recollection the more recent deaths of their own relatives, that lay buried so near us. Some had lost a parent, others a brother or sister; some perhaps had lost all these, and were committed to the mercy of their neighbors, as fatherless and motherless orphans. Such circumstances," he observes, "were occasionally useful to excite tender emotions, favorable to serious impressions" (213–14). Richmond is so gratified by his success with Little Jane that he claims her for his own: "If the first-born child in nature be received as a new and acceptable blessing," he asks, "how much more so the first-born child in grace? I claim this privilege . . ." (211). Later, after a poignant bedside scene with the dying girl, he reports: "My heart was filled with thankfulness for what I had seen and heard. Little Jane appeared to be the first-fruits of my parochial and spiritual harvest. This thought greatly comforted and strengthened me in my ministerial prospects" (238).

Richmond thus finds a "new and acceptable blessing" in "the pale, wasting consumption which is the Lord's instrument for removing so many thousands every year from the land of the living" (108). The Lord's instrument provides excellent opportunities to confirm a minister's vocation and to amplify his persuasive force, motives that betray themselves at high points of pathos. Most of Richmond's conversations with dying converts seem utterly scripted: "Were you not soon convinced," he asks the dairyman's daughter, "that your salvation must be an act of entire grace on the part of God, wholly independent of your own previous works or deservings?" (117). Such questions are doctrinal prompts, so few of the answers are unexpected. Interestingly, however, the most powerful scene in *The Young Cottager* features a telling swerve from correct doctrine. Richmond asks Little Jane who brings the good news of the gospel. "Sir," she replies, "*you* brought it to *me*." He continues, "Here my soul melted in an instant, and I could not repress the tears which the emotion excited. The last answer was equally unexpected and affecting. I felt a father's tenderness and gratitude for a first-born child" (237). The correct answer, of course, would be "Jesus." By substituting the reverend narrator for her savior, the little girl flatters his ministry; it is just after this interview that he recognizes her as the firstfruits of his harvest and feels comforted in his prospects.

The flattery extends as well to all those other literal and figurative ministers whose imitation of Christ is enjoined by such a story. Thus the Reverend John Ayre, whose "Sketch of the Life" is prefixed to later editions of the *Annals,* confesses:

I can *venerate* the high and exalted piety of the "dairyman's daughter," who, with a masculine strength of understanding, had ever her word of counsel even for the minister; but I *love* the little, backward, neglected, retiring child, who starts forth at once in all the moral beauty of Christian attainment. (16)

Ayre's response to Little Jane turns out to be anchored in just those "affecting" moments that trouble the orthodoxy of the text:

The scene, for example, where Mr. Richmond, on his first visit to her, while speaking of the good news of the gospel, inquires, "Who brings this good news?" and is answered, "Sir, *you* brought it to *me*," I know not who can read unmoved. Her parting benediction too—"God bless and reward you!"—when with an unexpected exertion she threw her arms around him and expired, is inexpressibly affecting. (17)

Richmond and Ayres are thoroughly equivocal witnesses whose emotional response to the child's death is self-interested and self-indulgent. But their unconscious egotism, however morally unattractive, is not a merely personal failing, nor does it detract from the narrative's power "to excite tender emotions, favorable to serious impressions." On the contrary, these swervings from perfect religious truth point to the real source of the narrative's emotional and imaginative force, which lies in the kind of narcissism that the text pretends to sacrifice in its devotion to "the truth as it is in Jesus."

Wendy Lesser has well described the sentimentality such scenes depend on. Their essence lies in

> a kind of alienation: a separation between viewer and object which allows the viewer to indulge in self-pity at a distance, to expend the kind of emotion that he would be afraid to expend on himself, for fear of deep pain and an ultimate sense of loss. Sentimentality allows us to feel a kind of superficial pain which closely resembles pleasure. It allows us not to substitute ourselves for another (as the empathy experts would have it), but to substitute another for ourselves as a sacrifice to feeling. (197)

When Richmond's own natural children died, he was unable to sustain the alienation on which his ministry depended.[10] He repeatedly claims to feel a father's affection for Jane as his "first-born child in grace" (211), but the comfort and strength he too easily gathers from her pious death lend his repeated references to "the first-fruits of my parochial and spiritual harvest" (238) an uncomfortable resonance, reminding us that their conventional language echoes scriptural passages in which Yahweh demands not just the Israelites' firstfruits but also their firstborn sons. Lesser's description of the sympathetic object as "a *sacrifice* to feeling" could scarcely be more apt, for it points to the ways in which the ancient symbolic economy of filial sacrifice passes into the structure of the modern subject, there to reemerge in the emotional dynamics of sentimentality.

10. Ayres reports that when Richmond's second son died of consumption in 1825, followed six months later by his eldest son's death at sea, the minister's health declined rapidly, his spirits grew somber, and he died not long after (19–20).

## Dickens and Moloch

The religious tracts of the late eighteenth century grew out of a popular tradition reaching back to *The Book of Martyrs*. One indispensable way of studying this tradition is represented in a recent essay by Eirwen Nicholson, who points to the need for historical bibliography to be more scrupulous in documenting specific paths of transmission.[11] I would urge that the cultural history to which this tradition belongs must also be grasped as a symbolic economy. Within this economy, the sacrificial child may be a Carthaginian offering to Moloch, a Marian martyr at the stake, or a consumptive schoolgirl on the Isle of Wight: all pass through a sacrificial fire that in some sense remains the same. The recuperative force of such an economy gathers the arbitrary particularity of *what happens* back into established forms even as it recasts these forms in the process, stretching the familiar to accommodate the new. Probably neither God nor the Lacanian Symbolic dispatched an epidemic of tuberculosis across Europe in the late eighteenth and early nineteenth centuries to enlarge the scope of charitable ministries, but once the epidemic came along, cultural practices determined the range of things it could mean, whether as the fashionable disease of artists or the feverish burning of sacrificial children.[12] By the end of the nineteenth century this last symbol had emerged in almost pure form in "the dream of the burning child," reported by Freud in the final chapter of *The Interpretation of Dreams*. In this celebrated passage, a child who has died after an illness returns in a dream, beseeching, "*Father, don't you see I'm burning?*" (547–48). In effect, this haunting question thinks its way *back through* the cultural history that turns the fires of fever into those of martyrdom, tracing them to their scriptural prototype in child sacrifice. From this perspective, what the dream reveals is not the personal unconscious of the unknown dreamer, but the sacrificial economy of patriarchy, which operates in the Western cultural tradition as a distinct, semiautonomous system, shaping and informing individual subjects.

Dickens unfolds this sacrificial economy most explicitly in his Christmas books, especially the last and least admired of the series, *The Haunted*

11. Nicholson stresses the need for a more precise description of the way Foxe's influence was disseminated through a wide range of "abridgements and cheap pamphlet and broadside derivations" that he refers to as "the 'bastard' versions" (149).

12. McGrew writes, "In 1815, Thomas Young, a medical authority who had just completed a review of the writings available on tuberculosis, claimed that the disease had brought a 'premature death' to at least a quarter of Europe's population" (339). The epidemic began in the seventeenth century, reaching its first peak between 1650 and 1675, then declining sharply until 1730, rising again by 1750, and identified by 1800 as the most prevalent and dangerous of all diseases.

*Man,* published in 1848. The impulses of satire and hectoring sentimentality are ill-sorted in this work, but its artistic failure makes it useful in measuring the distance between *Annals of the Poor* and a major achievement like *Dombey and Son.* In this story Dickens illustrates the dynamics of the sacrificial economy through the simple expedient of imagining its undoing. *The Haunted Man* therefore provides what we might call a negative analysis of this economy's capacity to produce surplus spiritual value in the form of Christian charity. In this way it traces something like a Dickensian "genealogy of morals." The last of the "descriptive headlines" added to *The Haunted Man* in the edition of 1868 proposes a scientific analogy: it labels the essential principle of this economy "Christian Chemistry" (361). Whether we think of it as gift exchange or chemical reaction, the principle in question identifies remembered personal suffering with the present suffering of others, and so converts gall into the milk of human kindness. By imagining the undoing and then the restoring of this chemical-spiritual reaction, Dickens's fictional experiment deduces the sacrificial formula that can trigger an exchange of suffering between persons that resembles the exchange of constituents between substances heated in a glass beaker.

*The Haunted Man* is the story of Redlaw, a celebrated professor of chemistry who leads a brooding, isolated existence. His youthful hopes for romantic fulfillment and domestic comfort have long since been blighted by the treachery of his closest friend, Longford, who won the love of Redlaw's sister and then of his intended bride before abandoning them both to pursue a course of unspecified depravity. Redlaw's bitterness over these memories haunts him literally in the form of a ghostly double, a "Phantom" who resembles him exactly and, in the opening chapter, mocks him with a first-person recitation of his sorrows:

> "Look upon me!" said the Spectre. "I am he, neglected in my youth, and miserably poor, who strove and suffered. . . ."
> "I *am* that man," returned the Chemist. (266)

In the book's first chapter, "The Gift Bestowed," the Phantom offers Redlaw the gift of forgetfulness, erasing both his memories and the pain they cause. This ironic Christmas gift is itself a phantom; not a thing, certainly not a commodity, it is rather a spreading pool of oblivion that soaks up all consciousness of suffering. Its effect is to destroy empathy, affection, forgiveness, and other forms of fellow feeling in everyone it touches. Redlaw's neo-Faustian bargain and its terrible consequences form the core of the narrative, as indicated in its three chapter titles: "The Gift Bestowed," "The Gift Diffused," and "The Gift Reversed." The story's theme, epitomized in the motto "Lord, keep my memory green," is that the roots of Christian charity lie in the memory of past wrongs and sufferings. As it passes from Redlaw to the other characters, circulating *like* a commodity, this almost Nietzschean "faculty of oblivion" allows Dickens to explore the symbolic economy of filial sacrifice by imagining its undoing, or what Freud would call its *Ungeschehenmachen*. These effects are reversed, and the sacrificial economy is reinstated, only when the memory of suffering is found nestling in the maternal bosom of Milly Swidger.

Although Milly and Mr. William are childless, there is nevertheless (as he puts it) "a motherly feeling in Mrs. William's breast that must and will have went." The story that follows unfolds this pun, revealing that the present flowing forth, or venting, of motherly feeling from Mrs. William redeems a past loss, a motherly feeling that "went" with its brief object into death. For now, we know only that Milly, although she has never nursed a child of her own, acts as "a sort of mother to all the young gentlemen that come up from a wariety of parts, to attend your courses of lectures at this ancient foundation" (253). As this sublimated maternity arouses the narrator to an almost hysterical pitch of moral idealism, he declaims with reference to her bosom, "To whom would its repose and peace have not appealed against disturbance, like the innocent slumber of a child!" (255). Only this charismatic bosom, giving "went" to maternal tenderness as it pillows the slumber of a fantasy child, has the power to reverse the Phantom's gift in chapter 3.

In the final pages of the story, we learn that this child is not a fancy but a memory. Mr. Swidger prepares us for the revelation by repeating his earlier asseveration, "There's a motherly feeling in Mrs. William's breast that must and will have went!" (349). This time he continues:

> "It happens for the best, Milly dear, no doubt," said Mr. William, tenderly, "that we have no children of our own; and yet I sometimes wish you had one to love and cherish. Our little dead child that you built such hopes upon, and that never breathed the breath of life—it has made you quiet-like, Milly." (349)

From this revelation the story moves quickly to its conclusion. Milly explains to Mr. William that she thinks of her dead child constantly, but is "very happy in the recollection of it" because it has become "like an angel" to her, attending her from day to day and transfiguring her experience of the world:

> "For poor neglected children, my little child pleads as if it were alive, and had a voice I knew, with which to speak to me. When I hear of youth in suffering or shame, I think that my child might have come to that, perhaps, and that God took it from me in His mercy. Even in age and grey hair, such

as father's, it is present: saying that it too might have lived to be old, long and long after you and I were gone, and to have needed the respect and love of younger people." (350)

In Milly, then, we encounter nothing less than Dickens's *Pietà*, fused so deeply with the aging boy that they seem inseparable.

Redlaw is quick to recognize the Madonna and child so thinly veiled in Milly's serene response to infant mortality. Falling to his knees "with a loud cry" he thanks God in a language of pure typology for the "gift" of remembered suffering:

> "Oh Thou," he said, "who, through the teaching of pure love, has graciously restored to me the memory which was the memory of Christ upon the cross, and of all the good who perished in His cause, receive my thanks, and bless her!" (351)

In effect, then, and after his own fashion, Dickens has traced the genealogy of morals back to its sacrificial basis. The Father exists in this rendition only as an archaic pronoun, but the symbolic economy he graciously superintends does circulate his seminal gift of suffering, embodied in the Madonna and child. The sacrificial son emerges in this analysis as the primal gift underlying all empathetic exchange, or—in the story's other metaphor—as the reagent without which "Christian Chemistry" cannot transmute sorrow into charity.

One thing that sets Dickens apart from many nineteenth-century purveyors of sentimentality is his gift for incorporating wicked parodies of his loftiest themes and most touching figures. In *The Haunted Man* the Tetterbys serve this noble end, as Johnny and his infant sister, Sally, travesty both the central theme of empathy and the role of the mortal infant as its avatar. Consider the following exchange between Johnny and Mr. Tetterby:

> "Johnny, my child, take care of your only sister, Sally; for she's the brightest gem that ever sparkled on your early brow."
>
> Johnny sat down on a little stool, and devotedly crushed himself beneath the weight of Moloch.
>
> "Ah, what a gift that baby is to you, Johnny!" said his father, "and how thankful you ought to be! 'It is not generally known,' Johnny," he was now referring to the screen again [i.e., quoting from newspaper clippings pasted on a partition], "'but it is a fact ascertained, by accurate calculations, that the following immense per-centage of babies never attain to two years old; that is to say—'"
>
> "Oh don't, father, please!" cried Johnny. "I can't bear it, when I think of Sally." (281)

The mortality of children in Victorian London was no joke; it is "a fact ascertained" that almost half the funerals held in London in 1839 were for children under the age of ten.[13] What Dickens mocks is not the fear or sorrow that infant mortality inspires in almost everyone, but the *use* of such prepossessing emotions, the calculated playing upon them with an eye to some advantage. In other words, he is parodying the central imaginative tendency of his own fiction.

This parody is unusually explicit in its invocation of child sacrifice: "Tetterby's was the corner shop in Jerusalem Buildings," the narrator tells us, and among the relics to be found in the shop window is a lantern containing "a heap of minute wax dolls, all sticking together upside down, in the direst confusion, with their feet on one another's heads, and a precipitate of broken arms and legs at the bottom" (278). The suspiciously "archaeological" feel of this image is a subtle effect.[14] But the parody's most inspired moment comes in its conspicuous reversal of the sacrificial motif on which the whole story turns, as the narrator renames baby Sally:

> It was a very Moloch of a baby, on whose insatiate altar the whole existence of this particular young brother was offered up a daily sacrifice. . . .
> Yet Johnny was verily persuaded that it was a faultless baby, without its peer in the realm of England, and was quite content to catch meek glimpses of things in general from behind its skirts, or over its limp flapping bonnet, and to go staggering about with it like a very little porter with a very large parcel, which was not directed to anybody, and could never be delivered anywhere. (277)

This package reaches its symbolic destination at the close of the story. The Tetterbys are suffering from the terrible effects of Redlaw's "gift," which has transformed their domestic scene from its initial state of cheerful chaos (lapsing now and then into exasperation) to a dreary hostility in which even little Johnny has begun to detest his baby sister. All this changes at the approach of Milly Swidger:

> "Here! Mother! Father!" cried Johnny, running into the room. "Here's Mrs. William coming down the street!"
> And if ever, since the world began, a young boy took a baby from a cradle with the care of an old nurse, and hushed and soothed it tenderly, and tot-

13. Peter Ackroyd reports in *Dickens* that "in 1839, for example, almost half the funerals in London were conducted for children under the age of ten, carried off by sickness or malnutrition" (320).

14. I have not located a specific source for the image of the melted wax dolls, but suspect that one exists. The mapping and excavation of the basin between the Tigris and Euphrates rivers was a major project of Victorian orientalism, and many of the principals involved (men like Austen Henry Layard) belonged to Dickens's circle of acquaintance in London.

tered away with it cheerfully, Johnny was that boy, and Moloch was that baby, as they went out together! (335)

The package may be said to arrive late, for the story naturally concludes with a Christmas dinner hosted by Mr. Redlaw, at which Johnny and Moloch are the last to appear, too late for the beef. And yet we are not to take *this* sacrifice too seriously, for "that," confides the narrator, "was customary, and not alarming" (352).

Dickens may have helped us to see more than he intended, for in tracing the symbolic economy of his own moral vision, and with it that of his culture, back to a sacrificial basis, he demonstrates that what is customary—above all, Christmas, and the ethos of suffering it celebrates—is also profoundly alarming. We may suspect that he senses as much; we may even detect his effort to fend off this knowledge in the rhetorical questions—punctuated not as questions but as exclamations—with which his narrator rhapsodizes over Milly Swidger's "little bodice so placid and neat":

> Who could have had the heart to make so calm a bosom swell with grief, or throb with fear, or flutter with a thought of shame! To whom would its repose and peace have not appealed against disturbance, like the innocent slumber of a child! (255)

One measure of Dickens's greatness, even in a work as flawed as *The Haunted Man,* may be found in the way his writing provokes the disturbance this apotropaic rhetoric would ward off. He is indeed, as the *Atlas* reviewer so perfectly phrased it, "a dead hand at a baby."[15]

## Dombey and Son

From the first sentence of *Dombey and Son,* Dickens shows a sly awareness that his novel has, as it were, a sacrificial prehistory. There are no chortling references this time to Moloch or Jerusalem, but the very symbol of family life, the hearth, doubles as a human oven:

> Dombey sat in the corner of the darkened room in the great armchair by the bedside, and Son lay tucked up warm in a little basket bedstead, carefully disposed on a low settee immediately in front of the fire and close to it, as if his constitution were analogous to that of a muffin, and it was essential to toast him brown while he was very new. (49)

15. Qtd. in Slater, "Introduction to *The Haunted Man,*" in Dickens, *The Christmas Books* 237.

Little Paul Dombey may be slightly surprising as an avatar of the burning child, but long before we hear that he is "old-fashioned" it seems clear he is overcooked. Dickens doesn't miss a trick: having introduced Paul in the form of a snack, he quickly invokes the allegorical figure of Time with his scythe, and through him, a mythographic tradition in which the cosmic reaper snaps up children like muffins.[16]

Dombey "exulting in the long-looked-for event" is linked to this figure: he "jingled and jingled the heavy gold watch-chain that depended from below his trim blue coat, whereof the buttons sparkled phosphorescently in the feeble rays of the distant fire" (49). An emblem of impatience, he wants to devour the instant. He "loved his son with all the love he had," the narrator tells us, "though not so much as an infant, or as a boy, but as a grown man—the 'Son' of the Firm. Therefore he was impatient to advance into the future, and to hurry over the intervening passages of his history" (151). These motifs are taken up again when we meet Dr. Blimber, his clock, and his "forcing" method of education. In Brighton on Sunday evenings "the Doctor's dark door" stands "agape to swallow [Paul] up for another week" (229); and there too, as he grows more and more "old-fashioned," Paul each evening offers "his morsel of a hand" to Dr. Blimber (256).

In our glimpse of Dombey triumphant, Time the reaper is linked (by way of the watch chain) to a "distant fire" dancing in the father's coat buttons. The connection is no more than a flash of phosphorescence. Yet we may recall it when Dr. Blimber appears as a garden-variety Moloch, to whom parents eagerly pass their children through fire:

> In fact, Doctor Blimber's establishment was a great hothouse, in which there was a forcing apparatus incessantly at work. All the boys blew before their time. (206)

> In short, however high and false the temperature at which the Doctor kept his hothouse, the owners of the plants were always ready to lend a helping hand at the bellows, and to stir the fire. (234)

Repeatedly in such passages Dickens throws a sardonic glance toward the sacrificial prehistory of his scenes, elaborating his sympathy for the children with variations on the rhetoric of filial impertinence. Repeatedly as well, however, he invokes comic incongruities as a way of sliding back toward the tones of fatherly indulgence. There is, for example, an odd joc-

---

16. Time the reaper is traditionally identified with Saturn, and Saturn with Chronos, who swallowed his young. On the recurrence of this figure in Dickens's fiction, its possible derivation from *Sartor Resartus,* and its link to the motif of "oral sadism" in *Dombey and Son,* see Lukacher, esp. 298–313.

ularity in the way he reports the suicidal thoughts of "Poor Briggs," the most dispirited of the doctor's victims. Joining the others one day for a walk before tea, Briggs "looked over the cliff two or three times darkly" (223); later in the evening he remarks "that he should wish himself dead if it weren't for his mother, and a blackbird he had at home" (225). Finally, we are told when vacation time arrives that "friends of the family (then resident near Bayswater, London) seldom approached the ornamental piece of water in Kensington gardens, without a vague expectation of seeing Master Briggs's hat floating on the surface, and an unfinished exercise lying on the bank" (251). Like the opening simile that compares the newborn baby to a muffin toasting on the hearth, such moments temper melodrama and empathy with gallows humor. *You, too,* they seem to tell us, can take pleasure in this spectacle. *You shall be as gods.*

Dombey Senior takes on the full burden of this temptation, untempered by any of the narrator's whimsy. Critics have observed that there is a Dombey theology of sorts. "A.D." translates as "Anno Dombei" in this dispensation, for

> The earth was made for Dombey and Son to trade in, and the sun and moon were made to give them light. Rivers and seas were formed to float their ships; rainbows gave them promise of fair weather; winds blew for or against their enterprises; stars and planets circled in their orbits, to preserve inviolate a system of which they were the center. (50)

Dombey speaks of "the House" in language borrowed from God—language that would be mystical were it not emptied out by the blandness of his arrogance:

> Paul and myself will be able, when the time comes, to hold our own—the House, in other words, will be able to hold its own, and maintain its own, and hand down its own of itself, and without any such common-place aids. (102–3)

The vision of a self-reproducing corporate body able to "hand down its own of itself," without such "common-place aids" as women, pregnancy, or infancy, is a fiction inherited from medieval theology and law, where it defines the deity and the crown respectively. Dombey's tendency to consume infancy is a satiric exaggeration of this perspective: like the royal body politic as defined by the Tudor jurist Edmund Plowden, the "Son" of the Firm is "utterly void of Infancy, and old Age, and other natural Defects and Imbecilities, which the Body natural is subject to" (qtd. in Kantorowicz 7). In Dr. Blimber, Dickens offers a wickedly funny parody of this theoretical incapacity of the law: "the Doctor," he writes, "in some partial confusion of his ideas, regarded the young gentlemen as if they were all Doctors, and were born grown up" (233).

Dickens later speaks of Dombey as "the removed Being" (647). In the same chapter, Carker declares to Edith: "Dombey and Son know neither time, nor place, nor season, but bear them all down" (611). Susan Nipper, confronting Dombey at last over his neglect of Florence, recognizes what she is up against:

> ". . . she's the blessedest and dearest angel is Miss Floy that ever drew the breath of life, the more that I was torn to pieces Sir the more I'd say it though I may not be a Fox's Martyr." (703)

Later she protests that "ordering one's self lowly and reverently towards one's betters, is not to be a worshipper of graven images, and I will and must speak!" (705). At such moments, the Nipper looks like a burlesque of Shakespeare's Paulina, stripped of aristocratic status and maternal dignity but left with her determination, her truth, and her passing similarity to a Foxe's martyr: "It is an heretic who makes the fire, not she who burns in't."

Mistaking himself for God, Dombey endures the full consequences of his error, sacrificing his only begotten son to the symbolic identity they share in "the Firm." First, his impatient failure to acknowledge his son *as a child* hastens Paul's death. Then, as the miserable father looks on, helpless to prevent the death he has unconsciously willed, he is punished with exquisite precision by the dying boy's reciprocal failure to recognize him. His most cherished illusion has been that "I am enough for him, perhaps, and all in all," to which he adds, "I have no wish that people should step in between us" (103). So Polly Toodle is instructed in no uncertain terms, "It is not at all in this bargain that you need become attached to my child, or that my child need become attached to you. I don't expect or desire anything of the kind. Quite the reverse" (68). Miss Tox is "elevated . . . to the godmothership of little Paul, in virtue of her insignificance" (103); Florence, by contrast, is cast out precisely because she seems always to be there between Dombey and his significant others. He broods intently over the image of Florence embracing her mother, her brother, and eventually Edith, always feeling himself excluded from what he sees. While watching over Paul's deathbed, he is astonished to discover how utterly excluded he is:

> But this figure with its head upon its hand returned so often, and remained so long, and sat so still and solemn, never speaking, never being spoken to,

and rarely lifting up its face, that Paul began to wonder languidly, if it were real; and in the night-time saw it sitting there, with fear.

"Floy!" he said. "What *is* that?"

"Where, dearest?"

"There! at the bottom of the bed."

"There's nothing there, except Papa!"

The figure lifted up its head, and rose, and coming to the bedside, said:

"My own boy! Don't you know me?"

Paul looked at its face, and thought, was this his father? (294)

If Dickens had set out consciously to reverse Leontes' inspection of Mamillius in *The Winter's Tale* (complete with its buried allusion to Hamlet's contemplation of Yorick), he could hardly have done so with more precision.[17] Mistaking his father for a specter of death, the boy is, in fact, recognizing with devastating accuracy what Dombey has turned himself into. This reversal plays itself out in the novel's conclusion, as Dombey, broken and childlike, stands by the seashore with his grandchildren listening to the sound of the waves. Little Paul never does become a man; instead, the man who thought he was God turns into the little boy he failed to recognize.

As these scenes suggest, Dickens understands the fundamental role of witnessing in securing the meaning of filial sacrifice. Mr. Dombey, "the removed Being," does not know how to let himself *be seen,* and as a result he is never able to find his proper distance from little Paul. We find him lurking to watch his son from shadows and corners, lingering on the edge of the scene yet bristling if anyone appears between them. Florence should be the novel's Milly Swidger, the Madonna in the Dombey *pietà*. She wants desperately to play this role, mediating, absorbing conflict, reconciling witnesses to the spectacle of the son's death. Alexander Welsh describes her as an "Angel of Death," recalling that "in Genoa in 1844 Dickens dreamt of Mary Hogarth in the blue drapery of the Madonna . . . when he tried to ask her a leading question—whether she agreed that the form of religion did not matter as long as 'we try to be good'—she rather provokingly recommended Roman Catholicism" (177).[18]

Like the Catholic Madonna, the mourning mother-daughter in Dickens takes shape in response to the primary spectacle of the son's sacrifice. The faintly morbid sweetness that shrouds Florence Dombey may be similarly traced to her precocious deathwatch, first over her mother and then over

---

17. For discussion of this scene from *The Winter's Tale,* see chapter 3.

18. On the "Angel of Death" and the Dickens heroine, see especially Welsh, chaps. 10 and 11.

her brother Paul. Mr. Dombey, however, cannot acknowledge Florence any more than he can recognize Paul. Unable to discern in her the outlines of an acquiescent Madonna, he cannot respond properly to the sacrificial spectacle of his son's death. Dickens presents this inability to "read" the domestic *pietà* as the central knot of Dombey's character, the moral and psychological key to his failure as a husband and a father.

This failure makes Mr. Dombey the novel's haunted man; his inability to witness sacrifice has the same effect as Redlaw's oblivion, dissolving bonds of family and community that depend on the "gift" of suffering. He bitterly resents the crepe that Mr. Toodle wears in mourning for little Paul:

> To think of this presumptuous raker among coals and ashes going on before there, with his sign of mourning! To think that he dared to enter, even by a common show like that, into the trial and disappointment of a proud gentleman's secret heart! To think that this lost child, who was to have divided with him his riches, and his projects, and his power, and allied with whom he was to have shut out all the world as with a double door of gold, should have let in such a herd to insult him with their knowledge of his defeated hopes, and their boasts of claiming community of feeling with himself, so far removed: if not of having crept into the place where he would have lorded it, alone! (353)

In chapter 18, when little Paul's casket is carried out to the hearse waiting in the street, Mr. Dombey shows the crowd no sign of his grief. Nor does the narrative point of view take us into his feelings. It is as if Dombey, cutting himself off from human sympathy, has alienated his inner life from the solicitude of Dickens's art, and so for the moment has rendered his emotions inaccessible. The narrator turns instead to the wife of a juggler whose performance has been interrupted: "closer to her dingy breast she presses her baby" when the coffin is brought forth; and after the procession moves off "she is less alert than usual with the money-box, for a child's burial has set her thinking that perhaps the baby underneath her shabby shawl may not grow up to be a man, and wear a sky-blue fillet round his head, and salmon-coloured worsted drawers, and tumble in the mud" (311). In such passages Dickens evokes the *communicable* power of the child's death as a fantasy at once fearful and compelling. It exerts a strong mimetic pull, tempting the responsive witness to repeat the fantasy for herself, elaborating it with details from her own dreams. The ordinariness of these dreams, so literal and humbly specific, renders them more rather than less poignant in contrast to the grandeur of Dombey's plans for little Paul.

At such moments Dickens is subtly fictionalizing what Lesser describes as "a community of moral agreement" (192). Comparing newspaper ac-

counts of court cases involving maternal child abuse, one from the middle
of the nineteenth century and another from 1901, Lesser shows how
differences in tone and rhetoric reflect sharply contrasting assumptions
about social community and inter-subjective distance; she then convinc-
ingly relates these assumptions to the difference between Dickens's sentimentality and Joseph Conrad's irony. Dickens uses the juggler's wife to
show us how Dombey's proud isolation breaches the mid-Victorian community of moral agreement; the narrative point of view, meanwhile, remains subtly true to that community, withholding itself from Mr.
Dombey's inner world while passing easily, with affectionately mocking
condescension, into that of the juggler's wife.

Dombey's refusal of community contrasts sharply with the "personally
affectionate relationship" Dickens cultivated with "his public" (*Letters*
8:539). There is, however, an underlying similarity, for if Dombey unwittingly pays the price for playing God, so does his creator. The man who
murders Little Nells, little Pauls, and Tiny Tims for the sake of a good
story ends up replaying in his own person the dilemma projected onto
God and Dombey: he both destroys the children he loves, and bears witness to their destruction. While writing the death of Little Nell in *The Old
Curiosity Shop,* Dickens told George Cattermole, "I am breaking my heart
over this story, and cannot bear to finish it." To Macready he wrote, "I am
slowly murdering that poor child, and grow wretched over it. It wrings
my heart. Yet it must be." He added: "I am, for the time being, nearly
dead with work—and grief for the loss of my child" (Ackroyd 318). This
sounds for all the world like real grief—the words could as easily be those
of Freud, mourning the death of his beloved daughter Sophie in 1919.
The inevitability of Nell's death adds poignance to her loss, making her
somehow more his own, his Perdita. It is as if a lost child were there already in Dickens's heart, waiting for Nell to grow incorporate. Yet as Ackroyd remarks, "The grief is mingled with exaltation: 'I think it will come
famously,' he said in the same letter in which he described his grief." "In
fact," Ackroyd adds, "there is no doubt that he worked himself up into a
state of pity and holy terror in order to write of this death with the proper
sympathy—that is why he had begun thinking once more of the death of
Mary Hogarth, almost as if he were relishing the pain of loss" (318).

The fate that says "Yet it must be" has several layers. Nell died to redeem *Master Humphrey's Clock,* which was losing circulation and needed a
Dickens story to win its readers back; in John Ruskin's famous phrase, she
"was simply killed for the market, as a butcher kills a lamb" (275). Her
death was formally and thematically necessary to the narrative in more
specific ways, of course. But it was also necessary to the sacrament of
pathos, as Dickens sought through public discourse to weave an intimate

*domestic* relationship with his readers. In the 1848 preface to *Dombey and Son*, he casts the separate acts of writing and reading as a single shared experience of mourning:

> I cannot forego [*sic*] my usual opportunity of saying farewell to my readers in this greeting-place, though I have only to acknowledge the unbounded warmth and earnestness of their sympathy in every stage of the journey we have just concluded. If any of them have felt a sorrow in one of the principal incidents on which this fiction turns, I hope it may be a sorrow of that sort which endears the sharers in it, one to another. This is not unselfish in me. I may claim to have felt it, at least as much as anybody else; and I would fain be remembered kindly for my part in the experience. (41)

Dickens alludes with coy gravity to the occasion of all that warmth and earnestness, the death of little Paul. Given the extravagant public and private grief occasioned by the fifth number of the serialized *Dombey and Son*—and the significance of that grief as the shape of a beleaguered writer's brilliant success—the "if" of "if any of them have felt a sorrow" has the egregiously self-effacing manner of a mortician. The author, however, proceeds with disarming candor to wish that he may be "remembered kindly" as a sharer in this sorrow. Dickens reinforces this claim in the preface of 1867, describing how he wandered "a whole winter night about the streets of Paris . . . with a heavy heart, on the night when I had written the chapter in which my little friend and I parted company" (43).

Dickens is quietly finding a seat among the mourners, as if taking their side, like the good fellow he is, against the severity of his own executive role. At the same time he seems to be playing with the duplicity of that role, for as he adopts Paul's dying wish to be remembered kindly by everyone, he slips innocently into the voice of Blimber:

> The Doctor was sitting in his portentous study, with a globe at each knee, books all around him, Homer over the door, and Minerva on the mantleshelf. "And how do you do, Sir?" he said to Mr Dombey, "and how is my little friend?" Grave as an organ was the Doctor's speech; and when he ceased, the great clock in the hall seemed (to Paul at least) to take him up, and to go on saying, "how, is, my, lit, tle, friend? how, is, my, lit, tle, friend?" over and over and over again. (209–10)

Taking up the clock's refrain, Dickens rather impishly contaminates his identification with Paul. The clock in the hallway at Blimber's is only the most portentous of many timepieces in the story that officiously tick down the seconds of Paul's brief life. These watches and clocks (associated with the child-swallowing Chronos) are representatives within the fiction of that mixed necessity, the "fate" of the beloved child. The stylistic ambivalence of the 1867 preface thus indirectly confesses, even as it seeks to build a community of mourning between the author and his readers, that this necessity is brought to bear *by*, as well as *on*, the author. When he writes to Miss Angela Coutts, Dickens employs the predominant tone of the prefaces, with their careful mingling of intimacy and formality and their whimsical pretense that the characters are real: "Between ourselves—Paul is dead. He died on Friday night about 10 o'Clock; and as I had no hope of getting to sleep afterwards, I went out, and walked about Paris until breakfast time next morning" (*Letters* 5:9). A very different voice, scarcely audible in the Prefaces, declares in private correspondence to John Forster: "Paul, I shall slaughter at the end of number five" (Ackroyd 519).

Beneath the strained jocularity of such a remark lies something close to Yahweh's moment of greatest candor, as reported by Ezekiel: "I defiled them through their very gifts in making them offer by fire all their firstborn, that I might horrify them; I did it that they might know that I am Yahweh" (20:26; trans. Green 175). After reading his Christmas story *The Chimes* to Macready, Dickens wrote to his wife, Catherine: "If you had seen Macready last night—undisguisedly sobbing, and crying on the sofa, as I read—you would have felt (as I did) what a thing it is to have Power" (Ackroyd 446). What a thing it is, one might almost say, to be Yahweh. The confession is a piece of gloating as undisguised as Macready's tears; more insidious is the complicity it seeks from Catherine. *You too* must have felt this way, it urges her; *you too* would identify with the gods at that terrible moment when they see their own divinity reflected in the abjectness of human suffering.

## The Witness of Style

Of all the memorable characters Dickens invented, the most engaging may well be his own narrative voice. Like the author, the narrator in Dickens finds his complement, almost his fetish, in the ingénue: together they bear witness to the sacrificial scene. But where the "angel of death" tries to absorb conflict, offering herself (and through herself, the transcendent Father) as a resting place beyond the siege of contraries, the narrative voice shifts perspectives and juggles motives in the play of style. The contrast between Dickens and Dombey is also a clash of styles—Dombey the stiff and formal embodiment of all things patriarchal, Dickens the playful and benevolent public witness who would redeem fatherhood by humanizing it, turning it toward the well-intentioned paternalism of the liberal state. These contrasts have important moral and ideological dimensions, but we grasp them best by treating Dickens first as a stylist and storyteller, approaching his morality and politics through his fiction rather than approaching the fiction through them.

The importance of style in particular can be seen from the start. *Dombey and Son* opens with a witty flourish of antithesis, entering father and son in the lists of opposing parallel clauses:

> Dombey was about eight-and-forty years of age. Son about eight-and-forty minutes. Dombey was rather bald, rather red, and though a handsome well-made man, too stern and pompous in appearance, to be prepossessing. Son was very bald, and very red, and though (of course) an undeniably fine infant, somewhat crushed and spotty in his general effect, as yet. (49)

Here the gap between *Dombey* and *Son* is, literally, the space of stylistic performance. In this set piece Dickens is sporting with the problem of filial mimesis—as we have seen, the very fault line of patrilineal patriarchy. The very name "Dombey" encrypts this problem, for it is an anagram of "embody" (Newsome 199). The son in this system must somehow imitate the father, and the artist's challenge is to imitate that imitation: to represent a relation that cannot be seen, a patrilineal "body" that does not exist. Resemblance, as Shakespeare's Leontes discovered, only pretends to take the place of this missing, "inimitable"[19] object—the nothing that, if it were a thing, would link father to son. Dickens mocks this polite fiction, turning the fault line into a language game and so foreshadowing, in the play of his style, the main conflict of the narrative to come.

This stylistic mingling of youth and age plays across the gap between deep, irreconcilable identifications with the father and the sacrificial son. Dickens's satire boasts many of the rhetorical qualities of a gratifying oath. At the same time, his characteristic tone of lofty moral idealism and frequent exhortation lend the Dickens narrator an insistently patronizing mode of address, a rhetoric of fatherly indulgence proposed to the world at large. The brilliance of Dickens as a stylist is his surprising, endlessly resourceful invention of pleasure in the friction between these motives. As an author he reopens within himself, within his voice and agency, the split between the father's witness and the community of mourning gathered around a sacrificial son. At the same time he casts himself as the public voice of conscience—a fellow mourner of the good, a trustworthy witness of society's failure in the paternal role. In this he plays Horatio to his own Hamlet, even as the Hamlet-like brio of his performance transforms the sacrificial polarity, releasing its tensions in the play of style.

---

19. Dickens's nickname: "The Inimitable."

In chapter 47, "The Thunderbolt," the domestic melodrama reaches its climax: Edith Dombey flees, leaving Mr. Dombey in a blind rage so galling he strikes Florence to the ground and orders her out of the house. As he builds to these scenes, Dickens pauses to ask whether Dombey's "master-vice, that ruled him so inexorably, was really an unnatural characteristic?" (737). A passage follows in the high declamatory style of the political sermon, reaching its crescendo in the visionary rendering of a liberal fairy tale:

> Oh for a good spirit who would take the house-tops off, with a more potent and benignant hand than the lame demon in the tale, and show a Christian people what dark shapes issue from amidst their homes, to swell the retinue of the Destroying Angel as he moves forth among them! For only one night's view of the pale phantoms rising from the scenes of our too-long neglect; and from the thick and sullen air where Vice and Fever propagate together, raining the tremendous social retributions which are ever pouring down, and ever coming thicker! Bright and blest the morning should rise on such a night: for men, delayed no more by stumbling-blocks of their own making, which are but specks of dust upon the path between them and eternity, would then apply themselves, like creatures of one common origin, owing one duty to the Father of one family, and tending to one common end, to make the world a better place! (738–39)

The fantasy that triggers such elevated rhetoric is, clearly, an image of collective conversion that would turn the public into a benevolent father, imitating the paternal deity in order to take his place as protector and redeemer of the social family.[20]

Here and throughout the passage, Dickens is preoccupied with the issue of public witnessing; straining toward prophetic urgency, he exhorts us to *see* realities that do not belong to the order of the visible. The imperatives of the passage summon all the senses: "Hear the magistrate or judge . . . follow the good clergyman . . . Look round upon the world of odious sights . . . Breathe the polluted air . . . have every sense . . . offended, sickened, and disgusted" (737). But the overriding emphasis is an appeal to the public gaze to envision what cannot quite be seen, the moral dimension of material squalor:

> if the noxious particles that rise from vitiated air were palpable to sight, we should see them lowering in a dense black cloud above such haunts, and rolling slowly on to corrupt the better portions of the town. But if the

---

20. On the relation between social paternalism, the idealization of the family, and the rhetoric of reform movements in the period, see Catherine Gallagher, *Industrial Reformation,* part 2, "The Family versus Society."

moral pestilence that rises with them, and in the eternal laws of outraged
Nature, is inseparable from them, could be made discernable too, how terrible the revelation! (738)

For all his imaginative power, Dickens cannot place the body of fatherhood before us; its absence, here as in the opening set piece of the novel,
is the very space in which the writer works. He labors in that empty space
to construct a mode of witness that will reclaim it. Invoking "tremendous
social retributions" bred by this body's absence, Dickens exhorts us to *become* the thing we cannot behold in response to the horrors we can.

Perhaps the strangest feature of this passage is its placement just before
the collapse of the Dombey household. Is the failure of Mr. Dombey's
marriage a "social retribution" for the wretchedness of the urban poor?
How does a passage that begins by asking about Dombey's pride turn so
quickly to a vision of the "moral pestilence" (738) that rises from the
slums of London? In a strange, not-quite-explained way, the passage
rhetorically superimposes scenes from opposite ends of the social scale, the
domestic misery of prosperous families and the "world of odious sights"
where "the unnatural outcasts of society" are bred (737). Somehow, the
good spirit of fiction will lift the roofs off the houses of the bourgeoisie to
reveal unseen urban ghettos "lying within the echoes of our carriage
wheels" (737). The connection between these things is not visible; it is
the moral reality Dickens wants to bring before his readers, the belief that,
as Forster put it, social and individual happiness rest "on the same foundations . . . which are mercy and charity not less than justice" (347).
Charity is the virtue Mr. Dombey lacks, and when Dickens turns to the
rhetoric of the pulpit, suddenly enlarging his frame of reference to super-
impose the ghetto upon the nursery, the implication is that England, too,
lacks charity. The poor are our abused children, our Florence Dombeys;
society must become the "good" father for which Florence yearns, or risk
the destruction about to be visited upon the unloving father in his pride.

In the stories of Little Nell and Oliver Twist, Dickens had already developed a powerful narrative strategy, a form of sentimental class romance
that sends its lisping protagonists on a descent into the economic underworld. Their embassy to the streets of London carries bourgeois domestic
sentiment *out* of the affectively hypercharged sphere of the family, rein-
vesting it in the larger social world (Spilka 170, 174). In *Dombey and Son*,
Dickens modifies this strategy. Elements of the Oliver Twist pattern remain: early in the novel, Florence is briefly lost and then rescued by Walter Gay; later, searching for his fugitive wife, Mr. Dombey descends into
the same dark rooms where Florence had her brush with the urban traffic
in female children. This is the dwelling place of Mrs. Brown and her

daughter, Alice Marwood, key figures in the unraveling of the plot. Dickens leans hard on the parallel between his mercenary mothers, Mrs. Brown and Mrs. Skewton, and their sexually commodified daughters, Alice Marwood and Edith Dombey; eventually he reveals that they are literally related, but he has insisted all along on moral proximity of their careers despite the differences in wealth and status that set them far apart (579). Nevertheless, in emotional weight and narrative prominence this engagement with the social underworld is not quite a counterpart to Oliver's descent. Much closer is the pious, highly sentimentalized death of little Paul. This death reverses the Oliver strategy: rather than follow a lost lamb into the urban wolves' den, *Dombey and Son* detects the lethal penetration of mercantile values into the nursery, where they commandeer the maternal breast and put the beloved son on an emotional starvation diet.[21]

The novel has been faulted for failing to carry its critique of market values back into the public world in the action of its plot. But the mise-en-scène of the return to public life in *Dombey and Son* is not *in* the novel, it *is* the novel—chiefly, the work of its style as it nests the intimate personal relation between Dickens and his readers in a charitable social contract. The author does not send Dombey back out, redeemed by the love of a pious daughter, to remodel the marketplace or to campaign for slum renovation, but he does bring the social world into the novel through his gift for mimicry. Moreover, through his propensity for melodrama, nightmarish exaggeration of effect, and the comic reduction of human character to a few sharply drawn, endlessly recycled gestures, Dickens brings this world before us as a place of heightened feeling and value. Malcolm Andrews shrewdly identifies the extravagance of Dickens's style as an element of childhood in the mixed persona of his narrator: "The voice of the child in Dickens's fiction," writes Andrews, "is privileged not only in those pas-

---

21. No doubt there are many reasons why the child proves such a powerful "hook" for "human interest." Berry analyzes the usefulness of child-victimization narratives to the growth of an elaborate administrative machinery of social welfare—in effect, the bureaucratic counterpart to Dickens's "good spirit," which really did seek to lift the rooftops off the houses. Berry's analysis of the child as a figure that reconciles various contradictions and tensions characteristic of the period may be extended to include a social fantasy of the child as what Nunokawa calls "inalienable property." The structural paradoxes of the commodity form lend to property an *exchange value;* it has value only insofar as it is conceived as always on its way elsewhere in the circulation of goods and services. Such property is structurally alienated from its possessor even if he retains it, for his ownership is defined as a right of exchange. Nunokawa describes the wife in Victorian culture as the privileged bearer of an imaginary counterpart to the commodity form, what he calls "the fantasy of inalienable property." We should recognize children, especially favored sons, as differently privileged bearers of the same fantasy. From one point of view, the effect of child sacrifice would be to reassert the child's status as a gift, not an extension of the parental self. God's command to Abraham could be understood from this perspective as demanding that the earthly father sacrifice the fantasy of the son as inalienable property.

sages where the child's-eye viewpoint is formally deployed as a narrative method, but in the mercurial, protean activity of Dickens's prose throughout" (174). Childhood is a world of powerful emotional forces and attachments; its characters repel us or they draw us in. Dickens sends his fictional children, loaded with domestic affect, into this overwrought fantasy of the material world. Eventually, he sends his own narrative voice into Paul's point of view as death approaches. But even in verbalizing a copious and stylized world for these children to inhabit, he has already drawn that point of view indirectly, diffusely, and intermittently into his voice.

Through this combination of strategies Dickens engages his readers in a complex and mature experience that is nevertheless grounded in a deeply pleasurable, infantilizing fantasy. He activates this fantasy, binding readers to the intimacy of his narrative voice and then leading them toward the father's witness, in order to stage the conversion of the social conscience by the liberal imagination. This achievement is open to critique. Anita Levy, for example, argues in *Reproductive Urges* that the purpose of a fictional character like Mr. Dombey is to create a social desire for his opposite. He thus belongs to a "cultural logic of failed masculinity" (98) that is, paradoxically, one of the ruses by which paternalism sustains itself. We can see this process at work in the novel, for if Dombey exists in order to create a readerly desire for the qualities he lacks, then the Dickens narrator and the social ideal he expresses offer themselves to satisfy that desire.

In his use of child sacrifice to set forth a secular vision of benevolent social fatherhood, Dickens does not resolve the contradictions we encounter so starkly in Richmond and other evangelical moralists. Rather, he *fictionalizes* them, acknowledging his imaginary scene of witness as the work of "a good spirit" associated not with the Bible but with exotic tales. Just where evangelical discourse is most vulnerable to a skeptical reading—that is, in its insistent and implausible denial of fictional technique and rhetorical design—Dickens tips his hand, acknowledging that the "truth" to which his narrative testifies is not religious but imaginative. Such moments register the difference between Dickens's secular, fictional communion and the religious models he is drawing on—a difference that appears again, more subtly, in the word *like,* as it slips almost unnoticed into the closing period. If men ever did "apply themselves, *like* creatures of one common origin, owing one duty to the Father of one family," would they be acting as what they already are, or only as what we wish they were? Would they be imitating a transcendent reality or a social fantasy? For Dickens this remains a question of filial mimesis. In the ringing conclusion to his sermon, the ambiguity of the word *like* carries the full weight of the old epistemological uncertainty about fatherhood, amplified now into a whisper of ontological doubt about the collective Father. We may recall that the semantics of the word *truth,* in Victorian usage generally and in Dickens especially, tend to locate it less in doctrine or in fact than in powerful emotion—the truth of "true feeling." In fictionalizing the conventions of evangelical tracts, Dickens shows them answering not to transcendental or objective realities but to the internal structure of the modern subject. In this way too he stands in a direct line of development from Shakespearean theater.

# Jonson, Freud, Lacan:      **5**
# This Moving Dream

O, could I loose all father, now.
> —Ben Jonson, "On My First Sonne"

Dickens found out what it's like to play God: you create a world, people it with children in your own image, and then find yourself bound by the laws of your own creation to sacrifice them. The mixture of anguish and triumph he experienced in writing the deaths of Little Nell and little Paul Dombey—the sense that killing these imaginary children was both something he was forced to do and proof of his immense power—is one version of the dilemma I am calling the father's witness. Homer projected this dilemma onto Zeus, Virgil onto Jove; the Hebrew scripture configured it in Yahweh's command to Abraham, while Christianity has tried for the most part to veil or displace it. Dickens, however, experienced it *in his own person*. He did so because he was an author—and because authorship, in the nineteenth century, was no longer one social role among many that a man might play. It was at once a prophetic vocation, secular but still elevated, and a personal identity, integral to the writing subject. Dickens saw himself as a major public representative of this cultural function; he took it upon himself to exemplify the dignity of his profession, but he also took it into himself—took into his core sense of personal being the imaginary ideal he sought to embody for his public. In these respects Dickens really is exemplary of the implicitly masculine author function as it has developed in English literature since the Renaissance. In him we see how filial sacrifice has become intrinsic to the act of writing, inescapably part of what it means to *be* an author.

In this chapter I turn to two other writers who, like Dickens, figure crucially in the history of modern authorship: Ben Jonson and Sigmund Freud. I propose to read two of their most celebrated texts, "On My First

Sonne" and the seventh chapter of *The Interpretation of Dreams*, in a cross-historical, cross-generic comparison intended to demonstrate how, for both, the act of writing—when it is that momentous kind of writing that *makes one an author*—is burdened with the dilemma of the father's witness. Because I am framing the question of authorship not simply as one of legal, economic, or discursive functions but also as a question about the psyche of the writing subject, I am focusing on the sacrificial son as he appears in the most intimately personal of texts, the dream narrative. But because I am also still concerned with the larger question raised at the outset of this study—how does the figure of the sacrificial son remain so central and enduring across time?—I am considering not only the significance the dream possesses for the dreaming subject, but also its haunting power, its ability to rematerialize in responsive witnesses. What makes it such a *moving* dream?[1]

Framing the question in this way lets me step back from the major emphasis of most contemporary work on the concept of authorship, which has shifted attention from the subject who writes to the historical contexts that inform acts of writing and publishing, the institutions that mediate them, and the material objects they produce.[2] Presumably, in the midst of so much investigation, it is not enough simply to pick this subject up and set him down in his new surroundings, dusted off but otherwise not much altered. How then can we read the effects of such social and historical dynamics back into the masculine writing subject? Not, surely, by rehabilitating the author as a distressed unity. Rather we need to follow the tangled workings of his struggle to generate, out of the dispersed and conflicting grounds of his social existence, imaginary effects of integrity and authority.[3] If we understand, now, why this subject never could be the

1. The idea of transferential effects in reading and writing has been developed in a substantial body of criticism. I am especially indebted to Gallop, Sprengnether (whose work prompted me to think about a "spectral son"), and the essays in Bernheimer and Kahane.

2. In the quarter century since Foucault's "What Is an Author?" and Barthes's "The Death of the Author" were first translated into English, the concept has been "interrogated" often. Rumors of its death proved exaggerated, however, for it continues to serve many of the purposes Barthes and Foucault identified. In literary study the monograph on a single author may be increasingly rare, but the author's name is nonetheless a charm to conjure well-tilled fields of inquiry out of the textual wilderness. It remains the most important way texts are gathered into chronologies and databases or stitched into social, technological, and other histories. But increasingly, and in spite of excellent work on the literary history of authorship, we find the concept examined most seriously in works of cultural history and critical bibliography—in theater history, for example, or in accounts of court culture, intellectual property, censorship, patronage, literary coteries, manuscript circulation, print, publishing, and the book trade—where it designates broad forms of symbolic capital as well as immediate forms of textual control for which interested powers and parties compete.

3. Barbour argues that "across a wide range of theatrical and literary venues, Jonson's achievement documents dialectical struggle between social subjection and personal agency"

mythic figure of authority and creative potency that modern criticism has abandoned, we may still wonder about the effects of the long-standing cultural demand that he *should* be.

The career of "self-creating" Ben Jonson (as Thomas Dekker called him) has been an important site for Foucauldian excavations, and should therefore be an excellent place to reconsider the effects of social and economic forces on the once-familiar figure who has been parceled out into so many functions and discourses. Freud, too, is exemplary: he represents for Foucault one of the main types of author function, that of creating not just a text but also a form of discourse; he sought to be the father not only of books but of psychoanalysis. As the prevailing modern discourse about subjectivity, psychoanalysis in turn creates the historical and discursive possibility for my own framing of the issues to be explored in this chapter, and has played a central role in my argument throughout this book. In Freud, therefore (and by extension in Lacan), this book circles back to a very old crossroads shaped like the letter Y. There it comes face to face with its origins, a "mirror stage" that, to put it mildly, somewhat complicates my own agency as an author.

## All Father

The authorial self that Ben Jonson created is conspicuously virtuous and "centered." The ostentatiously masculine features of his poems—his love of words like *straight, stand,* and *upright,* his rhetoric of disavowal and stubborn independence—can still tempt critics to describe his best verse with phrases like "manly simplicity" and "achieved being."[4] But increasingly criticism has also described early modern England as a crisis point in the history of masculine selfhood.[5] In this account, masculinity as a social

---

(499). Other important studies of authorship and literary production that take up Jonson's career include Orgel, *Illusion of Power;* Helgerson, *Self-Crowned Laureates;* Fish; Newton; Loewenstein, "Script"; van den Berg; and Brooks. (Loewenstein's forthcoming *Ben Jonson and Possessive Authorship* will extend arguments about "the bibliographical ego" broached in his 1985 essay.)

4. Following a long tradition of critical diction, Helgerson says of the panegyrical epigrams, "Their manly simplicity, their air of achieved being, bespeaks the goodness of both the poet and his subjects" (*Self-Crowned Laureates* 169); he also comments (with a nod to Greene) on Jonson's affinity for the language of uprightness (170). Fish likewise touches on many of the themes I invoke here, including the self-begetting strategies that pervade the rhetoric of Jonson's verse, the notion of writing as a figurative genealogy, and the implicit masculinity of the writing self. For example: "generation in the world of Jonson's poetry occurs not by sex, but by reading, by the reading of like by like, and it is essentially a male phenomenon in which the organ of begetting is the eye" (245). My emphasis falls on differences internal to what Fish names "Jonson's Community of the Same."

5. See, for example, Shuger; Orgel, *Impersonations;* and Breitenberg, *Anxious Masculinity.*

role and a cultural artifact lacked precisely the qualities of stability, security, and autonomy that Jonson claimed for his authorial persona. Rather than enumerate the emphatic attributes that mark his self-presentation, then, I explore the imaginary defenses and compensations that complicate Jonson's acts of poetic making. To do so I draw on the psychoanalytic notion of the trauma, an imaginary "event" that turns the act of writing (I argue) into a compensatory assertion of creative mastery.[6]

In the spring of 1603, Queen Elizabeth died and James VI of Scotland traveled south to London to be crowned. He arrived in May along with the bubonic plague. Ben Jonson, meanwhile, had left the city, ostensibly because of the king's progress rather than that of the pestilence. He was visiting the country estate of Sir Robert Cotton, at Conington in Huntingdonshire—an excellent place to be during the planning stages of the Jacobean succession. Cotton, knighted by James on May 11, played a central role in the cultural vanguard of the new regime, so if Jonson wanted to seize opportunity by the forelock there was no better way to position himself for royal patronage than by joining William Camden and others in Cotton's library at Conington. But Huntingdonshire was also a very good place to find oneself in a time of plague, when the mortality rate in neighborhoods like St. Giles, Cripplegate (where Jonson's wife and children remained) could easily exceed 50 percent (Riggs 94–95).

Leaving London to avoid the plague was a matter of social privilege: "Members of the lower classes," writes David Riggs, "were forbidden to leave the city; they had no choice but to remain and die" (95). Joshua Scodel quotes "the official prayer for plague in 1603" as prescribing fatherly care: "The chief remedy to be expected from man is that everyone would be a magistrate to himself and his whole family" (92).[7] This was a double-edged prescription, for as Riggs observes, "Any city dweller who had access to a country house could be virtually certain of escaping the disease by vacating the town. The mortality bills for the great epidemic of 1665, to cite an extreme case, list over 100,000 Londoners but do not include a single magistrate, courtier, or wealthy merchant" (93–95). In this sense Jonson was rather too much a magistrate to his family.

It may be unfair for modern readers to sit in judgment, removed as we conveniently are from the horror of bubonic plague on the one hand, and on the other from the combined pressures of ambition and low status in a

---

6. My approach is broadly compatible with that of van den Berg, although I do not draw on Winnicott and hence do not specify the origin of the trauma in separation from the mother.

7. "By contemporary standards," writes Scodel, Jonson "had neglected his patriarchal obligations." Brady notes, however, that the poet enjoyed a class status he had no power to extend to his family, adding that "the court injunction of May 29, 1603 ordered all gentlemen to leave the city" ("Jonson's Elegies" 215). Jonson left in late March.

literary system propped up by patronage. The more intriguing question about Jonson's motives is how *he* understood them, for he faced an impossible choice. Monarchs are crowned once in a lifetime. Royal patronage in the latter years of Elizabeth's reign had been scarce; the doors that opened in 1603 might close quickly and stay shut for decades. What would it accomplish to stay in London? A man might share his family's fate, but there was no way he could shape it except by leaving.

And yet, to leave a child in danger betrays the father's role as protector. In the same year, Jonson's friend John Florio published a translation of Montaigne that laid out yet another logic implicit in such a choice:

> There are few men given unto Poesie, that would not esteeme it for a greater honour, to be the fathers of *Virgils Ænidos,* than the godliest boy in *Rome,* and that would not rather endure the losse of the one than the perishing of the other. For, according to *Aristotle, Of all workemen, the Poet is principally the most amorous of his productions and conceited of his Labours.* . . . Nay, I make a great question, whether *Phidias* or any other excellent Statuary, would as highly esteeme, and dearely love the preservation, and successfull continuance of his naturall children, as he would an exquisite and match-lesse-wrought Image, that with long study, and diligent care he had perfected according unto art.[8]

Jonson had confronted this "great question" less explicitly the year before in the "Apologeticall Dialogue" added to *Poetaster,* in which he depicted himself spending "halfe my nights, and all my dayes, / Here in a cell, to get a darke, pale face, / To come forth worth the ivy, or the bayes" (Herford and Simpson 4.324, lines 234–35).[9] Since this was about the time

8. Montaigne 2:88 (the italics are Florio's, or the printer's). Critics and biographers regularly note that Jonson presented Florio with a copy of *Volpone* inscribed to him as "Loving Father, & worthy Freind [*sic*]" (reproduced in Herford and Simpson 1.56–57). Trimpi suggests the relevance of Montaigne's essay to Jonson's poem, noting that Jonson, "as if directly contradicting Plato's preference for children of the mind . . . firmly asserts that this child of the body is *his* 'best' piece of poetry—that is, the best thing *he* has made" (150). Winner also cites this essay but suggests that Jonson "collapses Montaigne's distinction." I am indebted to Winner's suggestive discussion of the pun on "poesis" as "a complex response to 'fathering,'" and to his perception that the poem's "impulses do not entirely coalesce. . . . Instead of holding conflicting views in suspension, [the wordplay] underscores their incompatibility" (116–17). Scodel follows Winner in arguing that "Jonson rejects Montaigne's crucial distinction and categories . . . by making the identity of his child-poem dependent on himself alone" (106); he sees Jonson as resisting separation from the dead child (104). I argue that Montaigne's distinctions do inform the poem, which both enacts and rejects the Platonic preference, because I see the idealizing union of poet-father and son-poem as haunted by the specter of filial sacrifice.

9. The "Apologeticall Dialogue," appended to Jonson's play *Poetaster* but suppressed after a single performance, was not restored until the Folio printing in 1616, in which it appears under the heading "To the Reader" (1.317).

that he separated from his wife, it is hard not to suspect, with Riggs, that "compulsive work habits" alienated Jonson from his family (93).[10] Florio's Montaigne offered both justification and consolation for such distress: "What we engender by the minde . . . are brought forth by a far more noble part, than the corporall, and are more our owne. We are both father and mother together in this generation" (85). In these terms, Jonson would have been sacrificing domestic fatherhood for a metaphysical paternity in which he and his writings, like God, comprised a nuclear family in one person.

The rhetoric of patriarchy offered a number of mutually reinforcing ways for Jonson to refigure his domestic loss. It was a mark of social status (the father as magistrate); it was a choice of spirit over flesh, art over nature, craftsmanship over passion, and godlike self-sufficiency over dependency and loss of control. Florio's language glances, too, at the ever-present fear of cuckoldry when it praises intellectual offspring as "more our owne"; the desire to be "father and mother together in this generation" may illuminate the panic with which Shakespeare's King Leontes separates Queen Hermione from their son in *The Winter's Tale*, proclaiming that she has "too much blood in him" (2.1.58). Florio's Montaigne is uncomfortably close to this irrational conviction that *all* fleshly generation is adulterous when weighed against the uncontaminated purity of male parthenogenesis.

The journey to Conington, however, brought Montaigne's "great question" home in a new way. Sometime after arriving, Jonson had a vision. Sixteen years later he described it to William Drummond of Hawthornden:

> When the king came in England, at that tyme the pest was in London, he being in the country at S[i]r Robert Cotton's house with old Camden, he saw in a vision his eldest son, th[e]n a child and at London, appear unto him w[i]t[h] the mark of a bloody cross on his forehead, as if it had been cutted w[i]t[h] a sword; at which, amazed, he prayed unto God; and in the morning he came to Mr Camden's chamber to tell him, who persuaded him it was but an apprehension of his fantasy, at which he should not be disjected. In the meantime comes th[e]r[e] letters from his wife of the death of th[a]t boy in the plague. He appeared to him, he said, of a manly shape, and of th[a]t growth that he thinks he shall be at the resurrection. (Donaldson 600–601)

Drummond's account suggests that the "vision" may have been a dream; Riggs, identifying the "bloody cross" on the boy's forehead with the red

10. Pigman concludes that "not enough evidence exists to say whether or not he was estranged from his wife" in 1603 (88).

cross nailed on doors in plague time to mark houses under quarantine, calls it "the 'day residue' of a Freudian dream analysis" (95). But whether dream or hallucination, the apparition must have struck Jonson as a harrowing accusation.[11] In a powerful and lucid condensation of images, the sign of the plague has been identified with the crucifix. It has also been identified with the *signum Dei,* the mark of God's servants in Revelation: "Then I saw another angel ascend from the rising of the sun, with the seal of the living God, and he called with a loud voice to the four angels who had been given power to harm earth and sea, saying, 'Do not harm the earth or the sea or the trees, till we have sealed the servants of our God upon their foreheads'" (7:2–3).[12] If the apparition is in one sense an accusation, in another it expresses a potent counter-thought, for "the hundred and forty-four thousand sealed" (7:4)—which include "twelve thousand sealed out of the tribe of Benjamin" (7:8)—will be protected from the plagues and other judgments to follow.

This comfort, however, remains within a sacrificial logic, for God's servants are saved by the blood of the Lamb. Drummond's phrasing also recalls the opening description of the Redcrosse Knight in Spenser's *Faerie Queene:* "But on his brest a bloudie Crosse he bore, / The deare remembrance of his dying Lord" (I.i.2.1–2). Even if the allusion to Spenser was as fortuitous then as (it seems) inescapable now, the imaginary sword that *cuts a cross* into the boy's forehead still marks him as clearly for sacrifice as for salvation. If you want to be a divine maker, the vision seems to say, here is what it will cost you. *This* is what it takes to be God. And worse: *this is what you have done.* In this fantasy, it is Jonson himself who has marked the boy. The vision does quite not say so, but its implication is clear: as Benjamin is the child of his father's right hand, his death is the work of his father's writing hand. In the irrational but imposing logic of this dreamwork, the father's literary vocation has caused his son's death.

Benjamin was, in his father's words, "exacted" by fate on the very day he became a boy for his culture: his seventh birthday. "In early modern England," Scodel reminds us, "seven was considered the crucial age of transition, the usual age that children became subject to gender-specific behavior and boys left the feminine, nurturing world of their mothers, nurses, and school dames in order to enter the masculine, disciplined world of fathers and schoolmasters" (97). He adds that "Jonson himself entered Westminster School and discovered his spiritual father, Camden,

---

11. Brady notes that "the extensive mention of the impact of Benjamin Jonson's death on his father in contemporary memoirs of the poet suggests just how far he was from being able to absolve himself of responsibility" ("Jonson's Elegies" 215).

12. On the relation of this *signum Dei* to the semiotics of the stigmata, see Lowell Gallagher.

sometime after he turned seven." It was at Westminster too that Jonson met Robert Cotton. In its detail, then, as well as in its larger significance, the trip to Conington would have evoked for Jonson that momentous day when the masculine world of learning and social advancement first opened to him. In Cotton's library he was returning to the scene of his nativity in manhood and letters—a threshold he was still trying to cross, in pursuit of a status his "corporall" begetting had not conferred. But he was resuming the passage to manhood on his *son's* seventh birthday. Meanwhile the younger Ben Jonson stayed behind, on the day he should have left home, in a venue that was lower-class, feminine, infantilizing, and deadly. And there he died.

In the vision he appears "of a Manlie shape." This comes as a comforting thought, balancing the somber news of death with a subdued glance at the Resurrection. The vision gains poignancy from the unstated counter-thought that this "growth that he thinks he shall be at the resurrection" is also the growth he should have attained in life—if only his father had been less amorous of his productions and conceited of his labors. In this way the boy's visionary manhood brings consolation, loss, and accusation together in a single form. In that specter the father would have found himself reflected with unsparing precision, confronting the unforgivable transgression of usurping his son's passage to manhood, the guilty fear that his wish to do so might be (as in the event it was) too literally granted, even guilty anxiety lest the son should return, magnified and vengeful, for a ghostly squaring of accounts. The boy attains not only a "Manlie shape" but also a menacing form, and the charge he brings, rising from the grave, is one the father must face at the end of time—for the thought of Resurrection brings with it that of the Judgment Day.

For Jonson the logic of this symbolism, inherent in the long-term mythic structures of Western patriarchy, resonated in minutely personal ways. His own father had died a month before he was born; these two events, his own birth and his father's death, are strikingly condensed in his description of himself as "Posthumous born" (Riggs 9). This unhappy conjunction of paternity with mortality comes back to haunt him now as though his son's death were the price of his own survival, just as his father's death had been the price of his birth—and as Christ's death is the price of his salvation. The bleeding incision on his son's forehead condenses these associations at once with the *signum Dei* and with the sign of the plague. It also evokes the ideas of writing and swordplay. In 1598, as he lay under sentence of death for killing Gabriel Spencer—with a rapier—Jonson had converted to Catholicism, renegotiating his relationship with the heavenly Father. He got off by pleading "benefit of clergy," but his thumb was branded with the letter T, "for Tyburn, where he

would have been hanged" (Riggs 53). Are the rapier and the T-shaped
brand not recollected in the thought of a cross "cutted with a sword" into
a grown boy's forehead?

Jonson's vision gains density and resonance from the range of personal
and cultural materials it distills with such economy. Its pathos and arresting force, however, are retroactive effects of the little boy's death. As a
premonition, the vision gives the eerie feeling of an effect that precedes its
cause. It can do so, of course, only if the event it heralds has already in
some sense taken place. There is evidence that, for Jonson in 1603, this
was true. In the first place, the "event" his premonition signifies is not the
mere fact of his son's death but his own responsibility for it. The death itself, that random, intransigent piece of reality, has not only been foreseen
by the father's anxiety—a reasonable and even inevitable fear, under the
circumstances—it has also been transformed by a distinctive fusion of
imaginary and symbolic elements. For it is not literally true that Jonson's
vocation caused his son's death.

Among the symbolic elements that figure in this transformation is the
literary topos of the *puer senex,* or aged boy. As a variation on this topos,
Benjamin's premature manhood in the vision suggests that the proper sequence of things has been violated. The year before, Jonson had used this
same motif to commemorate Salomon Pavy, attributing the boy's untimely death to his skill at playing old men. In the poem Sal projects an illusion stronger than fate, but far from enabling a triumph over death, his
artistic coup only hastens it. Riggs describes the bitter reality Jonson so
euphemistically laments: "Like many of the Chapel Children, Salomon
Pavy had been kidnapped by Nathaniel Giles, the Queen's choirmaster,
who forcibly abducted him into the company at the age of ten. The children and their parents had no legal redress—the boys were impressed on
the authority of the Queen. . . . Sal was old before his time; his life was a
performance wherein he was doomed to play a part devised by cynical
adults" (91–92). In Jonson's poem death completes and, as it were, per-
fects the premature adulthood forced upon children abducted for royal
art. The Fates simply reenact the choirmaster's abduction in the name of a
higher authority, and "Heaven," like the queen, "vowes to keepe him"
(Herford and Simpson 8.77).

The prematurely aged boy is a figure for this pattern of anticipation.
Virtually a second-order symbol for the conundrums of symbolism, he
embodies the proleptic repetition of an "event" that always precedes itself.
For Jonson this event took the form of an antecedent fantasy that drew
him repeatedly toward the imaginary figure of the dead child. "All his
life," writes Ann Barton, "Jonson responded with what for the sixteenth
and seventeenth centuries was abnormal intensity to the deaths of chil-

dren, those of other people as well as his own."[13] Riggs compares him to
Dickens: Jonson "could identify with lost children because he too had
known misfortune at an early age" (88). A very early age, if he was
"Posthumous born."

Riggs and Barton speculate that Jonson had a hand in revising *The
Spanish Tragedy*.[14] Whoever wrote the additions imagined a resonant
question for Hieronimo: "What is there yet in a son / To make a father
dote, rave or run mad?" (Kyd 125, lines 9–10). I take this question seriously no matter who wrote it, and would like to propose an answer. A son
is a symbolic mirror; in him a father sees reflected the trauma of masculine
identity. *Trauma* is a psychoanalytic term whose meaning changes over
the course of Freud's work (and again in Lacan's appropriation of Freud),
but two elements are crucial to my use of it here.[15] First, the trauma is an
"event" defined not by its objective features but by its effects on the
human subject; second, these effects are determined retroactively. Traumatic effects may be produced by any childhood experience of helpless-
ness or isolation that brings home the fact of dependency, any seemingly
random injury that registers as punitive, any blow of circumstance that delivers the existential shock of vulnerability. Such effects also may result
from a seemingly trivial incident that acquires a painful significance only
much later. What matters is that the trauma shatters the subject's sense of
self, and that this experience—precisely because it could not be mas-
tered—remains with the subject, who keeps trying illogically to go back
and master it in retrospect. In Lacan, the trauma is associated with "the
real" as that which resists symbolization. It does so, I think, not because it
is tied to some inexpressible mystery at the heart of reality but because its
decisive character as a subjective event is precisely that it was overwhelming and could not be assimilated.[16] Whatever it was, the trauma caught us
off guard. Our efforts to master it in retrospect are interminable because
"it" entailed a loss of mastery that destroyed the illusion of security on
which our self-possession normally depends.

13. Barton 19. Kay also remarks that Jonson's epigrams on the deaths of children "betray
a tenderness with which he is rarely credited. No other English poet in the period opened
himself so fully in his verse to the grief and sorrow which his children's deaths may have
caused him" (136). Matalene qualifies this emphasis by stressing "the premodern, patriarchal
nature of Jonson's father-feeling" (107).
14. But see Craig, who offers stylometric grounds for doubting Jonson's authorship of
the additions.
15. For an accurate synopsis of the term's provenance and development in Freud's writings, see Laplanche and Pontalis s.v. "Trauma." For Lacan's appropriation of the term, see
"Tuché and Automaton," in *Four Fundamental Concepts* 53–64.
16. For Lacan, the trauma is distinguished as a moment in which the subject encounters
the fact of its own split existence. The encounter is therefore an essentially "*missed* encounter" with the real of the unconscious.

The effort to symbolize this moment for ourselves—by assigning it a cause or reason, for example—is a way of assimilating it. What caused the event objectively matters less than the fact that we experience it, initially, as *uncaused*—it seems to come from nowhere. In the essentially subjective character of the traumatic event, then, the search for a cause is secondary. We find a place in the scheme of things for what has happened, and in the process we reassert our own place in the scheme of things, resettling ourselves in relation to a knowable reality. In the abstract, there may be no reason this process should be gender-specific. But most human societies make gender a fundamental coordinate of that relation to reality, one of the elementary ways we project ourselves into the world. I assume, too, that our patterns of response to traumatic experience are central to the processes of ego formation. So the shattering experience remains with us, a perpetual stimulus to rebuild the imaginary self-possession of which it deprived us, and our efforts to do so are gender-specific. In other words, masculinity as a way of being in the world is also a way of being in relation to the trauma.

Why does a father see this in his son? Perhaps because a son implicitly calls on him to *be* that masterful and deified figure no person can truly embody. In a patrilineal patriarchy authorized by a paternal deity, the son both makes him *a* father and shows him that he cannot be *the* father. To be a father in the patriarchal tradition is to bear witness to the destruction of the son and to see in his death at once the essence and the destruction of fatherhood itself.

From this perspective Jonson's failure appears twofold. There is, first, the father's archetypal inability to prevent his son's death. Since the father also personifies necessity or the law, this failure often appears reversed as his *demand* for the son's death—as in the legendary severity of the Roman consul Lucius Junius Brutus, the myth of the Crucifixion, or the guilty subtext of Jonson's own vision. This reversal plays out the sacrificial paradox that identifies the essence of fatherhood with the son's destruction. Jonson's absence from London, however, adds a second layer of failure, for unlike the gods and patriarchs of Calvinist and classical myth, he has not *witnessed* his son's death. This is an essential role—even the medieval Christian tradition honors and preserves it in the figure of Mary—because only the gaze of the proper witness can guarantee the dignity, pathos, and significance of the filial sacrifice. Jonson's vision at once points to this failure and corrects it, bringing the dead son before the father's gaze as a grievous and arresting portent. The subsequent narrating of this vision—to Camden, to Drummond, *by* Drummond—repeats both the accusation and the compensatory motive, at once summoning and trying to ward off the specter of the dead boy each time the story is retold. (If the narration is not subsequent—if the apparition is neither dream nor vision, but a ghost story—then the motives of guilt and compensation stand out, if anything, even more starkly.)[17]

This contradictory play of motives extends into Jonson's authorship of Epigram 45, "On My First Sonne." The opening lines of the poem are an impossible speech act addressed to the dead boy:

> Farewell, thou child of my right hand, and joy;
> My sinne was too much hope of thee, lov'd boy,
> Seven yeeres tho'wert lent to me, and I thee pay,
> Exacted by thy fate, on the just day.
> O, could I loose all father, now. For why
> Will man lament the state he should envie?
> To have so soone scap'd worlds, and fleshes rage,
> And, if no other miserie, yet age?
> Rest in soft peace, and, ask'd, say here doth lye
> BEN. JONSON his best piece of *poetrie*.
> For whose sake, hence-forth, all his vowes bee such,
> As what he loves may never like too much.
> (Herford and Simpson 8.41)

The poet's speech is marked by a yearning resistance to the mortal paradoxes of patriarchal fatherhood: when he writes "O, could I loose all father, now," the conditional verb betrays his longing to give up paternity even as it acknowledges, tacitly, his inability to do so.

Scodel describes the poem as compensatory in a number of ways. It provides the burial monument and ritual that the child, as a plague victim, probably did not receive. It makes Jonson imaginatively present at the scene from which he was absent—so present, in fact, that he excludes the mother who *was* there. It also makes him the agent of an action ("I thee pay") rather than the passive victim of an event he learns about only belatedly (94–97). But what is more, the poem makes Jonson the author of Benjamin's death, and thus, reflexively, of his own. "Farewell" is the first (not last) word of a poem in which Jonson proceeds to compose himself in the form of Benjamin's absence. Lauinger's comment on the epitaph for Mary applies to this one as well: "To submit fully to the will of heaven and to resign his local fatherhood in favor of the divine paternity must have seemed to Jonson like embracing his own extinction" (226). In "On My First Sonne" he not only embraces his own extinction, he also seeks to author it: he replaces the lost boy, who will no longer bear his name, with

---

17. Brady writes suggestively about Jonson's motives in confiding such personal episodes to Drummond ("Jonson's Elegies" 208–13). The essay also offers perceptive observations on the links between "On My First Sonne" and other poems in *Epigrammes*.

language so powerful it has forced the loss itself to carry his name past
death to future generations.

The poem presents Benjamin's death as his father's, not his own. It
punishes the father's sin; it deprives *him* of the secular immortality conferred by the son as bearer of the paternal name; and its *meaning* is the
conditional rather than absolute status of human fatherhood.[18] It also
turns the father back into a son, as he stands humbled before the absolute
master, reminded of the death-wound with which he was "Posthumous
born." The poem addresses its salutation to the boy, but the father's apostrophe to his son is quickly subsumed by his stance toward God. "I thee
pay," he writes—not I pay *to* you (as your due) the fatherly care you
lacked, but I pay *you,* like money or a gift, to the eternal paradigm of fatherhood in recognition of His absolute claim to the title "Father." Cast
in the second person, this sentence is as rigorous as fate: an implacable re-
minder that Benjamin is not a boy, but a dead boy, the child not of Jonson's marriage but of his right hand. At the same time, by invoking *fate* it
softens the accusation implicit in the vision: if the boy's death was sealed
from the beginning, then in a sense it was not altogether his father's
doing.[19]

The closing lines of the poem bring its transaction from heaven down
to earth as the son mediates between the father and a hypothetical asker,
but the child is still caught up in an exchange between others. The concluding message is addressed from the author to himself, "For whose sake,
hence-forth, all his vowes be such, / As what he loves may never like too
much." The fictional epitaph, meanwhile, is voiced only by the father who
tells a dead child what to say on that inconceivable occasion when it will
speak.[20] The formulaic tag of monumental inscription, "Here doth lye,"

18. Fike remarks that "in giving his first-born son his own name, Jonson seems to have indicated his hope for a temporal immortality through his son" (208). Cf. Pigman: "Jonson's
attachment is fiercely possessive: the child is his creation. The entire poem is centered on
Jonson; the son has no existence independent of his father" (88). Peter Sacks finely observes
that the first couplet's "identically delayed cesurae . . . give the last foot in each line ('and
joy,' 'loved boy') a fragile and tragic detachability" that presents the boy as "a vulnerably exposed and indeed severed extension of Jonson's 'line'" (120).

19. Winner notes that "the sense of right as 'conforming with justice' echoes ironically in
the phrase 'the just day,' as the idea of the 'right' nudges that of the 'just.' In the same vein,
the note of submission in 'I thee pay' is checked by the force of 'exacted,' which loses its
theological connotations by virtue of its subject—the impersonal 'thy fate'" (113). The loss
of theological implication, as the poet attributes his child's death not directly to God's will
but to the more abstract, classical notion of fate, subtly reinforces the submission of "I thee
pay" by discreetly veiling God's fiercer aspect. The ancient prophets could be less decorous:
cf. Ezekiel 20:25–26, "I defiled them through their very gifts in making them offer by fire all
their firstborn, that I might horrify them; I did it that they might know that I am Yahweh"
(trans. Green 175).

20. Bell compares these lines with Hamlet's repeated plea to the ghost of his father,
"Speak to me" (179).

reminds us with laconic force that death, writing, and the author-father have all in their ways preempted this phantom voice. Scodel observes that Jonson's use of the "ask'd, say" formula echoes Spenser's envoi to *The Shepheardes Calender,* and therefore "emphasizes that his seeming address to his son is really a figure for his confrontation with his own written words" (105). In this confrontation, the commonplace "here doth lye" is wrested, by the audacious substitution of poem for child, from the head-stone we imagine to the literal space of the page before us. As Milton in "Lycidas" will turn aside from the lost body of Edward King to contemplate the power of his own consolatory vision, Jonson here turns from the lost body of the dead boy to commemorate his own poem.[21]

This is the *other* meaning of "his best piece of *poetrie.*" The poem's rhetorical coup is to convince us (as it no doubt convinced Jonson) that what we hear in this language is a chastened father's diffidence toward art, not the gratified mastery of a Virgil or a Phidias admiring his own handiwork. And yet "On My First Sonne" *is* Ben Jonson's best piece of poetry. He knew this, and says so in spite of himself, with stunning candor. We know it too, even as we read the boast.[22] In this sense the lost boy really is buried in, and by, his father's language. Perhaps it would be more exacting to say that his loss is buried there, repudiated by the self-effacing strategy that lets the poem's language seem to be about the child and not itself. For it is only the gesture of apostrophe, with its paper-thin fiction of a dead boy who will speak, that enables this language to conceal the counter-poem hidden all over its surface—the counter-poem whose burden we find in Montaigne. In that poem, the "sin" to which Jonson confesses is not that his son pleased him too much, but one much harder to acknowledge: that he took too much pleasure in his other creations. The all-too-conventional (and convertible) analogy between books and children sustains this unacknowledged confession of artistic pride through to the poem's final line.[23]

21. Here, as often, Sacks describes the poem much as I do, but with one-sided emphasis on its consolatory power for the grieving father. His account of the poem concludes on a note from which I recoil: "And what finer destiny for the child of his right hand than to be assimilated to that voice and mask which the poet has in turn bequeathed to him—to become, after all, an eternally speaking 'piece of poetry'?" (124–26). To such aesthetic piety, which seems to endorse and so to repeat the poet's retroactive effort to *choose* loss, one can only reply that living long enough to grow up, or even to grow old, might have been a finer destiny.

22. Booth dissents from this view in the aptly titled *Precious Nonsense.* Playing the grumpy outsider with obvious relish, he argues for the superiority of "On My First Daughter."

23. Scodel links Jonson's "evident pride in the poem-child as the product of his hand, and his alone" to the "later proud declaration that *Volpone* came 'from his owne hand'" (99). Many commentators note that in echoing the etymology of the name "Benjamin," Jonson speaks not of "the" but of "*my* right hand" (emphasis added).

It would be hard to imagine a more tangled play of motives. Tilt the page slightly and the pious fiction about a humbled author-father and his "loved boy" turns into the guilty confession of a stricken author-father whose first love was his work. Stare at the page long enough and this guilty confession turns into the astonishing fait accompli of a "self-creating" poet who was always his own first son.[24] Epigram 45 performs the impossible act of inscription by which Jonson means to take possession of his own dispossession by death. He would name two sons "Benjamin," but only the children of his right hand would survive. His consolation would be that of Montaigne's exclusive maker, for his name lived on through the "Sons of Ben." These heirs of the letter were gotten, not begotten, through the textual inversions that enabled Ben Jonson, "Posthumous born," to become the retroactive author of his own death.[25] When he came back to the *signum Dei* in that context, his allusion to it would be deliberate, unambiguous, and controlled:

> First, give me faith, who know
> My selfe a little. I will take you so,
> As you have writ your selfe. Now stand, and then,
> Sir, you are Sealed of the Tribe of *Ben*.[26]

Ben Jonson's literary career embodies a powerful ideology of authorship. Within this ideology lurks an impulse to master fate. Imbued with this impulse, the act of writing becomes an effort to untie the temporal knot of the trauma by restaging its inversion of cause and effect. The author goes back, confronting again the blow for which he had been so unprepared.

24. It was also in 1603 that Jonson dropped the *h* from his patronymic, self-consciously adopting an idiosyncratic spelling. Riggs links this innovation with the motive of self-creation in the epitaph for Benjamin: "The new spelling proclaimed his uniqueness. . . . In a narrower sense, the change of name set him apart from his real father and his three children, all of whom had been Johnsons. The aggrieved parent who wrote 'On My First Son' had wished to 'loose all father, now'; the altered spelling, which appears in the first occurrence of his name after the death of his sons, reaffirmed that intention. 'Johnson' was an inherited name ('son of John') that connoted filial and paternal attachment; 'Jonson' was an invented name that implied autonomy" (114–15). Brooks notes that the new spelling appears in print for the first time on "the [1604] title page of Jonson's contribution to James's procession into London [STC 14756]" (88), a detail that ties the change decisively to the conjunction of circumstances surrounding the trip to Conington.

25. Brady reads *Discoveries* as evidence of "the period, late in life, when Jonson considered his status as a progenitor of poets—not only the Tribe of Ben, but generations yet unborn" ("Progenitors" 16).

26. "An Epistle Answering to One That Asked to Be Sealed of the Tribe of Ben," lines 75–78.

But now he takes possession of it by projecting himself as author into the empty space of the absent cause. He wants to be taken as one who knows and has written himself.

Needless to say, the unique and unrepeatable events of 1603 do not make up a general paradigm of authorship. In seeking to generalize about them we confront a milder version of the dilemma created by the traumatic "event," for as we gather specific incidents into broader patterns, they turn out (insofar as they fit the patterns) already to have happened. My argument cannot escape this quandary, but it does not need to: the quandary is the point. Jonson's creation of himself as an exemplary author is distinctive because he so powerfully fuses its private and idiosyncratic form (masculine identity-formation as retroactive resistance to a particular traumatic experience) with its broader form as an ever-present dimension of writing (reference is retroactively constitutive).[27] For Jonson, then, the passage to manhood and the creation of a public authorial self are the same struggle.

The form this struggle takes is *writing as symbolic fatherhood*. The literary and cultural traditions of early modern Europe are so thoroughly patriarchal that this development seems, in retrospect, to have been inevitable. The dominant conceptions of authorship and literary creation could only be masculine and procreative.[28] Decades of feminist scholarship have demonstrated the barriers these conditions presented to women who wrote, but such conditions were no unmixed blessing for men.[29] Lacan calls this force of tradition the symbolic; in Epigram 45 Jonson calls it "fate." He says this fate was Benjamin's, but it is his own. Death is arbitrary—Benjamin Jonson didn't *have* to die, he just did. What was not arbitrary but socially, culturally, and historically bound was his father's response. Early modern England demanded that a male author recast the choices and circumstances of his personal life, and even construct his sense of selfhood, in the terms its culture offered. His task was to achieve the inevitable—whatever it cost.

27. In *The Story of All Things* Marshall Grossman offers a magisterial account of the literary history to which this brief analysis belongs. Moving from Augustine to Milton, Grossman analyzes the narrative and rhetorical strategies that generate successive historical versions of a "canonical" and implicitly masculine literary selfhood. I am particularly indebted to his definition of a "literary-historical event" (16–18, 47).

28. This does not mean they were simply, unequivocally, or uniformly so. For an interesting discussion of male authors' figurative appropriation of female procreativity, see Maus, "A Womb of His Own."

29. Woods offers "a few preliminary comparisons and contrasts between Lanyer's and Jonson's approach to the authority derivable from the Jacobean patronage system," noting the gender advantage Jonson enjoys in a hierarchical system in which "all authority derived from the idea of the father" (15, 19).

## Freud as Laius

Almost three hundred years separate Jonson's dream from Freud's, yet the parallels between them are unmistakable. These include the figures of the dead child and the guilty father (present this time to witness the death, but still unable to prevent it); the question of voice, of who speaks or falls silent; the wound to the forehead; the topos of the *puer senex;* the temporal structure of the trauma, with its inversions of causal sequence; and the struggle to *write* the dream as a resistance to its uncanny priority.

*The Interpretation of Dreams* is a peculiar autobiography, filled with its author's fantasies yet marked by the reticence with which he divulges them. Often his dreams are intriguing in ways the analysis declines to pursue. Among the most intriguing, however, is a dream reported by one of Freud's patients:

> The preliminaries to this model dream were as follows. A father had been watching beside his child's sick-bed for days and nights on end. After the child had died, he went into the next room to lie down, but left the door open so that he could see from his bedroom into the room in which his child's body was laid out, with tall candles standing round it. An old man had been engaged to keep watch over it, and sat beside the body murmuring prayers. After a few hours' sleep, the father had a dream that *his child was standing beside his bed, caught him by the arm and whispered to him reproachfully, "Father, don't you see I'm burning?"* He woke up, noticed a bright glare of light from the next room, hurried into it and found that the old watchman had dropped off to sleep and that the wrappings and one of the arms of his beloved child's dead body had been burned by a lighted candle that had fallen on them. (547–48)

Freud uses this dream to open the seventh chapter of his study. Having set forth in detail the principles of dream formation, he seeks in the final chapter to explain the generic qualities that make dreaming so different from waking life. He does so by elaborating a speculative model of the mental "apparatus" together with a hypothesis about how this apparatus functions differently in dreams than it does in conscious perception. To introduce the discussion, he chooses a striking and enigmatic dream that nevertheless "raises no problem of interpretation and the meaning of which is obvious" (549). He needs a hook, something to catch the reader by the arm but not draw him off into a long interpretation—a dream, then, whose striking features will not be idiosyncratic but generic, since it is the generic qualities of dreaming to which the author wants to direct our attention. He needs a dream that belongs to no one in particular, but is everyone's: "this model dream."

It is a father's dream, but not Freud's. In fact it was reported to him by a woman patient—yet it was not hers either. She heard it in a lecture, and carried the dream from doctor to doctor. "Its actual source," writes Freud, "is still unknown to me." Then he adds: "Its content made an impression on the lady, and she proceeded to 're-dream' it, that is, to repeat some of its elements in a dream of her own, so that, by taking it over in this way, she might express her agreement with it on one particular point" (547). Freud says no more about this patient, so we can only wonder what sort of impression it made on her, which elements she redreamed, and why, or on what "particular point" she not only agreed but felt a need to *express* her agreement. Was the wish she expressed in any way bound up with the desire that carried her to a lecture on dream interpretation in the first place? Was that desire in turn bound up with her transference onto Freud, or with the countertransference?[30] Did she in any sense redream the dream in order to produce it for her analyst? If so, was she responding to a desire she sensed or imagined in him?

The content that "made an impression on the lady" concerns the death of a child as experienced by the father. Why does a woman in analysis redream a father's dream of loss in order to *express her agreement with it*? Does she do so to please the analytic father to whom she bears the dream? The father, perhaps, *for* whom she bears it? The father of dream interpretation as such, whose writing gave birth to an institution that, even more than his children, came to bear his name?

Freud does not answer these questions. In his account the lady vanishes, her secret mission accomplished. She does so in order for Freud himself to take over the narrative, expressing his agreement with it on one particular point. In this way the dream passes through a chain of dreamers: the unnamed lecturer from whom the woman heard it had already taken it over to make a point; Freud's patient does the same, and so again does Freud. All three are in agreement, too, for "the explanation of this moving dream is simple enough and, so my patient told me, was correctly given by the lecturer" (548). As it moves from dreamer to dreamer along a chain of corroboration, the dream leaves us wondering, finally, who is dreaming whom. What "peculiar feature" makes it so mobile and so apt to elicit agreement? For some reason Freud does not tell us; oddly, he defers

---

30. These questions are also raised by Gallop, who anticipates my argument in a more general way by discussing the dream interpreter's identification with the dreamer and by characterizing her own reading of Lacan as a "redreaming" (172, 183).

the exposition the dream was supposed to introduce. Something is deeply amiss in the argumentative sequence of chapter 7. No sooner has Freud identified the "new path" we must follow than he senses a need to be wary, "to pause and look around, to see whether in the course of our journey up to this point we have overlooked anything of importance." And indeed we have. A fearful obstacle arises, "a difficulty which we have not hitherto considered but which is nevertheless capable of cutting the ground from under all our efforts at interpreting dreams" (549). This mortal blow must be warded off. A long digression intervenes before we can resume our journey in the confidence of "having now repelled the objections that have been raised against us, or having at least indicated where our defensive weapons lie" (571).

Such is the path by which Freud approaches his model of "the mental apparatus." Now at last he can tell us the peculiar feature (peculiar, yet also generic) that "calls for explanation." The dream illustrates "the essential characteristics that differentiate dreams so strikingly from waking life": it possesses an eerie sensory intensity, the hallucinatory hyperreality so peculiar to dreams; and it represents an expected, hypothetical, or desired reality as *present,* invested with the full force of that intensity. Over and above the interpretation of the dream, this intensity "calls" for explanation: Father, it asks, don't you see I'm burning?

The problem is one of sequence. Freud warns us in introducing his model of the mind that although his metaphors give an impression of spatial order, the important point is the way an excitation passes through the various systems of the apparatus "in a particular *temporal* sequence" (575). This sequence begins with sensory perception and ends in motor discharge. Between perception and action occur memory and choice: memory follows perception, sorting its contents according to their logical relations, while consciousness precedes motor discharge, exercising voluntary control. But suppose that in sleep the daytime "advance" of this sequence from perception to motor discharge were blocked at the threshold of consciousness. Wishes arising from the unconscious might circumvent this by doubling back—reversing their flow, so to speak, through the grids of the memory system. As they moved backward through these grids, logical relations would dissolve and dream thoughts would turn into mental pictures, like a sentence rewriting itself in rebuses. Now the wish could move "forward" again *as perception,* evading the censorship this time by appearing not as thought but as the "raw material" of the senses.

This is how Freud derives the special quality of dreams. They know only the present tense because their regressive movement breaks down chronological relations as it translates thoughts "backward" into pictures. The resulting images have a hallucinatory intensity for two reasons. First, dream thoughts arise from infantile memories which in themselves retain a high degree of sensory vividness; second, these memories work like magnets, pulling blocked dream thoughts back through the mental apparatus. One reason, then, is regression, and the other is displacement. "In most dreams," writes Freud,

> it is possible to detect a central point which is marked by peculiar sensory intensity. . . . This central point is as a rule the direct representation of the wish-fulfillment . . . for, if we undo the displacements brought about by the dream-work, we find that the *psychical* intensity of the elements in the dream-thoughts has been replaced by the *sensory* intensity of the elements in the content of the actual dream. (600)

But if this is correct—if the sensory intensity of the dream image replaces the psychical intensity of the dream thought it translates—then the generic intensity of dreams is not separate from their interpretation after all. In his discussion of the burning child, Freud wanted to keep these issues separate. The work of interpretation was easy, he declared, it met with no obstacles, but it left the phenomenon of vividness unexplained. Many pages later, after strange displacements and regressions in the sequence of the argument, we learn that in fact the interpretation of a dream remains incomplete *until* it has translated sensory vividness back into psychical intensity. *Father,* says the dream, *I'm burning for you to see.*

What does Freud not see? He knows nothing about the original dreamer, and therefore cannot recover the infantile scene that, according to his theory, must be transferred onto the recent experience reflected in the dream, charging it with sensory intensity. But what could be the "actual source" of a dream that belongs to no one dreamer? Freud takes the dream over for his own purposes, yet once he has done so his account of these purposes immediately starts to behave like a dream, displacing the peculiar into the generic, then zigzagging back from the goal of the argument into an imagery of pathways, defensive weapons, and cutting away the ground.

Perhaps the "peculiar feature" about which Freud seems at once so insistent and so reticent in discussing this dream is its combination of sensory-emotional intensity with the *absence* of a motivating memory. Through this absence, the dream satisfies the author's wish for a text whose interpretation should seem at once blocked and without obstacle, at once circumstantially withheld and too obvious to require comment. But the absence of a motivating memory not only serves the immediate purposes of the argument; it also enables Freud, or anyone, to appropriate the dream—or to be appropriated by it—on a deeper level, supplying its missing origin from their own associations and then redreaming it so as to identify with its haunting question.

Perhaps, then, the dream enters into a deeper train of associations. Has Freud supplied its missing origin from his own experience? Decades later, he adds to the explanation of the mental apparatus a dream of his own. Inserted in 1919, it is a wartime dream about news from the front concerning his son, and it arises, as Freud discreetly says, from "the envy which is felt for the young by those who have grown old, but which they believe they have completely stifled" (599). If this envy has a sexual component, it amounts to a kind of reversed, belated Oedipal wish, a father's fantasy about replacing his son in the affections of the mother-wife. Again, a problem of sequence: if Ben Jonson imagined himself usurping his son's escape from the mother-wife, Freud imagines his son replacing *him* in her affections. In his 1933 lecture on "Femininity" Freud writes that it is in her maternal identification that a woman "acquires her attractiveness to a man, whose Oedipus attachment to his mother it kindles into a passion." Then he adds: "How often it happens, however, that it is only his son who obtains what he himself has aspired to! One gets an impression that a man's love and a woman's love are a phase apart psychologically" (*New Introductory Lectures* 134). This sounds like the trace of a *Laius* complex. Whose unconscious fantasy *is* the son's Oedipal desire?

The anxiety betrayed in this exclamation from the text of 1933 is already evident in Freud's wartime dream:

> Indistinct beginning. I said to my wife that I had a piece of news for her, something quite special. She was alarmed and refused to listen. I assured her that on the contrary it was something that she would be very glad to hear, and began to tell her that our son's officer's mess had sent a sum of money (5000 Kronen?) . . . something about distinction . . . distribution. . . . Meanwhile I had gone with her into a small room, like a storeroom, to look for something. Suddenly I saw my son appear. He was not in uniform but in tight-fitting sports clothes (like a seal?), with a little cap. He climbed up on to a basket that was standing beside a cupboard. I called out to him: no reply. It seemed to me that his face or forehead was bandaged. He was adjusting something in his mouth, pushing something into it. And his hair was flecked with grey. I thought: "Could he be as exhausted as all that? And has he got false teeth?" Before I could call out again I woke up, feeling no anxiety but with my heart beating rapidly. My bedside clock showed that it was two thirty. (597–98)

As in Jonson's "vision," the child in the dream has aged and has been wounded in the "face or forehead." When the dream occurs, there has been no news from the front "for over a week"; in the dream, Freud tries to give his wife "good news" which she, alarmed, refuses to hear. The day before the dream, he writes, he had received "a sum of money . . . derived from an agreeable occurrence in my medical practice" (598). This day residue appears in the dream invested with an unconscious wish for news of the son's death in battle. Freud's analysis traces this wish to an infantile memory, an accident dating back to his second year when, climbing "on to a stool in the store-closet to get something nice that was lying on a cupboard or table," he had fallen and been struck by the stool "behind my lower jaw; I might easily, I reflected, have knocked out all my teeth. The recollection was accompanied by an admonitory thought: 'that serves you right'; and this seemed as though it was a hostile impulse aimed at the gallant soldier" (599).

Reaching for "something nice," the child falls. It serves him right, too: he has overlooked the danger of his position, so the ground is cut out from under him and he is struck from behind. The dreamwork, in linking Freud's son to Freud *as* son, displacing the gallant soldier onto the greedy child, seems to recall and then to reverse this Oedipal punishment. It is as if Freud wants to pass along to his son the arbitrary blow of fate, together with the admonitory thought, "that serves you right." But it also seems as though the memory of this blow finds its way into the text that reports it, there to disturb the proper sequence of the exposition. Freud, *as he writes,* is still trying to ward off the blow he will later, in his wartime dream, pass on to the gallant soldier.

This dream has curious links to *Beyond the Pleasure Principle,* which dates from the same period. Derrida notices the way Freud's account of the "fort-da" game in that text aligns the father with the daughter in the absence of the son-in-law, who also is at the front (311–12). Freud's analysis of his wartime dream locates these same relatives, Ernst and his soldier-father, as links in the chain binding Freud to his grown son. Significantly, Freud is associated not with the soldier-father but with the resentful son: in *Beyond* he notes that Ernst "used to take a toy, if he was angry with it, and throw it on the floor, exclaiming: 'Go to the fwont!' He had heard at that time that his absent father was 'at the front,' and was far from regretting his absence; on the contrary he made it quite clear that he had no desire to be disturbed in his sole possession of his mother" (10). The central figure in both scenes is a woman, the mother-wife or daughter-wife in whose ambiguous affections father and son imagine themselves changing places. The feminine gaze is like a pivot on which the Oedipus complex reverses itself; and the problem is one of (generational) sequence. This reversibility, in which the son's resentment may begin as his father's preemptive fantasy, is suggested by the intriguing image from Freud's wartime dream of the boy as a *puer senex,* a young child whose "hair was flecked with grey." This is the image he associates with Ernst and the son-in-law, and ultimately with his own childhood accident.

In the sequence of the dream, the child takes his father's place. Freud has gone with his wife into "a small room, like a storeroom, to look for something," and there the son appears. He climbs up to reach the shelf— not to remove something, as in the accident Freud remembers, but "as though he wanted to *put* something on the cupboard" (perhaps to put it back?). The father, now an adult, returns to the scene of his Oedipal mishap, accompanied this time by the mother-wife whose possession he has since gained, though he may be losing her to a "gallant" young rival (how often it happens!). The son appears to have taken his place, as in the 1933 essay, obtaining what the father had aspired to, enacting the gesture of desire that triggered fate's punitive blow in the guise of an accident. The accident has already taken place, yet the grey-haired child may be try-ing not only to reenact it but also to undo it—his gesture, like the dream itself, a belated effort (always belated) to put back "something nice" that is missing from the maternal cupboard.

Much as Jonson's vision of his son seems to encode thoughts that are at once wishful and admonitory, Freud's dream appears to condense oppo-site versions of the same scene into a single image. In the dream, he re-members, "I called out to him: no reply." Is the failure to reply another sign of death? Or do the signs of wounding and premature aging that fol-low immediately in the dream constitute a reply of sorts? "Before I could call out again I woke up," says Freud, "feeling no anxiety but with my heart beating rapidly. My bedside clock showed that it was two thirty." After a dream so full of temporal dislocations, so preoccupied with aging, envious retrospection, castration, and premature death, the awakening glance at the bedside clock may register more than the hour. To whom is Freud calling out in the figure of the child—his son or himself? And what could he have been meaning to say? Is the cry a warning? Or is Freud him-self now the burning child who "calls" for explanation?

Freud does not explicitly connect his wartime dream with the one he used to open the chapter. Yet in his text the dream of the burning child joins a chain of associations leading back to the cupboard and the blow to the jaw. This dream too may be invested, then, with the father's intolera-ble wish to witness his son's death and to take his son's place in life. Yet side by side with the wish to bequeath castration, Freud's wartime dream expresses a wish to go back and undo it. After all, if chronology can be re-versed, if a son might die in his father's place, then perhaps one need not die at all. A father might evade death not only by trading places with his son but also by going backward (like a crab, says Hamlet) to undo its blow. This journey, backward in time, leads to a realm like the Elysian fields in Virgil—or in Catholic theology, the place called limbo. Lacan calls it the domain "of the *unborn*." The analogy is suggestive: the relation of repression to the unconscious, he says, "is the abortionist's relation to limbo" (*Four Fundamental Concepts* 23). If this is so, then to dream may be to reenter limbo in search of the prematurely mortal infant that is one-self, cut off by the threat of castration yet still urgent to be born. Perhaps this is where Virgil, journeying back to the mythic origins of Rome, means to lead his audience; perhaps it is what he means to show them in the pro-cession of already-dead, not-yet-born sons that pass before Father An-chises. Aeneas does, after all (as so many commentators have noticed) exit the underworld through the gates of ivory, or false dreams.

It may be at this level that the "peculiar feature" which draws Freud to the dream of the burning child is finally revealed. As we have seen, problems of sequence and regression are central to the argument of chapter 7, which seems troubled by the fear of a blow that will cut the ground away. They are at issue most obviously in Freud's insistence that, although the temporal se-quence of mental operations is irreducible, dreaming reverses it. They are at issue again as Freud worries over his use of the telescope and "reflex appara-tus" as figures for an unknown process: such reliance on visibilia in a theo-retical argument is equivalent to the regressive phase of dreamwork, which translates thoughts back into visual images. Freud's analogies seek to illus-trate, not dissolve, logical relations, but they cannot avoid spatializing time. He even illustrates the analogy to the reflex apparatus with a series of dia-grams (576–80). Concrete images of abstract processes are frequent in the volume and indeed throughout Freud's work, but these diagrams have no counterpart anywhere in *The Interpretation of Dreams*.

As the argument progresses, we learn that dreaming is "regressive" in more than a merely technical sense. Dreams not only reverse the sequence of mental operations involved in cognition, they do so by harking back to infantile memories. These memories are "primitive" in mode as well as content, and dreams not only reactivate the unfulfilled wishes for which the memories serve as "screens," they also resume the hallucinatory form of infantile wishing (606). This argument attains its most complex layer-ing of regressions when Freud, in his most striking anticipation of *Beyond the Pleasure Principle,* thinks backward to the evolutionary origins of the apparatus he has sketched and imagines that wishing began as the organ-ism's hallucinatory re-cathexis of memory traces left by a prior satisfaction (604–5). Motor functioning arises, he suggests, only because the halluci-natory "short path of regression" does not effectively reestablish the ob-jective conditions of satisfaction: to do that we must act upon the world. Freud's struggles with the progressive and regressive movements of his ar-gument, and his preoccupation with comparable movements in the mental apparatus, suggest that the idea of sequence, especially the difference between reversible and irreversible sequences, carries for him a powerful set of unconscious associations with the idea of his own death—*especially* with the idea of his death as premature, an accident that has already happened. He displaces the memory of this childhood accident onto his son in a mixed effort to evade death by passing it on and by undoing it.[31]

The dream of the burning child offers an extraordinary subtext for the argument to which it seems so casually, indeed so reluctantly, connected. The dream gains much of its pathos from the situation in which it occurs, the father keeping a sleepless vigil "for days and nights on end" at the sickbed of his dying child. On this level it serves a conscious, ethical, and sentimental purpose, dressing the dream thought in its exact opposite. The father's vigilance is helpless to prevent the child's death, however, and so he is forced to witness the most dreadful violation of proper sequence—what Freud, writing to Ludwig Binswanger about Sophie's death, would later call "the monstrous fact of children dying before their parents" (qtd. in Schur 329). Leaving an old man to watch over the dead body in his place, the exhausted father retires to sleep in the next room, *leaving open the door* that leads to the room where the body is laid out. A few hours later he is awakened by the dream, which harks back to his ordeal of helpless watching as the child whispers "reproachfully: *'Father, don't you see I'm burning?'* "

Let us go back now, one last time, to Freud's hypothesis about the mental apparatus—this, after all, is what he *says* he wants the story to lead us toward. Among the implications of his argument, he points out, is that the censorship, so often cast in a negative role as the agency of repression, the warden of conventional morality—even, in Lacan, the abortionist—"deserves to be recognized and respected as the watchman of our mental health" (606). Without it, unconscious fantasies would have access to the power of movement. This is crucial, for Freud then goes on to ask,

> Must we not regard it . . . as an act of carelessness on the part of that watchman that it relaxes its activities during the night, allows the suppressed impulses in the Ucs. to find expression, and makes it possible for hallucinatory regression to occur once more? I think not. For even though this critical watchman goes to rest—and we have evidence that its slumbers are not deep—it also shuts the door upon the power of movement. (607)

The father of the burning child goes to sleep with the door open. It is not the censorship but the dream itself that makes him stumble on the thresh-

---

31. Pontalis remarks that Freud's preoccupation with the date of his death during the period 1890–95 "indicates a desire for immortality, for nonirreversible time" (87).

old of awakening, as its flash of regression balks his return through the open door. The opening is why he wakes up: "The glare of the light shone through the open door into the sleeping man's eyes." This signals a failure of vigilance: the watchman has fallen asleep (the whole of Troy may be in flames). But the dream intervenes between the father's perception of the glare and his awakening into the power of movement. In *its* "zigzag" movement, the dream links the watchman's failure with the father's helpless vigil and the fever it could not prevent. Yet according to Freud's own theory, it must also hark back further, back to some infantile memory in which the father, it may be, occupied the place now taken by his dead child. Such a memory would have been revived by the contrary wishes that must have tormented the exhausted father: the wish to be able somehow to prevent the blow that has already fallen, but also the wish to evade that blow himself by trading places with the child, by *witnessing* the child's death. Not until his vigil has ended, not until he sees the child die, can the weary father at last give in to sleep. (Could he be as exhausted as all that?)

For Freud, the open door is a threatening signal. He seems to know on some level what lies suspended across its threshold, waiting to be born: an ancient ritual in which the son's death at once destroys and guarantees the father's identity. But closing the door will not quench the flames. Behind it the sacrificial fire, swallowed in moments of passionate grief and devotion, still burns with what Lacan calls "the most anguishing mystery" (34). So anguishing, our very mental health would be threatened if "this moving dream" ever crossed the threshold into "the power of movement"—as indeed it might if the censorship, that critical watchman, ever went to sleep without closing the door.

## Jacques Lacan and the True Formula of Atheism

> . . . no one can say what the death of a child is, except the father *qua* father, that is to say, no conscious being. For the true formula of atheism is not *God is dead*—even by basing the origin of the function of the father upon his murder, Freud protects the father—the true formula of atheism is *God is unconscious*.
>
> —Lacan, *Four Fundamental Concepts*

Luce Irigaray suggests that men, alienated from the masculine body, recover it as an erotic object in the pleasure of touching their infant sons.[32]

32. "Perhaps man and woman no longer caress each other except through that mediation between them that the child—preferably a boy—represents? Man, identified with his son, re-

There is something irresistible in the resilience of a child's body. When my oldest son was much younger, he would sometimes go to sleep lying on my chest. I would stroke his back lightly with my fingertips, and as sensual pleasure mingled with affection I would wonder whether the burning child might not be ignited by desire. One evening as he was drifting off I said, "I love you." With a trace of sleepy annoyance he murmured, "Why do you ask me that, when you already know I do?" Something in him overheard the demand spoken backward in my desire.

Freud puts the dream of the burning child into circulation on a grand scale. To rewrite Freud—to redream psychoanalysis, to go back and get it right, seeing what the father missed—has been a prevailing temptation of modern letters. The problem, said Lacan, is one of sequence: by a historical accident, a blow of fate, Freud was born too soon to avail himself of structural linguistics. We must therefore read him retroactively, loyal to his discovery of the unconscious, but recognizing it both as it would have been for Freud ("structured like a language") and as it will have been for us: according to "the true formula of atheism," the voice of God.

Lacan discusses the dream of the burning child in his 1964 seminar, *The Four Fundamental Concepts of Psychoanalysis*. He too redreams it, and it was the obscure lyric intensity of his remarks on the dream that left me burning with what he calls "the most anguishing mystery, that which links a father to the corpse of his son close by, of his dead son" (34). This is a well-known mistake: Freud writes not of a son but of a child, "das Kind." It seems strange that Lacan, who identifies the unconscious with the letter of the text and therefore often reads Freud hyperliterally, should commit such an obvious blunder. On the other hand, if my reading of Freud is correct, then Lacan's mistake follows the logic of the text, completing and making explicit, as it were, an identification lurking in the dreamwork of Freud's argument—unless it precedes and produces that logic. A problem of sequence: it was under the influence of Lacan's mistake that I went back to Freud. I wrote a draft on chapter 7 of *The Interpretation of Dreams* without once noticing that Freud writes "child," not "son," and was completely out of countenance when a friend pointed out the mistake. (Father, don't you see? Apparently not.) I have no idea now whether, in my reading, Freud's text produces

discovers the pleasure of maternal fondling; woman touches herself again by caressing that part of her body: her baby-penis-clitoris" (27). I read Irigaray here as implying that "man" identifies with his son as the object of fondling even as he assumes the maternal role of doing the fondling: the son in this way allows the masculine imaginary to close the gap between subject and object that opens within the symbolic as a result of the masculine tendency to identify exclusively with the subject position.

Lacan's mistake or Lacan's mistake produces Freud's text. Who is the father here, who the son? All of us, though, are produced by foreclosure
of the ungendered and elision of the feminine: Freud, Lacan, and Miller
all unwittingly transform a feminine or ungendered child into the specular son. In this way they (we) repeat the compulsive founding gesture of
masculinity. Dickens, meanwhile, has already diagnosed this error in Mr.
Dombey, who cannot forgive his daughter Florence for surviving her
dead brother. The stonemason commissioned to carve a headstone for
little Paul has to call the father's attention to a mistake in the inscription,
which reads "beloved and only child." Pointing to the word "child"
with his ruler (a fine touch), the mason asks if it shouldn't read "son"
(312).

In his discussion of Freud, Lacan introduces a dream of his own. Between introducing the dream of the burning child and returning to discuss what it reveals—repeating Freud's symptomatic gesture of delay—
he describes another dream of awakening. This time the door—the one
the first dreamer leaves open, the one Freud wants the watchman to shut
before going to sleep—is closed. And then someone knocks. Stealing a
nap in his office one day, Lacan is awakened by the sound. Between
hearing it and becoming conscious of it, he has a dream. He tells this
story to illustrate how the subject of consciousness, the "I" that knows
"that I am there, at what time I went to sleep, and why I went to sleep"
(56), is both subverted and constituted in the interval between perception and consciousness—that is, between the sensory-receptive and
motor-active ends of the diagrams in chapter 7 of *The Interpretation of
Dreams*.

Lacan never bothers to report the content of his dream—only that it
"manifested to me something other than this knocking." Exactly what it
manifested we cannot know, but we can guess at the desire it may have expressed. Lacan's discussion of the burning child, which precedes and follows the account of his dream like knock and awakening, contains other
slight inconsistencies. In his own case, he notes, "the knocking . . . is, to
all appearances, what woke me." Returning a moment later to Freud's
text, he declares that the dream of the burning child "is *also* made up entirely of noise" (57, my emphasis). For a moment he seems to confuse the
two dreams, forgetting the child's appearance in the dream Freud reports,
and his gesture of catching the father "by the arm." This oversight appears
to express impatience with the stages of argumentation, a proleptic leaping ahead to his conclusion. A problem of sequence—for Lacan is going
to insist that in either instance what shakes the dreamer awake is not the
external stimulus, the knock at the door or the glare of the flame, but an
encounter with the "real" of the unconscious—which touches him, inex-

plicably, where the fire has touched his son's body: on the arm.[33] For Lacan, however, what he calls the *tuché*—the always-missed encounter with "the real"—is not touch but sound, a reproachful and beseeching whisper. He cannot wait for the dreamwork to substitute this sound for the visual stimulus of the glare or the unnerving hand on the arm, so he anticipates and completes this substitution in his memory of Freud's text, declaring a little too hastily that the dream is "made up *entirely* of noise." He does this despite his insistence in principle on "the total distinction between the scopic register and the invocatory, vocatory, vocational field" (118).

Lacan seems to be repeating the dream in that second field, handing it over from the scopic register to "the invocatory drive, which is the closest to the experience of the unconscious" (104). It is there, in relation to the unconscious traces of spoken words, that Lacan places the baffling experience of *tuché*. For Lacan, the moment of awakening is the moment in which we glimpse the disappearance of this "real" as it retreats into the limbo of the unborn. In its place we grasp *only* our reflection, never ourselves: "after the awakening knock," he writes, I am "able to sustain myself, apparently only in a relation with my representation, which, apparently, makes of me only consciousness. A sort of involuted reflection—in my consciousness, it is only my representation that I recover possession of" (57). Consciousness, for Lacan, is always "Posthumous born."

The "vocatory" is also the vocational field, that of the psychoanalytic "calling." Always contemptuous of ego psychology, Lacan identified the psychoanalytic calling with the voice of the unconscious itself, aborted by repression, wandering in the limbo of the unborn (which Catholic theology placed between hell and purgatory), calling out to the Father who abides in the scopic register, urging him to *see* what he can only hear. "What we have in the discovery of psychoanalysis," writes Lacan, "is an encounter, an essential encounter—an appointment to which we are always called with a real that eludes us" (53). With a flourish of wit he transforms the analytic session from an encounter between patient and analyst into a "missed encounter" with the unconscious, the essential and anguishing mystery around which analysis, for Lacan, is always suspended.

---

33. Slavoj Žižek refers in discussing this dream to "the smell of smoke" (*The Sublime Object* 45), a detail not mentioned in Freud's text or Lacan's. The recurrent impulse to invent plausible external stimuli betrays each writer's desire to place himself at the trauma's scene of origin, bearing witness to its material truth. Žižek's larger point is consistent with my argument: the dreamer awakens, he says, because "the dream, the reality of his desire . . . is more terrifying than the so-called external reality itself. . . . He escapes into so-called reality to be able to continue to sleep, to maintain his blindness, to elude awakening into the real of his desire" (45).

This is precisely the transformation Lacan's unreported dream performs: in response to a knock at the door (announcing his next appointment?) the sleeping analyst first hears the true call of his vocation, summoning him not to consciousness but to "the real." So he dreams, zigzagging back toward a door that is already closing, toward a rendezvous with "the beauty behind the shutters" (134)—only to awaken, reluctantly it seems, to the "impatient knocking" at his office door (56). It is in terms of *this* scenario that he keeps misremembering details of Freud's text. In an earlier reference, we read: "As he is falling asleep, the father sees rise up before him the image of the son" (34). Freud says the father awakened "after a few hours' sleep" (547). It is Lacan whose dream awoke him from "a short nap" in response to "impatient knocking"— Lacan, then, who felt as if he were just falling asleep. Felt, perhaps, as if his falling asleep and his waking up had been unfairly *reversed,* calling him back from his rendezvous with "the real" to what may be merely a drowsy encounter with another ego. For when the ego knocks at the door, the analytic project founders: "To appeal to some healthy part of the subject thought to be there in the real . . . is to misunderstand that it is precisely this part . . . that closes the door, or the window, or the shutters, or whatever—and that the beauty with whom one wishes to speak is there, behind, only too willing to open the shutters again. . . . It is to the beauty one must speak" (131). The beauty: something other than this knocking.

Freud wanted to slow down, look back, find his defensive weapons. Lacan is in a hurry. Like Alice's white rabbit forever consulting a broken watch, he is always late for a very important date. The trauma is a date for which he can never be on time, since for Lacan it is an *essentially* missed encounter, a blow that fell before we were ready and to which we therefore always respond too late. Yet he cannot resist bearing personal witness to the originary moment, composing himself, like Jonson and Freud, as the *author* of the trauma:

> I, too, have seen with my own eyes, opened by maternal divination, the child, traumatized by the fact that I was going away despite the appeal, precociously adumbrated in his voice, and henceforth more renewed for months at a time—long after, having picked up this child—I have seen it let his head fall on my shoulder and drop off to sleep, sleep alone being capable of giving him access to the living signifier I had become since the date of the trauma. (63)

This child is only asleep, not dead, but for Lacan he is nonetheless the "burning child"—and the burning child is a son. The father here repeats the gesture of Jonson and Freud, making the mother-wife at once marginal to his recognition and yet strangely central to it, since her attenuated presence hovers between father and son as the medium of perception. Like the holy ghost in an Oedipal trinity, she exists only as an adjective modifying the noun of her spiritualized mediation. Yet by this mediation she gives the father access to the originary scene. Only she can open his eyes to the trauma.

## The Eucharist of the Unconscious

The dream of filial sacrifice insists like a symptom within each effort to rewrite it. What gives it the power to sustain this migratory witness, disclosing itself in one dreamer after another and retying its knots of emotion in each? One answer seems to be that the sacrificial son configures for the fantasy the male subject's traumatic and compulsively repeated assumption of an impossible gender identity. There may be other answers as well; there are other dreamers, including women—Freud's unnamed patient, or more recently Jane Gallop. But for Jonson, Freud, and Lacan the dream seems to repeat the lived contradiction of masculinity.

Judith Butler argues that gender identity, or what Stoller calls the "gender core," is constituted not only by the incest taboo and the Oedipal crisis it precipitates, but also, and prior to these, by the taboo on homosexuality, which *creates* the heterosexual desires presumed by the Oedipal model (Stoller 11–14, Butler 24).[34] This prior repression of homosexuality appears in Sophocles' treatment of the Oedipus myth, which "forgets" that in earlier versions, "the tragic sequence is initiated because Oedipus' father, Laius, loved a beautiful youth, Chrysippus," and so drew down upon Thebes the wrath of Hera, guardian of marriage (Dollimore 204). Freud has recourse to the truncated, Sophoclean version of the story. Retracing the path that leads from his 1917 essay "Mourning and Melancholia" to the account of ego formation in *The Ego and the Id* (1923), Butler suggests how the theory of gender acquisition might look if we assumed a primary taboo on homosexuality. The prohibition against desire for the same-sexed parent, she argues, would differ crucially from the prohibition against desire for the parent of the opposite sex. The second prohibition does not require renunciation of the desire itself, but only of its primary object; the desire may be deflected toward a secondary, exogamous object, rather than renounced. But the prohibition against homo-

34. On gender as a knot tied by the trauma, see Lacan, "Meaning of the Phallus": "What we are dealing with is an antinomy internal to the assumption by man (*Mensch*) of his sex: why must he take up its attributes only by means of a threat, or even in the guise of a privation?" (75).

sexual incestuous desire extends its taboo over the desire itself, and not just its primary object. Since the desire is forbidden to pursue non-incestuous alternatives through displacement, Freud's theory suggests that it may instead be fixed and internalized through the dynamics of melancholia. Thus "gender identification is a kind of melancholia in which the sex of the prohibited object is internalized as a prohibition" (63).

Freud distinguishes mourning from melancholy in part by whether the object of loss is consciously recognized.[35] If it is recognized, then it can be sustained internally while the ego lets go, reviewing one by one the ties of association now severed by loss, dissolving them gradually in preparation for new attachments. The ego retains the imprint of the lost object, but it also mourns and moves on. If the loss is *not* consciously recognized, however—or perhaps we should say, more realistically, *to the extent* that it is not—then the identification remains fixed. In this case, ties of attachment are not available for conscious review and dissolution. Desire for the same-sex parent will then be melancholic, unavailable for mourning because it undergoes a prior and more thorough repression than heterosexual desire: hence Butler's suggestion that melancholy is the mechanism by which gender imprints itself, making the body its "living signifier." Identification in this model takes the form of incorporation, which "*literalizes* the loss on the body and so appears as the facticity of the body, the means by which the body comes to bear 'sex' as its literal truth" (68).

This argument need not assume a primary bisexuality, although it might appear to do so. It does assume that gender and sexuality as such are *retroactively* organized and imprinted in the body through the interplay of prohibition, identification, and incorporation. Thus, even if prohibition begins as a twofold taboo on homosexual aims *and* objects, there is no need to imagine such desires as already existing fully formed in the infant. They may crystallize within a primary flux of infantile fantasy and sensation as possibilities defined in the moment of denial, desires given form and emphasis by the very act of repression that erases them from awareness. Butler's use of the term "literalize" makes it clear that she defines melancholy incorporation as a trope—a kind of unconscious Eucharist in which the infant *becomes a subject* by saying to itself, "This is my body." This hypothetical speech act installs the grammatical distinction between subject and object, together with the act of predication that links them, at the originary moment of human identity. Again, this moment is "originary" because it *creates* the loss it is literalizing: until the infant recognizes in some form the prohibition that forbids it to desire the body of the

35. Enterline offers a lucid discussion of Freud's essay in relation to a wide range of psychoanalytic theory in the introduction to *Tears of Narcissus;* see esp. 15–23.

same-sex parent, there is no sexual differentiation within the primary presence of the Other.

Psychoanalysis typically uses the word *maternal* to name the phantasmic body associated with pre-Oedipal fusion between parent and child, but when we do this we are in a sense committing a politically loaded anachronism. This anachronism takes the form of a deferred interpretation: it is only in *retrospect*, after all, that the phantasmic body comes to be gendered, and identified as the mother's. When that happens we are carrying Oedipal distinctions back into the pre-Oedipal domain, misnaming its objects. Children are more precise. When my oldest son (an object of mourning only in that he is now a teenager) was about two, he used the term *mommadaddy* for either parent without distinction. He showed classic anger and denial when eventually forced to confront the differences internal to the body of mommadaddy, and this anger did, predictably, emerge in a repudiation of femininity. But what disturbed him most seemed to be the presence, not the loss, of the maternal body. What he lost was a purely imaginary body, unsplit by difference.

In that hypothetical (or anecdotal) moment when the pre-Oedipal body is given its Oedipal determination, a lot can get lost—everything excluded by the Oedipal logic of a patriarchal culture, including female voice, agency, and desire. I want to suggest another loss present along with these others, mingled with them so deeply it can scarcely be sorted out: the pre-Oedipal father. We haven't heard a lot about him, for he seems to be much more lost than his maternal counterpart—*so* lost, in fact, that he never existed in the first place. Babies are never incorporated into their fathers' bodies: paternity never has a bodily form. It remains purely testimonial, legal, or symbolic (fatherhood is language). The pre-Oedipal father, the *bodily* form of fatherhood, crystallizes, then, only as an excluded possibility, a negated idea, cast out of the symbolic order in the moment that order is instituted. The absence of this body persists, however, as a fundamental embarrassment for patrilineal patriarchy. Any social system that privileges a relation which cannot be seen must of force commit itself to an endless project of representation. It has to go on tirelessly symbolizing the thing it cannot point to.

My argument in this book has been that although the body of fatherhood remains an impossible concept, produced only in the moment of its negation, it nevertheless belongs to what Lacan describes as "the real," and it exercises considerable force. In *The Winter's Tale*, Leontes inspecting Mamillius is distraught to find no bodily link joining him to his son; he is clinging not only to the pre-Oedipal mother but also to the impossible and nonexistent father she screens from view. Within Hermione's imagined demand, "Remember mine!", I still hear that father's ghostly cry, "Remember me!" Hermione herself, for all the fluidity of her desires, may yearn for a recovery of the paternal. Recall the odd moment at her trial when she wishes her father, the emperor of Russia, were alive to witness the scene. She disavows any desire for revenge, which of course suggests a powerful aggressive impulse in denial. But perhaps she does want his pity more than his vengeance, and his witness more than either. The inaccessibility of the father *as father,* even to himself—perhaps most of all to himself—may be as devastating as maternal separation, even to the mother.

To give the originary object a single, definitive name is impossible, since it has always already been transformed by the taboos through which we gain access to speech. Diffracted by language, it will have as many configurations as there are erotic dispositions. If I insist on a particular name (still harping on fathers), the reasons are historical: we have lived under the rule of the fathers since ancient times, so the absence of the paternal body has a special significance. Freud's theory suggests that if the lost object could become conscious, it would then be available to mourning: knots are loosened when we acknowledge the "nots," the prohibitions, that have tied them. Can we hope, then, in Jonson's phrase, to "loose all father"?

This question reminds me of one more dream, the last one recorded in Freud's analysis of "Dora." In it she wanders the streets of an unfamiliar town, then enters the place where she lives to find a letter from her mother saying that Dora, having run away, can now come home. Her father is dead. After some difficulty finding her way, she is greeted at the door by a maidservant who announces that her mother and "the others" are at the cemetery. Dora, however, does not join them. She has finished mourning the father, and her self-exile is over. She sees herself climbing the stairs: "I went to my room, but not the least sadly, and began reading a big book that lay on my writing table" (114). The father's death frees Dora to come home, but instead of mourning she mounts the stairs to her room and opens a book. Whatever the name of the "big book" on Dora's writing table, it is the mother's "letter" and not the father's that summons her to read it. We can be fairly sure it was not *The Interpretation of Dreams.*

What text might *we* begin to read if the phantom of patriarchy were laid to rest? Unnamed perhaps because not yet read, the book Dora takes up at the end of her dream offers a tempting blank space in which to write utopia. Such a gesture would be suspect, though: that volume belongs to Ida Bauer, her "best piece of poetrie." In a sense it really isn't blank—it carries the traces of a specific life history, traces according to which it should be read as the dreams of Jonson, Freud, and Lacan have been. My argument does, however, leave open a space for hope. For although the knots of gender are tied long before we learn to read—a problem of sequence—if their effects extend into reading, perhaps we may yet engage them there. In the space where texts elicit our fantasies, we may seek to loosen the knots of filial paternity. To do so, however, we, too, would have to *finish* mourning the body of patriarchy, which still makes "living signifiers" of us all.

# Mourning Patriarchy:          6
# A Return to the Crossroads

There is no story that is not true.
   —Chinua Achebe, *Things Fall Apart*

## From the Crucifix to the Crossroads

In the introduction to this book, my point of departure for understanding blood sacrifice was the work of the anthropologist Nancy Jay. Her description of the ritual as a social technology for the creation of patriliny offers advantages whose value, I hope, has been demonstrated in the preceding chapters. Does the description also carry drawbacks? We know that traditional ethnology runs into methodological quandaries it cannot resolve because its accounts of ritual societies are written by observers, not participants. American and European social scientists have their own tribal customs and beliefs; as academic visitors from "modern" societies they are not disinterested recorders of fact but actors whose interests are shaped by disciplinary and institutional forces. Even if this were not true, to "objectify" social reality, transforming it into data, is still to alter its nature fundamentally in the process of recording it. There is a crucial difference between understanding social practices through observation and analysis and understanding them experientially, modes of apprehension that are incommensurable even though an individual may pass between them.

At the same time, the very distinction between "insiders" and "outsiders" can prove misleading if we imagine ritual societies as pastoral enclaves, innocent of "sophisticated" responses such as alienation or skepticism. In taking Jay's theory as a point of reference, my argument has implicitly tended to abstract and idealize the notion of a "ritual culture" in contrast with the world-historical conflicts of imperial Rome and modern Europe. As I noted in the introduction, anthropological models presume *relatively* stable social settings for the practice of ritual. This does not mean, however, that the tribal societies in question are either unchanging or free of conflict. Their relative stability is better described as a delicate balance of contending forces, an equilibrium that cannot be static because the community must adjust and adapt. Like a tightrope walker, the ritual community maintains its poise through a constant play of small self-correcting movements—or it falls.[1]

The difficulties that ethnology encounters in the observer-participant crux were addressed in the realm of fiction as novelists in the nineteenth and early twentieth century refined techniques for orchestrating point of view and cultivating the play of diverse styles and voices in narrative. Presumably this is why one significant response to the critique of ethnology has been to seek methodological inspiration in Bakhtin's theory of the novel as a "dialogic" mode of representation. Fiction is not social science, but it does offer an ideal medium for nuanced descriptions of the encounter between tribal communities and the emissaries of Western society. This is the challenge taken up by Chinua Achebe in *Things Fall Apart*, the story of a Nigerian village society overtaken by Christianity, writing, and gunpowder.[2] Achebe's novel lets me turn the disciplinary tables at the close of this study by using fiction to approach anthropological questions. Because filial sacrifice plays such a conspicuous role in the story, a discussion of *Things Fall Apart* also permits me to raise once again a recurring set of questions about the scope and persistence of this motif, and about its functions in the symbolic economies of ritual and modern cultures. Consideration of Achebe's work has the advantage as well of letting me step back briefly from the Eurocentric focus of the preceding chapters to gain a different vantage on questions about the ideological value of literary forms.

Colonial situations break down the distinction between insiders and outsiders because they overlap alien cultures within a single milieu, forming subjects in the fold between traditions. This recognition has become a central theme in work on European colonialism, which now speaks of

1. Like a tightrope walker, or a dancer, or a woman who walks from the stream back to her village bearing a jar of water on her head. Russell McDougal, drawing on Robert Farris Thompson's study of African art, examines the theme of cosmic, social, and personal balance expressed as an aesthetic of bodily movement, especially in the activities of walking and dancing, in "Okonkwo's Walk: The Choreography of Things Falling Apart."

2. Achebe has suggested calling the Igbo people a "nation" rather than a "tribe"; see *Home and Exile* 3–6. There is no single term for the social and political organization of the Igbo, who lived in autonomous clusters of villages linked by multiple dialects of a common language and a network of marketplaces. Achebe has addressed the question of his relation to the anthropological tradition (briefly) in the essay "Colonialist Criticism"; see *Morning Yet on Creation Day* 4–7.

"hybridization" as a feature of colonial situations going back to the late Middle Ages. In Ireland during the sixteenth century, for example, there was already an "Anglo-Irish" aristocracy that saw itself as neither English nor Irish. Even the Elizabethan poet Edmund Spenser, who did not arrive in Ireland until 1578 or 1579, is less likely now to be seen as unproblematically "English," for during the two decades in which he established himself as a landed gentleman in Ireland, his poetic address to the English court was increasingly characterized by an identification with his adopted (or appropriated) land. Thus the "home" of his 1595 poem "Colin Clouts Come Home Againe" (an allegorical account of the poet-shepherd's visit to the court of Gloriana) turns out to be Ireland, not England.[3] Achebe approaches colonial experience from the other side. And yet, as an African writer with an English education, casting his story not only in the language of the conquering people but also in European literary forms, he cannot be seen as speaking simply from "within" Igbo village culture.

Achebe describes himself as having grown up "at the crossroads of cultures," the son of an evangelist and church teacher surrounded by adherents of traditional Igbo customs and beliefs. His description of this "crossroads" is remarkable for the way it appropriates and transvalues the dominant symbol of European religion:

> On one arm of the cross we sang hymns and read the Bible night and day. On the other, my father's brother and his family, blinded by heathenism, offered food to idols. That was how it was supposed to be anyhow. But I knew without knowing why that it was too simple a way to describe what was going on. . . . I do not remember any undue distress. What I do remember was a fascination for the ritual and the life on the other arm of the crossroads. And I believe two things were in my favor—that curiosity and the little distance imposed between me and it by the accident of my birth. The distance becomes not a separation but a bringing together like the necessary backward step which a judicious viewer may take in order to see a canvas steadily and fully. (*Morning Yet on Creation Day* 119–20)

If his Europeanized background imposed a "little distance" between Achebe and traditional Igbo culture, his transformation of the crucifix in this passage gives him a complementary distance from his father's adopted religion, a "necessary backward step" that locates the writer inside neither religion but, instead, at their point of convergence, in the historical process unfolding in eastern Nigeria before World War II.

This crossroads provides an apt figure for Achebe's literary achieve-

---

3. The best place to begin on the large body of work concerning Spenser's literary career in Ireland is the important contribution of Louis A. Montrose, "Spenser's Domestic Domain."

ment. His appropriation of European literary forms demonstrates in a
striking way that their powers of representation are not bound by the cultural traditions in which they first developed. Achebe uses the openness of
novelistic discourse to incorporate African storytelling, myth, and proverb
while he employs the classic structure of tragedy to endow his deeply
flawed protagonist, the Igbo tribesman Okonkwo, with heroic dignity.
Achebe turns the narrative techniques of the modern novel toward an exploration of the social and intersubjective nuances of village culture, nuances to which Okonkwo himself remains oblivious. In the process,
Achebe appropriates the English language as well: a number of critics have
noted that his stylistic mastery creates an "African vernacular English" capable of delineating variations of individual feeling and attitude within a
shared cultural horizon, or what Wendy Lesser, writing about nineteenth-
century British fiction, calls "a community of moral agreement."[4] The
striking gesture by which the novel's title, *Things Fall Apart,* is wrested
from Yeats's poem "The Second Coming" epitomizes this strategy of appropriation: the "ceremonies of innocence" drowned in violence are not,
now, the aristocratic traditions of Western Europe but the village culture's
community of moral agreement, evoked in all its fragility as a continually
renegotiated balancing of group interests and individual dispositions.
Igbo tradition is the ceremonious past that "falls apart" when the mis-
sionary zeal and military force of British imperialism take up the role of
rough beast slouching toward Bethlehem.[5]

Initially this strategy of appropriation looks like a rhetorical equivalent
of the crossroads, a chiasmic exchange that uses European terms to figure
African experience and African terms to figure European or American experience. In a similar vein Achebe recalls greeting James Baldwin for the
first time "in the jungles of Florida" with the words "Mr. Baldwin, I presume" (Ezenwa-Ohaeto 213–14). But the novelist's appropriation of European cultural forms and symbols is more radical than simple reversal. He
does not associate village traditions with the coherence mourned by Yeats
in order to idealize the tribal past. The "little distance" that separates him
from Igbo culture makes him a "judicious viewer," and the echo of
Matthew Arnold's injunction to "see life steadily and see it whole" in
Achebe's reference to seeing "a canvas steadily and fully" reinforces the
sense that Western culture is an important means of achieving this creative
distance. The complexity of the writer's historical position is captured in
the rhetorical complexity of his prose: he describes his detachment from

4. For the phrase "African vernacular English," see C. L. Innes, "Language, Poetry, and
Doctrine in *Things Fall Apart*" 111; for the quotation from Lesser, see chapter 4, this volume.
5. See A. G. Stock, "Yeats and Achebe."

Igbo culture—"not a separation but a bringing together"—by detaching the preeminent symbol of Western culture, the crucifix, from its inherited significance. Reimagining the cross as a figure not of sacrifice but of convergence—balancing detachment and engagement, participation and observation, things coming together rather than falling apart—Achebe does not simply reverse its meaning, as he might, for example, if he were to see Africans as the sacrificial victims of a neo-Roman empire. Instead, his writing *performs* the cultural convergence he is describing, using each tradition to observe the other with the intimacy of a participant in both.

Two of Achebe's novels take their titles from modern English poems, both of which imagine the Nativity of Christ as a cultural trauma that strands the speaking subject between great colliding forces. *Things Fall Apart* is the first; the second is *No Longer at Ease,* the title of which comes from T. S. Eliot's poem "The Journey of the Magi." As Lloyd W. Brown observes, Achebe is once again transvaluing his European model: "Whereas Eliot, the orthodox Christian, sees the conflict between the old paganism and the new Christianity in clear moral terms, Achebe the African insists that the 'old dispensation,' as well as Christianity, had its own beauty and human dignity" ("Cultural Norms" 26–28).

Implicit in Achebe's strategy is, once again, a dislocation of the sacrificial motif, not only because these allusions reenact the characteristic transaction of the crossroads, viewing each culture in terms of the other, but also because Achebe so consistently uses the myth of Christ to evoke this transaction. "The Second Coming" and "The Journey of the Magi" are poems about the Nativity, not the Crucifixion, but as we saw in chapter 1, the whole career of Christ is implied within each of its episodes; the Nativity already contains a death. This is why Michelangelo's evocation of it in his first *Pietà,* although astonishingly original, is also thoroughly conventional: it restates an iconographic commonplace in reverse by glimpsing the joyous birth so poignantly in the sorrowful tableau of death. Achebe sees the Nativity differently, of course, but with a similar sense of it as prefiguring the Crucifixion. He takes it over from Yeats and Eliot as an image of radical dislocation, and the subject who lives through this dislocation, like the magus in Eliot's poem, seems to experience the Crucifixion in it:

> I had seen birth and death,
> But had thought they were different; this Birth was
> Hard and bitter agony for us, like Death, our death.
> We returned to our places, these Kingdoms,
> But no longer at ease here, in the old dispensation.[6]

6. *The Complete Poems and Plays* 69 (no line numbers given in this edition).

Achebe's novels repeatedly confront the tragic dimension of this clash: the protagonists of *Things Fall Apart, Arrow of God,* and *No Longer at Ease* are all destroyed in the collision between old and new dispensations, between a tribal order that has fallen apart and a national order that has not yet come together.[7]

In *Things Fall Apart,* Achebe makes filial sacrifice the turning point in both the career of his tragic protagonist, Okonkwo, and the collective life of Umuofia. The "sacrificial son" of the novel is a fifteen-year-old boy named Ikemefuna, given as hostage when "a daughter of Umuofia," having traveled to market with a neighboring clan, is killed there by the boy's father (11).[8] Ikemefuna, we are told, "belonged to [Umuofia] as a whole, and there was no hurry to decide his fate" (12). He is placed in Okonkwo's household; "no one thought it would be as long as three years," but the clan's elders "seemed to forget all about him as soon as they had taken the decision" (27). When his death is eventually decreed, one of the oldest and most respected of these elders visits Okonkwo to deliver the news:

> "That boy calls you his father. Do not bear a hand in his death." Okonkwo
> was surprised, and was about to say something when the old man continued:
> "Yes, Umuofia has decided to kill him. The Oracle of the Hills and Caves
> has pronounced it. They will take him outside Umuofia as is the custom,
> and kill him there. But I want you to have nothing to do with it. He calls
> you his father." (57)

The elder, Ogbuefi Ezeudu, stresses his injunction to Okonkwo, not only repeating it but beginning and ending with it as well. Nevertheless, Okonkwo ignores Ezeudu and accompanies the execution party. At the last minute, he repeats the gesture familiar to us from classical epic: "As the man who had cleared his throat drew up and raised his machete,

---

7. "Christmas in Biafra (1969)," the title poem of Achebe's 1973 collection *Christmas in Biafra and Other Poems,* is also a Nativity scene heavy with death: "Jesus plump wise-looking and rose-cheeked" in a crèche set up by hospital nuns is "the heart of the divine miracle," in contrast with the "infant son flat like a dead lizard" whose mother comes to join in the adoration. Yet as the speaker of the poem (Achebe's magus?) sardonically testifies, the dying Biafran child, "his arms and legs / cauterized by famine was a miracle / of its kind" (27).

8. David Carroll writes perceptively of the passage describing Ikemefuna's death as "a turning point in the novel. The guardianship of the boy was a mark of Okonkwo's hard-won status and the highest point of his rise to power. The execution of Ikemefuna is the beginning of Okonkwo's decline, for it initiates the series of catastrophes which end with his death. But this event is not only a milestone in the career of the hero. The sympathetic rendering of Ikemefuna's emotions as he is being marched through the forest to his death had wider implications." *Chinua Achebe* 48–49.

Okonkwo looked away" (61). But he is not permitted the divine privilege of evasion:

> He heard the blow. The pot fell and broke in the sand. He heard Ikemefuna cry "My father, they have killed me!" as he ran towards him. Dazed with fear, Okonkwo drew his machete and cut him down. He was afraid of being thought weak. (61)

In a flash, the evasive maneuver of Zeus gives way to the human predicament of Abraham, and this time there is no descending angel to stay his blow.

Achebe leaves no doubt that the analogy to the *aqedah* is deliberate. When Okonkwo's eldest son, Nwoye, converts to Christianity he takes the name Isaac, signifying his identification with the adopted brother, Ikemefuna, who was killed. His conversion is driven not just by his father's harshness but also by the twinned horrors of infanticide and filial sacrifice. When Nwoye first learns of Ikemefuna's death, "something seemed to give way inside him, like the snapping of a tightened bow. He did not cry. He just hung limp" (61). He had felt the same way once before:

> They were returning home with baskets of yams from a distant farm across the stream when they heard the voice of an infant crying in the thick forest. A sudden hush had fallen on the women, who had been talking, and they had quickened their steps. Nwoye had heard that twins were put in earthenware pots and thrown away in the forest, but he had never yet come across them. A vague chill had descended on him and his head had seemed to swell, like a solitary walker at night who passes an evil spirit on the way. Then something had given way inside him. It descended on him again, this feeling, when his father walked in, that night after killing Ikemefuna. (61–62)

When Nwoye converts to Christianity, he is "captivated" not by the theology but by "the poetry of the new religion, something felt in the marrow":

> The hymn about the brothers who sat in darkness and fear seemed to answer a vague and persistent question that haunted his young soul—the question of the twins crying in the bush and the question of Ikemefuna who was killed. He felt a relief within as the hymn poured into his parched soul. (147)

Achebe, who clearly disapproves of Christianity's exclusivity and its aggressive, proselytizing aims, nevertheless makes strategic use of it to criti-

cize Igbo traditions.[9] As C. L. Innes and others have observed, the new religion's power lies in its music and imagery because they are "felt in the
marrow": they speak to the unarticulated sorrow and alienation created
within Igbo culture by the cruelty of its own religious practices ("Language, Poetry, and Doctrine" 118–19).

*Things Fall Apart* does not, however, achieve critical distance on the
traditional Igbo religion by assuming an external, explicitly Christian perspective. It does so from within, by exploring the suffering, conflict, and
confusion "felt in the marrow" of the African characters. Nwoye is not
alone in questioning tradition. Okonkwo's closest friend in the village,
Obierika, will not lead Ikemefuna to his death in the forest, and he challenges Okonkwo for taking part:

> "You know very well, Okonkwo, that I am not afraid of blood; and if
> anyone tells you that I am, he is telling a lie. And let me tell you one thing,
> my friend. If I were you I would have stayed at home. What you have done
> will not please the Earth. It is the kind of action for which the goddess wipes
> out whole families."
>
> "The Earth cannot punish me for obeying her messenger," Okonkwo
> said. "A child's fingers are not scalded by a piece of hot yam which its
> mother puts into its palm."
>
> "That is true," Obierika agreed. "But if the Oracle said that my son
> should be killed I would neither dispute it nor be the one to do it." (67)

Obierika's refusal makes him a more sympathetic character than
Okonkwo, but it does not resolve the issues they face. Like Zeus, Obierika
would look away, submitting to the sacrificial demand even though he
does not embrace or internalize it.

We see this impasse elaborated in a later passage. Okonkwo must be
driven out of the village after his gun explodes during the funeral ceremony for Ezeudu, accidentally killing one of the dead man's sons.
Obierika ruminates doubtfully on the justice of this punishment:

> Obierika was a man who thought about things. When the will of the god-
> dess had been done, he sat down in his *obi* and mourned his friend's

---

9. In the autobiographical essay "Named for Victoria," quoted earlier, Achebe writes,

The bounties of the Christian God were not to be taken lightly—education, paid jobs, and
many other advantages that nobody in his right senses could underrate. And in fairness we
should add there was more than naked opportunism in the defection of many to the new
religion. For in some ways and in certain circumstances, it stood firmly on the side of hu-
mane behavior. It said, for instance, that twins were not evil and must no longer be abandoned in the forest to die. Think what that would have done for that unhappy woman
whose heart, torn to shreds at every birth, could now hold on precariously to a new hope.
(115–16)

calamity. Why should a man suffer so grievously for an offense he had committed inadvertently? But although he thought for a long time he found no
answer. He was merely led into greater complexities. He remembered his
wife's twin children, whom he had thrown away. What crime had they committed? The Earth had decreed that they were an offense to the land and
must be destroyed. And if the clan did not exact punishment for an offense
against the great goddess, her wrath was loosed on all the land and not just
on the offender. As the elders said, if one finger brought oil it soiled the
others. (125)

Tribal customs do change: we learn, for example, that the punishment for
Okonkwo's offense had once been death, but was softened to a term of
exile. Presumably, the doubts we see passing through Obierika's thoughts
might lead to further humanization of tribal customs. But the arrival of
Christian missionaries forecloses that possibility. Internal points of resistance that might have led to self-correcting adjustments within Igbo society serve instead as openings for a powerful wedge, a proselytizing mission that rejects the traditional culture in its entirety.

Umuofia will not be mended but destroyed, and because Okonkwo
struggles to embody his world unreservedly, banishing from his thoughts
and feelings every tremor of ambivalence, he must be destroyed along
with it. Like Abraham, he finds no refuge from the law. Abraham might be
said to come face to face with the divine will because God personally di-
rects his action, whereas Okonkwo obeys his own relentless spirit—but
what is Okonkwo's will except a deeply internalized, rigidly enforced version of divine law? He responds to the familiar logic of the law, the cate-
gorical imperative: as he tells Obierika, "Someone had to do it. If we were
all afraid of blood, it would not be done. And what do you think the Oracle would do then?" (67).

Both the *aqedah* and the story of Okonkwo zero in on filial sacrifice because it crystallizes the inescapable contradiction between fatherhood and
the law of patriarchy. But where the *aqedah* averts tragedy with further divine intervention, reaffirming the covenant with Yahweh, *Things Fall
Apart* presses on to destroy both Okonkwo and the deities he serves. It is
Obierika, once again, who voices the connection between Ikemefuna's
sacrifice and Okonkwo's suicide. He has come to Mbanto to visit
Okonkwo in exile, having harvested his friend's yams and brought the
money:

"I do not know how to thank you."
"I can tell you," said Obierika. "Kill one of your sons for me."
"That will not be enough," said Okonkwo.

"Then kill yourself," said Obierika.

"Forgive me, said Okonkwo, smiling. "I shall not talk about thanking you any more." (142)

Obierika's macabre jest turns on a sharp contrast between human and divine gifts, between the act of human sustenance performed out of friendship and the harsh covenant that makes children's lives the price of the Earth's bounty. Through this mordant counterstatement, Obierika is voicing a message like that of Jesus: "I desire mercy, not sacrifice" (Matthew 9:13). But he is also voicing a more far-reaching critique of filial sacrifice, implying that the father's destruction follows from the son's. And so it does, in a logic as inexorable as the divine will itself: the same unyielding identification with the law that drives Okonkwo to sacrifice Ikemefuna leaves him dangling from the branch of a tree when Umuofia capitulates to white rule. Like the adopted son he both loved and cut down, Okonkwo in death embodies the contradiction that turns identification with divine law into desecration: "It is an abomination for a man to take his own life. It is an offense against the Earth, and a man who commits it will not be buried by his clansmen" (207).

Obierika cannot think his way through this impasse. The alternative he is unable to imagine finds no direct expression in the novel, but it is realized *as* the novel, which embodies the principle of the cultural crossroads in its very language and form. The alternative to Okonkwo's tragic and implicitly sacrificial death, in other words, is the novelist's vision of that death, with its faultless integration of sympathetic understanding and critical detachment. This complex act of representation embodies an African aesthetic of balance but extends that ideal into the uncertain space *between* cultures, inviting an exchange of values that might further humanize both Christian and Igbo traditions. One version of this exchange appears in the passage quoted earlier from *Morning Yet on Creation Day,* in which the intersection of cultures becomes not a place of sacrificial death, like the Christian crucifix or the Y-shaped intersection where Oedipus meets his fate, but a place where "I do not remember any undue distress."

Achebe's memoir looks forward to the resonant close of his last published novel, *Anthills of the Savannah.* This novel tells the interwoven stories of four main characters. The two men, Christopher Oriko and Ikem Osodi, are close friends whose education and abilities place them in the ranks of cultural and political leadership. The two women, Beatrice Nwanyibuife and Elewa, are very different—Beatrice a convent-educated government employee, Elewa marked by her pidgin speech and lack of surname as poor and uneducated, the daughter of a market woman. Once again the male protagonists are destroyed, but this time the story ends with a new beginning, a naming ceremony for Elewa's baby girl, fathered by Ikem Osodi before his assassination. The ceremony is a tribal ritual reinvented on the spot, improvised by Beatrice "on a sudden inspiration" (201). The result is a latter-day Nativity scene, complete with "a baby born into deprivation" surrounded by "the same handful of friends who had kept together around [Beatrice] like stragglers from a massacred army," their very presence "an eloquent tribute to the potency of lost causes" (201, 202). These friends are Muslim and Christian, Igbo and ag-nostic, members of different generations and social classes; the scene as it unfolds calls up intense sorrow for the men who were killed but then transmutes this grief into a celebration of new life. Baldly summarized in this way the event may sound contrived, but in it I believe Achebe has re-alized a powerful culmination not only of the novel's action but also of the concerns that shape his whole body of work. The result is a vision of the transformation prefigured in his childhood memoir and implicit in most of his fiction and poetry. Like the St. Peter's *Pietà*, this vision turns the Crucifixion—particularly the tragic, self-sacrificing death of "Chris" in *Anthills*—back into a Nativity; but it also turns *the* Nativity, the Christian myth, into a personal and cultural crossroads where things that have fallen apart may once again converge, a place of innovation and exchange where it becomes possible to imagine the birth of something radically new.

The ethical imperative to which Western readers are summoned by Achebe's writing is, in effect, to lay aside the crucifix and meet him instead at this crossroads to join in a christening of the future. To name the future is also, however, to rename the past, a past that reasserts itself even in the word *christen*. Achebe captures the play of un-naming and renaming *within* acts of naming in the autobiographical essay whimsically titled "Named for Victoria, Queen of England." The author reports that he was baptized "Albert Chinualomogu," but "dropped the tribute to Victorian England when I went to the university. . . . So if anyone asks you what her Britannic Majesty Queen Victoria had in common with Chinua Achebe, the answer is, They both lost their Albert!" (118). In the manner of sar-donic counterstatement so characteristic of his style, Achebe is "named" for Victoria through the loss of his "Christian" name, and his essay is "named" for this un-naming by way of a punning reversal. This onomas-tic crossroads is a place in and of language, but not for that reason "merely verbal": it is, after all, the place where words perform their most powerful ritual, the naming of the world. This crossroads can be a dangerous place, as Achebe acknowledges, because "a man might perish there wrestling with multiple-headed spirits, but also he might be lucky and return to his people with the boon of prophetic vision" (119).

If my argument in this book has any force, it should be clear that letting go of the crucifix and renaming the past cannot be a simple gesture. No matter of conscious choice alone, it calls for an exploration of the past that is also a self-searching and a labor of discovery. The critique of Western cultural traditions according to utopian political norms will not be sufficient if it makes history no more than a foil to our own enlightenment. What stands in need of correction, or better, of re-creation, is our own engagement with the past as it continues to shape us, and for such a task we require the same balance of sympathy and detachment achieved in powerful works of realist fiction. Achebe has described *Things Fall Apart* as "an act of atonement with my past, the ritual return and homage of a prodigal son" (123). But that homage is complicated, as we have seen, by a pervasive critical and historical distance, registered here in the irony of a "prodigal son" whose apostasy was the Christian religion, and whose atonement carries with it a powerful drive, borne out of that apostasy, to undo the cruelties of the past by going back to seek within it an internal resistance to the ritual sacrifice of human life.

In Achebe's hands the "new religion" produces a strategically powerful rereading of the Igbo traditions. Perhaps one way for us to meet him at this crossroads is to seek, in our own qualified homage to the Western cultural past, a rereading of *its* sacrificial elements. Does European literature have its equivalents to Obierika's doubt, to Ikemefuna's terrible cry, "My father, they have killed me!" or to the voices of the twins crying in the Evil Forest? My answer has been that they do. Ikemefuna's appeal— not to be saved, for he speaks of himself already in the past tense, but to be seen and heard, to be *witnessed*—echoes backward through our literary history, from *"Father, don't you see I'm burning?"* to "I am dead, Horatio" to "My God, my God, why have you forsaken me?" If my argument is correct, if the call that surfaces at such moments has somehow been "there" all along—not only in the Evil Forest but also in the canonical works of European literature—then it wouldn't be surprising if we found that Milton had heard it, too, in the seventeenth century. Early in *Paradise Lost* there is a catalogue of devils, and it starts with "Moloch, horrid king, besmeared with blood / Of human sacrifice, and parents' tears; / Though, for the noise of drums and timbrels loud, / Their children's cries unheard, that passed through fire / To his grim idol" (1.392–96). Milton records not only the children's cries but also the strange resistance of the parents, whose ritual with drums and timbrels drowns out an insupportable sound that their tears nonetheless acknowledge. The line re-creates this resistance: it too says "children's cries" first and only then declares them "unheard," as if the trailing adjective took up the force of the missing verb, acting out the ear's repression of what it has already taken in.

The small movements of Milton's verse often sketch great matters. For a seventeenth-century Protestant poet, the cries of these burning children would be typologically linked to the moment in the Passion when a forsaken Christ calls out to God. By extension, the resolute *unhearing* of those cries might well be linked to Milton's own avoidance of the Passion in the major works of his maturity. One might suppose that the appropriate companion piece to a poem about the Fall would be one about the Crucifixion, especially since Protestant typology links the two scenes in an extensive network of parallels and repetitions. But in *Paradise Regained* Milton chooses to represent the salvation of man through the Temptation in the Wilderness rather than the Passion; in *Samson Agonistes* he seeks out its antetype. Why does he avoid the Crucifixion through such displacement in his major works? I don't mean to suggest a single reason, or a simple one.[10] But one thing Milton's displacements accomplish is to "unhear" the purely human appeal of the forsaken son.

What happens to a cry so resolutely unheard? Perhaps it comes back in the silence of dreams, and in what Keats (struggling to unhear Milton) calls the "unheard melodies" of verse. It may also come back in reverse—for example, in the "pretty babe all burning bright" of Robert Southwell's Christmas vision:

> As I in hoary Winters night
>    Stood shivering in the snow,
> Surpris'd I was with sodaine heate,
>    Which made my hart to glow;
>
> And lifting up a fearefull eye,
>    To view what fire was neare,
> A pretty Babe all burning bright
>    Did in the ayre appeare;
>
> Who scorched with excessive heate,
>    Such floods of teares did shed,
> As though his floods should quench his flames,
>    Which with his teares were fed:
>
> Alas (quoth he) but newly borne,
>    In fierie heates I frie,
> Yet none approach to warme their harts,
>    Or feele my fire, but I;
>
> My faultless breast the furnace is,
>    The fuell wounding thornes:

10. For an illuminating discussion of the question, see Grossman, "'In Pensive Trance.'"

> Love is the fire, and sighs the smoake,
>     The ashes shame and scorns;
>
> The fewell Justice layeth on,
>     And Mercie blowes the coales,
> The metall in this furnace wrought,
>     Are men's defiled souls:
>
> For which, as now on fire I am
>     To worke them to their good,
> So will I melt into a bath,
>     To wash them in my blood.
>
> With this he vanisht out of sight,
>     And swiftly shrunk away,
> And straight I called unto minde,
>     That it was Christmasse day.
>
>                                     (15–16)

In reading "The Burning Babe" we may recall that immolation was a common fate for heretics in the sixteenth century (although Southwell himself would be hanged, disemboweled, and beheaded). We might especially remember that it was the fate of Perotine Massey's burning child, described in a highly controversial episode from Foxe's *Acts and Monuments,* and pictured in one of the volume's most notorious woodcuts. To recall these precedents may help us appreciate the strangeness of lines 13–16, in which the newborn cries out from the fire to lament—not because "none approach" to put out the flames but because none come to "warme their harts" at the bonfire he provides.

Is it implausible to think of "The Burning Babe" as forcefully unhearing a horror that echoes from Isaiah through the *Book of Martyrs* to *Paradise Lost*? The same elements described by Foxe and imagined by Milton are featured in the poem—the fire, the blood, the tears, the sacrificial child—but they programmatically deny themselves. Nightmare images of Herod and Moloch yield to an abstract theology: "The fewell Justice layeth on, / And Mercie blowes the coales." The child is there, "scorched with excessive heate" and shedding "floods of teares," and he poses essentially the same question: *Don't you see I'm burning?* But his tears are for us, and his question has been turned around—no longer a plea, now, but a lament, offering rescue instead of asking for it. His blood does not smear or stain—it washes away guilt. "Love is the fire." Freud argued that dreams evade the censorship by translating abstract thoughts into sense perceptions; this poem borrows the power of an insupportable spectacle and then bribes the censorship by translating sense perceptions into abstract thoughts. The poem thus forms a more powerful counterstatement to the spectacle in Foxe than any of the explicitly polemical responses offered by his Catholic critics.

Ben Jonson told William Drummond of Hawthornden he "would have been content to destroy" many of his own poems "so he had written that piece of [Southwell's] 'The burning babe'" (Donaldson 599). Perhaps we are now in a better position to guess at the impulse that lies behind such a remark. As we saw in chapter 5, he also told Drummond that in 1603 (the year after Southwell's poem was written) his own firstborn appeared to him in a vision fully grown, "with a bloody cross on his forehead, as if it had been cutted w[i]t[h] a sword." The morning after this dream he learned that the boy had died. The result was his finest poem, the epitaph "On My First Sonne." We know the horror Jonson represses by pretending to tell a dead boy to recite his own epitaph. But through what obscure channels does this ancient horror pass from prophecy to poetry, from poetry to nightmare, from nightmare into fact, and then from fact back into poetry? To whom *does* the dream of the burning child belong?

## Mourning Patriarchy

Academic historicism will tell us there is not one burning child, but many. The sacrificial children of Hebrew scripture, Ascanius with his halo of fire, the *delicatus* Glaucias in Statius' funeral elegy, Southwell's burning babe, little Paul Dombey toasting by the hearth, the Reverend Legh Richmond's feverish "Young Cottager," the unnamed children in Freud and Foxe—each must be understood in the context of contemporary material interests and social practices. To see them as manifestations of a single phenomenon is to posit an essence that somehow transcends local circumstance. Myth criticism fails this test, unable to explain the recurrence of its archetypes without falling back on discredited notions of a universal human imagination. Literary history, art history, and intellectual history, by contrast, adapt the methods of philology to pursue specific topics, or *topoi*, the recurrence of which can be explained as a matter of conscious imitation within historical traditions. Poststructuralist theory transforms the study of *topoi* by resituating the notions of intention, imitation, and tradition within the field of "intertextuality," where many of the assumptions on which these concepts depend are called into question. In its more recent forms, historicism modifies the abstractness of this intertextuality with a return to materialism and a renewed interest in notions derived from economics: scholars now study the history of the book, for example, its modes of production and circulation and the cultural practices that make use of it.

None of these critical approaches can explain the repetition of specific figures in widely divergent historical contexts spanning two or three millennia. For all it can tell us about Foxe's martyrs or Virgil's Ascanius, historicism has little to say about the connection between them. In this book I have pointed to many such recurrences: not only the figures of the burning child and the sacrificial son, the motif of the father's witness, and the topos of the boy/old man, but also (for instance) the peculiar reappearance of the *signum Dei* in both Jonson's and Freud's dreams about their sons' deaths. These repetitions are especially compelling because they do not occur in isolation: the wound to the boy's forehead in Jonson and Freud reappears *along with* the aged-boy motif, the father's guilty conscience, the question of who speaks, the inverted temporal structure of the trauma, and writing as an effort to resist the uncanny priority of the dream. Nor has the force of these topics dwindled: many of them reappear in J. K. Rowling's popular series of Harry Potter books. Harry, a version of the sacrificial son, bears a lightning-shaped scar on his forehead, the mark of a failed effort to kill him in his infancy. Perhaps Rowling is deliberately alluding to the mark of the Lord's servants in the Book of Revelation, but if so the reason is probably not that she is attempting religious allegory. (If she is, her readership seems rather to have missed the point; evangelical parents in many parts of the United States have sought to keep her books out of public school classrooms and libraries.) Instead she seems, like Dickens before her, to be rediscovering within the conventions of popular fiction elements of an enduring symbolic repertoire.

What calls for explanation in all this is not just the persistence of individual motifs, then, but the power *and* persistence of their ensemble. Dickens's *Dombey and Son* offers the most impressive evidence of this trait. In his drive to gather the world's own plenitude into an encyclopedic form, Dickens not only combines the motifs of filial sacrifice and the burning child with every conceivable variation on the *puer senex* topos; he also follows *The Winter's Tale*'s use of romance to reform tragedy, meanwhile mocking academic veneration for Roman culture and parodying the "beloved son" motif that elevates younger brothers in the Hebrew scripture. When the dying boy gazes uncomprehendingly on his father ("'Floy!' he said. 'What *is* that?'"), *Dombey and Son* reverses Leontes' inspection of Mamillius with pointed irony: "Paul looked it in the face, and thought, was this his father?" (294). Then, when Mr. Dombey mistakenly writes "child" for "son" in Paul's epitaph, the text even manages to anticipate Lacan's misremembering of Freud, a feat of prophecy it is hard to put down to artistic intention.

I proposed in the introduction that the persistent clustering of these motifs is best understood as the effect of a symbolic economy. This supposition is compatible with academic historicism as I have described it, for it envisions literary and artistic signification as effects of cultural transactions through which meanings are circulated, pleasures exchanged, and social roles acted out. It thereby helps us to imagine cultural repetition and continuity as including traditions of conscious imitation without being limited to them, for the symbolic economy itself, operating as a social system, will carry its structural demands forward through time to be rediscovered in comparable ways by artists who need not have studied one another. These demands are not unchanging; on the contrary, the artists most likely to achieve preeminence are those who manage to recast the symbolic economy most forcefully and comprehensively in the face of political, economic, and technological change. Viewing such creative achievements as responses to epochal disruptions of the social order enables us to reckon with long-term continuities as well as with local conditions, for it locates the act of artistic innovation at the stress point where these forces meet. There is nothing aesthetically pure about such a view, for this stress point is also the place where daily life unfolds. The challenge of literary history is not to transcend the local, but to locate it meaningfully within the *longue durée* of Western history and culture.

In the twenty-first century, the accelerating rate of social, economic, and technological change threatens the study of literary and cultural history with an increasingly marginal role, not only in public life but even within the curriculum (and the budget) of the modern research university. This does not mean that the old symbolic economy has at last been shattered, its power broken. Far from it. Rather, the sacrificial economy has adapted more successfully than scholarship and poetry have to the environment taking shape around us. The danger in this situation is not that we will lose touch with our past, but that we will fail to recognize its hold on us. Academic historicism is indispensable to the work of knowing, perhaps even shaping, how our past extends through the present and into the future. My purpose is not, therefore, like Nietzsche in *Untimely Meditations,* to attack it in the name of some "suprahistorical" ideal. But historicism *itself* is a product of the past it studies, as the example of Virgil's *Aeneid* may suggest. I would argue that the temporal fold made explicit in Virgil's epic is nothing less than the unavoidable structure of *any* narrative retrospect, which "historicizes" the past by fitting it into a causal chain that leads to the present. "Hindsight as foresight," in Auden's phrase, not only makes sense, it is the principle of historical sense-making par excellence. Virgil objectifies this doubling of perspective in the figure of "father" Anchises. In doing so he calls attention to the ideological impulse seldom acknowledged in supposedly more objective historical narration: the impulse to construct and employ an imperial gaze, looking back across the centuries to tell the story of our own advent.

Nietzsche saw this historicism as corrosive. Human as opposed to animal existence, he argued, begins in the "untimely," or the historical sense, but it also depends on vital and organic powers that can be destroyed by too much historical study:

> It is true that only by imposing limits on this unhistorical element by thinking, reflecting, comparing, distinguishing, drawing conclusions, only through the appearance within that encompassing cloud of a vivid flash of light—thus only through the power of employing the past for the purposes of life and of again introducing into history that which has been done and is gone—did man become man: but with an excess of history man again ceases to exist, and without that envelope of the unhistorical he would never have begun or dared to begin. (64)

Nietzsche's attack, published just as Hegelian academic historicism was being institutionalized in the universities, is a telling critique of the scientific pretensions to which professional history is prone. He characterizes the consequences for life of "historical culture" (102) by taking over the trope of the *puer senex* and reversing it much as Dickens had done, satirizing the effects of education on the young. Forced to learn history before they know life, they are spiritually diminished by "the awareness of being a latecomer and an epigone, in short of being born grey-haired" (102). Nietzsche contrasts the "premature greybeardedness of our present-day youth" (116) with the organic vitality that characterizes "the first-born of all ages, even though they may have also come last" (107)—again paralleling Dickens as he links the trope of the *puer senex* to the biblical motif whereby a younger son is preferred before his elder brothers.

In celebrating the possibilities of such a reversal, Nietzsche revives yet another motif as old as Plato and Virgil: the rejuvenation of time by which old age, like a crab, travels backward. He attributes this regress to the somewhat mystified energetics celebrated throughout his essay in the opposition of strength and weakness (a polarity proper to organic life). This power of reversing both history and historicism to rejuvenate the culture is simply *there* in "strong" natures; Nietzsche cannot tell us how to acquire or gain access to it except by celebrating "the instinct of youth" (117). His extravagant and hortatory style, however, offers a rhetorical counterpart of the vitalism he is urging. By a deconstructive turn after Nietzsche's own fashion, we might well see this thematics of force and energy in the argument as an existential projection of the style itself—a pro-

jection of the author's verbal energy into the world by sheer force of elo-
quence. For as we have seen, the rewinding of chronological time involves
the wishful projecting onto nature of a reversibility proper to language.

It seems to me that Achebe's play with the retroactive force of naming-
as-unnaming engages the reversibility of language in a less mystified way
than Nietzsche's vision of the "victorious second nature" that "will become a first" (77). As an imaginative model for cultural history, Achebe's
wordplay suggests that renaming the past is a reciprocal way of renaming
ourselves. Within the European tradition, one important text that seems
close in spirit to this insight is Freud's essay "On Mourning and Melancholia." Freud presumably had no intention of crafting a historiographical
meditation, but his essay has proven fruitful in unanticipated ways. As a
historiographical model, it emphasizes the critic's retrospect rather than
the illusion of a prospect situated in the past. Like a bereaved person sorting through the memories and associations that link her to a lost object,
the critic tries to understand her relation to forms of social life no longer
in existence, to artifacts and expressions from a world long gone. The aim
of this labor is not simply to surrender the object, freeing the cultural ego
once and for all from its attachment to Shakespeare or the Bible. It is
rather to transform the attachment, surrendering one *conception* of the
object in favor of another. Something very much like the work of mourning as Freud describes it is integral to this labor, for its imperatives

> are carried out bit by bit, at great expense of time and cathectic energy, and
> in the meantime the existence of the lost object is psychically prolonged.
> Each single one of the memories and expectations in which the libido is
> bound to the object is brought up and hypercathected, and detachment of
> the libido is accomplished in respect of it. (245)

As a critical practice, this detachment of the libido works not on the object
itself but on those things *in* it which have perished—a version of our history, culture, or values that is ideologically moribund. This labor frees the
libido to form new attachments with the same object, based on a revised
understanding of ourselves and of the history that joins us to it.

Freud's discussion points toward the complexity of a relationship that
includes unconscious as well as conscious ties, hostility as well as love, and
an uncertain dimension of meaning—for as his most famous formulation
has it, the melancholic "knows *whom* he has lost but not *what* he has lost
in him" (245). This sentence pinpoints the overlap of the two concepts
Freud seeks to distinguish—for although he never quite says so, his description of the terms *mourning* and *melancholia* suggests finally that they
are not mutually exclusive alternatives but phases of a single complex pro-

cess. Melancholy understood in this way marks the limit of mourning's ability to let go; melancholy incorporates what mourning cannot relinquish. This incorporation is bodily because its rhetorical form is that of a "literalizing" trope, an internalization of the eucharistic speech act ("this is my body").

Patriarchal imperatives attach this speech act embedded in the individual unconscious to an impossible corollary—a collective identification, not just with a male or female body, but with a *fatherly* body. Because it corresponds to nothing in nature, this body was never anything *but* what Freud calls "a loss of a more ideal kind" (245). Sacrificial practices, narratives, rhetoric, and imagery have been marshaled in endless combinations to represent this "lost" body as the collective form of social being, in a process that structurally resembles melancholy incorporation: the ego, in this case the self-image of an entire society, identifies with the lost object and substitutes for it. In the analogy I am describing, criticism seeks to bring this melancholy fixation to consciousness so that it may be acknowledged and mourned. That is one way of understanding the aim of this book, especially in its reliance on close readings of canonical works. Textual commentary can be a way of bringing up "each single one of the memories and expectations in which the libido is bound to the object," "hypercathecting" them in preparation for letting go of elements that still bind us to the fantasy of the father's witness. Needless to say, such a labor must ultimately be collective, like the processes it tries to engage. No one book can hope to detach modern culture from this structure of identification; to review our ties to the past, renaming ourselves in relation to it, must be a challenge shared by practitioners in many fields. I hope this book can contribute to such a project, for indeed, much current research in the humanities and social sciences might be thought of as an academic work of mourning for the dead body of patriarchy.

## The Self as Crossroads

The account I have constructed takes Virgil as a powerful early model. From a position inside Roman imperial culture, the *Aeneid* objectifies a symbolic economy that joins filial sacrifice to imperial history, the father's gaze, and the "biform" *puer senex,* and it reveals the melancholy formation in which the trauma of loss becomes fixed as the pattern of desire. Virgil's achievement is not to have revolutionized this economy but to have elucidated its workings passionately and comprehensively. The *aqedah* in the Book of Genesis is another paradigmatic text, demonstrating with a starkness borne of extremity how the patriarchal covenant can use narrative to capitalize on its own underlying contradictions, forcing them to a point of crisis and resolution. The Gospels turn this narrative pattern upside down: withdrawing the father from view, they anchor themselves in the son's perspective. This shift does revolutionize the sacrificial economy, for it converts the father's lethal demand into the son's loving deed, replacing the cruelty of ritual killing with the pathos of self-surrender. Yet although the Gospels transform the sacrificial economy radically, they still seek an effect comparable to that of the *aqedah,* amplifying and reaffirming a covenant with the father's law. Their representational strategy, epitomized in Michelangelo's first *Pietà,* is to let the father be present only in the bodies of the acquiescent mother and son, who constitute the visible form of his law. Even more powerfully than the *aqedah,* this strategy deifies fatherhood, binding male parenthood to secular and divine authority by way of the most powerful emotions at its disposal.

In Shakespeare we see two related transformations of this economy. There is, first, the shift from a ritual to a theatrical mode of witness, precipitated by the fracturing of religious community. In the culture wars of the Tudor Reformation, the central ritual of bearing witness to God's fatherhood was re-created as a horrifying public spectacle; in the decades that followed, the function of witnessing was itself scattered into various secular venues of which the professional theater was one. *Hamlet* reflects in a profound way on the destabilizing of the sacrificial scenario that results from this scattering. Like the Gospels, *Hamlet* views filial sacrifice from the son's perspective, but unlike them it seeks in vain for a witness that can ensure the meaning of the son's deed. All action, even the act of self-sacrifice, has passed irremediably from ritual into theater; as such, its meaning is no longer given but instead is subject to the contending perspectives of rival social witnesses. In this context the son cannot secure the meaning of his sacrifice—and since its meaning is, finally, the reality of fatherhood, the cornerstone of patriarchal culture appears to be in crisis.

The second development we see in Shakespeare, represented in the arc that leads from *Hamlet* to *The Winter's Tale,* takes us from the son's perspective back to the father's. If Hamlet shows what happens when the son cannot know the father and therefore cannot know himself *as son,* then *The Winter's Tale* shows us the same dilemma from the other side: Leontes cannot know his son and therefore cannot know himself *as father.* The madness of Leontes resumes and intensifies Hamlet's sexual and epistemological malaise, but it does so in order to seek, within the resources of theater itself, a redemptive mode of witness. In the process, Shakespeare dramatizes with increasing clarity the emergence of a traumatic masculinity, a form of subjectivity developed, as Debora Shuger has argued, through the cultural program whereby the Reformation enjoined its subjects to *internalize* the sacrificial spectacle, making it the template of an unstable, self-punishing ego.

Shakespeare's theater also reflects a newly secular economy of spectatorship, in which different media use their representational resources to make the image of the boy *signify* the reality of fatherhood. This spectatorial economy is organized with reference to an adult witness who, whether male or female, is a delegate of the fatherly gaze. Within this economy, masculinity is a mimetic desire perpetuated by the complementary demands that the boy take up the role of the "little man" and that adult witness flatter him with indulgent admiration. The style and content of this mini-manhood may change drastically without altering the essential structure of the cultural transactions through which it circulates.

Dickens, however, like Shakespeare, responds to a profound shift in this structure by renewing the gospel strategy, returning to the son's (more broadly, the child's) point of view to bear witness to the lethal implications of the demand for precocious adulthood. Little Paul Dombey is sacrificed to this demand, embodying in himself the unity of the *puer senex* and the sacrificial son. Dickens achieves this transformation of the sacrificial economy partly by taking advantage of fundamental alterations in the public sphere, including the spread of literacy to the working poor and the industrialization of publishing. These social and economic developments set the stage for a new imaginative synthesis in which Dickens forges the nucleus of fantasies that define modern liberalism: a paternalistic concern for the poor, focused on the pathos of the suffering child, which is presented in a melodramatic bid to shape the reading experience as a secular "conversion." This model of reading draws on a psychology of sentimentality, which activates pity for the child-victim by covertly arousing and then borrowing from the reader's store of self-pity and self-love. This process emerges in a recognizable way from the conventions of evangelical literature, where its complacency is more obvious. Dickens's appropriation of these conventions links him to a tradition of popular martyrdom that reaches back to Foxe. In taking them over for the novel, he is arguably following a path laid down by Shakespeare and the Elizabethan professional theater as they emerged from the eucharistic crisis and the polemical manipulation of sacrificial spectacle in the mid-sixteenth century. Where Shakespeare represents the transfer of the father's witness from God to the audience, Dickens represents its further transformation into a "public sphere" constituted partly by the novel and anchored in the social fantasy of a benevolent paternalism.

These developments accompany changes in the cultural construction of subjectivity, and hence of that special kind of subject called an "author." If sentimentality depends on an internalization of the sacrificial scenario that began in the sixteenth century, so too does the form of authorship that we see fully realized in Dickens. This model of authorship, implicitly both masculine and sacrificial—and therefore, like tragic manhood in Shakespeare, deeply traumatized—can also be observed in Ben Jonson and Sigmund Freud, for whom the act of writing turns out to recapitulate the sacrificial economy. In their efforts to take up the godlike role of the writing subject, both men find themselves forced, like Dickens, to return to the scene of filial sacrifice, repeating the trauma in their very efforts to rise above it.

Literature and other works of art are by no means the only instances of cultural practices as broadly defined and far-reaching as those I am calling the symbolic economy of filial sacrifice. They are especially revealing instances, however, not only for the combination of intense pleasure and imaginative insight they offer, but also because they tend to operate socially at the point of interpellation, the point at which individual subjects are shaped by and fitted into a social and cultural order. Such works represent this process, but they also belong to it, and in the most ambitious instances they seek to reshape it. The history I have just summarized is neither comprehensive nor definitive; it is highly selective and altogether speculative, though I hope not unpersuasive. It needs to be tested and extended by critics and scholars in other fields, and doubtless revised in the process. With these provisos in mind, I want to conclude not with a sweeping assertion, but with a final speculation, one focused on the most intimate dimensions of the topic. The question that motivates my curiosity is the one raised earlier in connection with Achebe's work: what would it mean for us to accept his implied invitation, to break with this history, lay down the cross, and journey to meet him at the crossroads?

My argument proposes that the normative models of modern Western selfhood are residually but still very deeply sacrificial: gender itself, as I suggested with reference to the work of Judith Butler, may be assumed by our literalizing internalization of the eucharistic speech act, "this is my body." The idea of undoing, or even modifying, such a fundamental element of personal identity may seem utopian or fantastic. It is characteristic of the therapeutic culture that developed in the twentieth century, seeking to realize the ancient myth of rejuvenation by finding time reversed in the psyche: the "inner child" is our modern *senex puer.* My recourse to these notions does not, however, presume a therapeutic program; rather, it follows from the assumption that we are historical creatures, fashioned by dreams, fantasies, and social practices. If this is so, then we can be refashioned by them as well. The question is how. The selfhood I have described is still patriarchal, still sacrificial. What might a post-patriarchal self look like? A self in which the sacrificial cross and the

Oedipal crossroads have been reconceived as a scene not of filial agony or patricidal rage, but of un-fathered convergence and exchange? In particular, how might this self be reimagined at that most radical point of interpellation where we identify with our own body images?

When I started to work on this book, my point of departure was subjective and intuitive; it was the moment in which a question takes on urgency. I call this moment subjective rather than personal because I believe it to be somehow "there" for any of Yahweh's subjects to experience—a structural possibility latent in human subjectivity as constituted in patriarchal cultures. At the same time, it feels intensely personal, and this may be a measure of its power. For me it arose when I encountered the question asked by the dead child in Freud's dream book: *Father, don't you see I'm burning?* This question strikes me at once with the enormous sadness of a disregarded plea and the cutting force of an accusation. In this way it takes me back, emotionally, to the scene of sacrifice, and there it divides me— for I seem to identify at once with the father and the child.

Perhaps this residual sadness and guilt reveal a bit of what it means to exist in a culture founded by Abraham and refounded by Jesus on the sacrifice of the son's body to the father's word. My response is undoubtedly inflected by the fact that I am not only a subject in this culture but, more pointedly, also a son and a father of sons. Yet all subjects in a patriarchal system are in some way defined by their relation to fatherhood, and are bound, in however complex or negative a fashion, to the symbolic father (it was a woman who reported the dream of the burning child to Freud). So I imagine that to be a subject in our culture means in some way to find oneself drawn at once to both positions, that of the father and that of the child. Perhaps the father is what Lacan says he is: law, language, the symbolic domain of identity and conscious selfhood. The child would then be the body, desire, the unconscious that Lacan identifies as the authentic subject of being. Together these two figures would make up the barred subject of Lacanian theory, with sacrifice figuring the split between them: the Oedipus complex sacrifices the subject *of* infantile desire in constituting a person subject *to* the law of the father. On this reading the burning child would be an imaginary figure whose pathos evokes our mourning for a primary, always-lost love object composed by the imaginary union of the pre-Oedipal parent with the amorous child.

I don't know whether to believe this Lacanian allegory. Critics like Judith Butler, extending Foucault's critique of psychoanalysis and its "repressive hypothesis," would argue that the primary love object I have described is not recollected but produced by the law and the discourses in which it is embedded, including the discourse of dreams. The burning child is, after all, a seductive figure; there may be pleasurable tremors in the shudder of horror aroused by that haunting plea. Doesn't Yahweh himself tell us, with stunning, godlike candor, that the purpose of child sacrifice is to restore the law by polluting the sacrificial community? Such sacrifice builds community by instilling in its members a horror that can then be converted to piety: *I did it that they might know that I am Yahweh.* But even if the sacrificial fantasy is not originary, it still figures the law's deepest reach into the recesses of the self, and is thus an appropriate point at which to seek a transformation in the self's relation to the law. What if the Other we encounter at this imaginary crossroads were not the Father? What if it were not the Other at all, but simply someone else?

On the hills north of La Jolla, the campus of the University of California at San Diego overlooks the ocean to the west and a freeway running through the canyons to the east. The scene includes some impressive buildings; on one hilltop, the university's Geisel Library, with its stepped and cantilevered upper layers stacked on a concrete pedestal, looks as if it might just have touched down after a long interstellar voyage. The Mandell Weiss Forum, by contrast, is unimposing. Approaching at street level you can just see the top of the building over a long wall of glass panels the size of billboards (figure 8). These panels form a reflective surface, giving back to the gaze a tree-lined expanse of gravel lined with footlights, holding the mirror up to nature quite literally (and quite theatrically).

To enter the forum you turn and follow a walkway down the wall of glass. The effect is to make you a furtive and self-conscious spectator before you even get inside. Do you ignore the spectacle beside you, implausibly pretending not to notice? If you do look, where do you aim your gaze? At yourself, or at others as they file past? And where do they look? Do you catch them stealing a glance at you, or at themselves? Do they catch you watching? The impulse to look, combined with the unnerving prospect of being caught in the act, prevents you from settling down at one "end" or the other of a Lacanian Gaze, secure in your role as either the subject or the object of vision. This is a little like the trick that Purdy's photomontage plays on the adult witness, opening his hiding place to view by revealing that the child is a mirror. Our laughter at Purdy's image comes with a faint shock in which recognition and estrangement are combined.

Estrangement is part of this experience because the moment of surprise, when you find yourself watched from an angle you failed to anticipate, is *not* a moment that pegs you haplessly to your bodily image. It is just the reverse, a Humpty Dumpty moment that reveals the bodily image to have been propped up on a fantasy of seeing yourself from the outside. Mirrors collaborate with this fantasy, reassuring you that the carefully tended

**Figure 8.** Mandell Weiss Forum, University of California, San Diego. Reproduced with permission from the University of California, San Diego.

image they give back is the one you present for the world's admiration. But no mirror can totalize the field of vision; there is always another position from which to be seen. When such a viewpoint takes you by surprise, it ruptures the protective fantasy in which you say to yourself, *I know how I look,* and so it knocks the prop out from under your self-possession. The result is a moment, trivial or devastating, in which the cocoon of seeing and being seen falls away. The loss of self you abruptly rediscover at such moments is a version of the phantasmic event psychoanalysis calls the trauma.

The path that leads to the Mandell Weiss Forum conducts the theatergoer into an artificially traumatic moment. At first it teases your vanity with anxiety as you try to settle down in the crossfire of real and imagined gazes set into play by the collective reflection. At this point, the shock of dispossession still lurks as one possibility within an intersubjective intrigue. The mousetrap springs shut only after you turn through the entryway in the glass wall. Crossing an open patio toward the box office, you see all at once that what had been a mirror is now a window. Looking back through it you see that you were unwittingly on stage the whole time, faked out by a two-way mirror that re-creates the proverbial "fourth wall" of the proscenium arch, behind which the theater audience hides to watch a performance. Your hide-and-seek game with the mirror was exposed all along to an audience of those who came before you in line.

To realize this is a bit like discovering that you're Malvolio. But the special quality of the revelation is not just that it makes you an object of the gaze all over again. It is rather that it places you—almost, but not quite, simultaneously—on opposite ends of the *same look,* a hidden perspective before which the ego in its furtive vanity is laid bare. Literally of course it is someone else, not you, whose uncomfortable negotiations with the mirror are now on display, and this is a crucial part of the experience. Only by identifying with that other person can you retroactively glimpse yourself an instant ago. This splicing of another into the repeating loop of narcissism makes a considerable difference—enough to deconstruct the whole fantastic dynamic of the Gaze, based on the illusion of a witness who sees everything but is never seen. This subject, whether imagined collectively as "the world" or transcendentally as God, is the paternal witness tacitly assumed by a rhetoric of laying bare the ego or hoping (however whimsically) for its redemption. Such phrases allude to an imaginary subject greater than the abject personal ego, a watching presence in whose eyes the ego falters and might seek redemption.

The forum entryway demystifies this Other by demonstrating that the superior awareness it enjoys is purely structural *and cannot be the attribute of a subject.* If the person on the other side of the mirror is imaginatively equivalent to you as you were a moment ago, then who is the subject before whom you were exposed, if not the imaginative equivalent of you as you are now? The entryway's revelation splits you between these two positions, demonstrating in the most intimate way that the same subject cannot occupy both at once. Turning the corner you assume the voyeur's privilege, but the first thing you recognize in doing so is your own instantaneous, retroactive displacement from the imaginary social space in which you had situated yourself. You are in this manner divested of yourself by the act of assuming a privileged point of view. The subject before whom you were exposed was similarly dispossessed by the act of perceiving you—and since your exposure retroactively dispossessed him, or her, just as someone else's is now doing to you, it was never merely *your* exposure. If the first recognition is disconcerting ("A moment ago, I was exposed to the point of view I have just stepped into"), the second one should come as a relief ("The person who saw me then was seeing *in* me his or her own retroactive exposure, just as I am now seeing mine in someone else"). If the first recognition dispossesses you of your imaginary self, then the second *should* dispossess you of your imaginary Other—for if your ego doesn't entirely belong to you, then neither does its abjection.

To be dispossessed of the Other: what kind of relation between subject and spectacle does such a possibility hold out? I suspect it is one in which, to paraphrase Cusanus, we would no longer exist by means of the Other's seeing. Perhaps then, freed from this Other who demands our sacrifice—guaranteeing our bodily existence only if we first guarantee His—we might manage the encounter prefigured in the architecture of the forum, and so come to know ourselves in relation not to the Other, but to others.

# Bibliography

Achebe, Chinua. *Things Fall Apart.* 1959. New York: Anchor, 1994.
——. *Christmas in Biafra and Other Poems.* New York: Doubleday, 1973.
——. *Morning Yet on Creation Day: Essays.* Garden City, N.Y.: Anchor/Doubleday, 1975.
——. *Anthills of the Savannah.* New York: Anchor/Doubleday, 1988.
——. *Home and Exile.* New York: Oxford University Press, 2000.
Ackroyd, Peter. *Dickens.* 1991. New York: Harper Perennial, 1992.
Adelman, Janet. *Suffocating Mothers: Fantasies of Maternal Origin in Shakespeare's Plays, "Hamlet" to "The Tempest."* New York: Routledge, 1992.
Agnew, Jean-Christophe. *Worlds Apart: The Market and the Theater in Anglo-American Thought, 1550–1750.* Cambridge: Cambridge University Press, 1986.
Albright, W. F. "The Names *Shaddai* and *Abram.*" *Journal of Biblical Literature* 54 (1935): 193–203.
Andrews, Malcolm. *Dickens and the Grown-up Child.* Iowa City: University of Iowa Press, 1994.
Auden, W. H. *Collected Poems.* Edited by Edward Mendelson. New York: Random House, 1976.
Bacon, Francis. *The Works of Francis Bacon.* Edited by James Spedding, Robert Leslie Ellis, and Douglas Denon Heath. 14 vols. London: Longman, 1868–90.
Baldwin, T. W. *William Shakspere's Small Latine & Lesse Greeke.* 2 vols. Urbana: University of Illinois Press, 1944.
Ball, Robert. "Theological Semantics: Virgil's *Pietas* and Dante's *Pietà.*" In *The Poetry of Allusion: Virgil and Ovid in Dante's "Commedia,"* edited by Rachel Jacoff and Jeffrey T. Schapp, 19–36. Stanford: Stanford University Press, 1991.
Bandera, Cesário. "Sacrificial Levels in Virgil's *Aeneid.*" *Arethusa* 14 (1981): 217–39.
Barber, C. L., and Richard P. Wheeler. *The Whole Journey: Shakespeare's Power of Development.* Berkeley: University of California Press, 1986.
Barbour, Richmond. "Jonson and the Motives of Print." *Criticism* 40 (1988): 499–528.
Barchiesi, Allesandro. "Virgilian Narrative: Ecphrasis." In Martindale 271–81.

Barkan, Leonard. " 'Living Sculptures': Ovid, Michelangelo, and *The Winter's Tale.*"
 *English Literary History* 48: 639–67.
Barthelme, Donald. *The Dead Father.* 1975. New York: Penguin, 1986.
Barthes, Roland. "The Death of the Author." In *Image, Music, Text: Essays Selected and
 Translated by Stephen Heath,* 142–48. New York: Hill and Wang, 1977.
Barton, Ann. *Ben Jonson, Dramatist.* Cambridge: Cambridge University Press, 1984.
Bell, Ilona. "The Most Retired and Inmost Parts of Jonson's 'On My First Sonne.' "
 *CLA Journal* 29: 171–84.
Bellamy, Elizabeth J. *Translations of Power: Narcissism and the Unconscious in Epic His-
 tory.* Ithaca: Cornell University Press, 1992.
Benveniste, Emil. "La blasphémie et l'euphémie." In *Problèmes de linguistique générale,*
 2:254–57. 1966. Paris: Gallimard, 1974.
Bernard, John D., ed. *Virgil at 2000: Commemorative Essays on the Poet and His Influ-
 ence.* New York: AMS, 1986.
Bernheimer, Charles, and Claire Kahane, eds. *In Dora's Case: Freud—Hysteria—Femi-
 nism.* New York: Columbia University Press, 1985.
Berry, Laura C. *The Child, the State, and the Victorian Novel.* Charlottesville: University
 Press of Virginia, 1999.
Bicknell, E. J. *A Theological Introduction to the Thirty-Nine Articles of the Church of En-
 gland.* 3d ed., rev. Edited by H. J. Carpenter. London: Longmans, 1959.
Blum, Virginia L. *Hide and Seek: The Child between Psychoanalysis and Fiction.* Urbana:
 University of Illinois Press, 1995.
Boose, Lynda. "The Father's House and the Daughter in It: The Structures of Western
 Culture's Daughter-Father Relationship." In *Daughters and Fathers,* edited by
 Lynda Boose and Betty S. Flowers, 19–74. Baltimore: Johns Hopkins University
 Press, 1989.
Booth, Stephen. *Precious Nonsense: The Gettysburg Address, Ben Jonson's Epitaphs on His
 Children, and Twelfth Night.* Berkeley: University of California Press, 1998.
Boothby, Richard. "Altar-Egos: Psychoanalysis and the Theory of Sacrifice." *Journal of
 Psychoanalysis in Culture and Society* 1 (1996): 47–61.
Bowra, C. M. "Some Characteristics of Literary Epic." In Commager 53–61.
Box, Terry J. "Young Paul Dombey: A Case of Progeria." *Artes Liberales* 9 (1983):
 17–21.
Boyarin, Daniel. " 'This We Know to Be the Carnal Israel': Circumcision and the Erotic
 Life of God and Israel." *Critical Inquiry* 18 (1992): 475–505.
Brady, Jennifer. "Jonson's Elegies of the Plague Years." *Dalhousie Review* 65 (1985):
 208–30.
———. "Progenitors and Other Sons in Ben Jonson's *Discoveries.*" In Hirsh 16–34.
Brady, Jennifer, and W. H. Herendeen, eds. *Ben Jonson's 1616 Folio.* Newark: University
 of Delaware Press, 1991.
Breitenberg, Mark. "The Flesh Made Word: Foxe's *Acts and Monuments.*" *Renaissance
 and Reformation* 13 (o.s., 25) (1989): 381–407.
———. *Anxious Masculinity in Early Modern England.* Cambridge: Cambridge Univer-
 sity Press, 1996.
Brenk, Frederick E. "*Aurum Spes et Purpurei Flores:* The Eulogy for Marcellus in
 *Aeneid* VI." *American Journal of Philology* 107 (1986): 218–28.
Brooks, Douglas. " 'If He Be at His Book, Disturb Him Not': The Two Jonson Folios
 of 1616." *Ben Jonson Journal* 4 (1997): 81–101.
Brower, Reuben A. *Hero and Saint: Shakespeare and the Graeco-Roman Heroic Tradi-
 tion.* New York: Oxford University Press, 1971.
Brown, Cedric C., and Arthur F. Marotti, eds. *Texts and Cultural Change in Early
 Modern England.* New York: St. Martin's, 1999.

Brown, Christopher. *Van Dyck*. Ithaca: Cornell University Press, 1983.

Brown, Lloyd W. "Cultural Norms and Modes of Perception in Achebe's Fiction." In Innes and Lindfors 22–36.

Bruster, Douglas. *Drama and the Market in the Age of Shakespeare*. Cambridge: Cambridge University Press, 1992.

Budick, Sanford. "The Prospect of Tradition: Elements of Futurity in a Topos of Homer and Virgil." *New Literary History* 22 (1991): 23–37.

——. "The Experience of Literary History: Vulgar versus Not-Vulgar." *New Literary History* 25 (1994): 749–77.

Burkert, Walter. "Greek Tragedy and Sacrificial Ritual." *Greek, Roman, and Byzantine Studies* 7 (1966): 131–74.

——. *Homo Necans: The Anthropology of Ancient Greek Sacrificial Ritual and Myth*. Translated by Peter Bing. Berkeley: University of California Press, 1983.

——. "The Problem of Ritual Killing." In Hamerton-Kelly 149–76.

Burrow, Colin. *Epic Romance: Homer to Milton*. Oxford: Clarendon, 1993.

Burt, Richard. *Licensed by Authority: Ben Jonson and the Discourses of Censorship*. Ithaca: Cornell University Press, 1993.

Butler, Judith. *Gender Trouble: Feminism and the Subversion of Identity*. New York: Routledge, 1990.

Buttrick, George Arthur, et al., eds. *The Interpreter's Dictionary of the Bible: An Illustrated Encyclopedia*. New York: Abingdon, 1962.

Bynum, Carolyn Walker. *Holy Feast and Holy Fast: The Religious Significance of Food to Medieval Women*. Berkeley: University of California Press, 1987.

——. "The Body of Christ in the Later Middle Ages: A Reply to Leo Steinberg." In *Fragmentation and Redemption: Essays on Gender and the Human Body in Medieval Religion*, 79–117. New York: Zone Books, 1991.

Carroll, David. *Chinua Achebe*. New York: Twayne, 1970.

Cavell, Stanley. *Disowning Knowledge in Six Plays of Shakespeare*. New York: Cambridge University Press, 1987.

Chaucer, Geoffrey. *The Complete Poetry and Prose of Geoffrey Chaucer*. Edited by John Hurt Fisher. New York: Holt, Rinehart, 1977.

Clay, William Keatinge, ed. *Liturgical Services in the Reign of Queen Elizabeth*. Cambridge: Cambridge University Press, 1847.

Collinson, Patrick. "Biblical Rhetoric: The English Nation and National Sentiment in the Prophetic Mode." In McEachern and Shuger 15–45.

Commager, Steele, ed. *Virgil: A Collection of Critical Essays*. Twentieth Century Views. Englewood Cliffs, N.J.: Prentice-Hall, 1966.

Conrad, Joseph. *Heart of Darkness*. Edited by Robert Kimbrough. Norton Critical Edition. 2d ed. New York: Norton, 1971.

Conte, Gian Biagio. *The Rhetoric of Imitation: Genre and Poetic Memory in Virgil and Other Latin Poets*. Edited by Charles Segal. Translated from the Italian. Ithaca: Cornell University Press, 1986.

Craig, D. H. "Authorial Styles and the Frequencies of Very Common Words: Jonson, Shakespeare, and the Additions to *The Spanish Tragedy*." *Style* 26 (1992): 199–220.

Curtius, Ernst Robert. *European Literature and the Latin Middle Ages*. Translated by Willard Trask. Bollingen Series, 36. Princeton: Princeton University Press, 1953.

Davila, Juan, and Paul Foss. *The Mutilated Pietà*. Surry Hills, NSW, Australia: Artspace, 1985.

Davis, Robert Con. *The Paternal Romance: Reading God-the-Father in Early Western Culture*. Urbana: University of Illinois Press, 1993.

de Grazia, Margreta, Maureen Quilligan, and Peter Stallybrass, eds. *Subject and Object in Renaissance Culture*. Cambridge: Cambridge University Press, 1996.

Dekker, Thomas. *The Dramatic Works of Thomas Dekker.* Edited by Fredson Bowers. 4 vols. Cambridge: Cambridge University Press, 1953–61.

Derrida, Jacques. *The Post Card: From Socrates to Freud and Beyond.* Translated by Alan Bass. Chicago: University of Chicago Press, 1987.

de Tolnay, Charles. *The Youth of Michelangelo.* Princeton: Princeton University Press, 1943.

——. *Michelangelo: Sculptor, Painter, Architect.* Princeton: Princeton University Press, 1975.

Dickens, Charles. *Dombey and Son.* Edited by Peter Fairclough. 1970. New York: Penguin Classics, 1986.

——. *The Christmas Books,* vol. 2: *The Cricket on the Hearth, The Battle of Life, The Haunted Man.* Edited by Michael Slater. 1971. New York: Penguin Classics, 1985.

——. *The Letters of Charles Dickens.* Pilgrim Edition. Edited by Madeline House, Graham Storey, and Kathleen Tillotson. Vol. 5, 1847–49, edited by Graham Storey and K.J. Fielding. Vol. 8, 1856–59, edited by Graham Storey and Kathleen Tillotson. Oxford: Clarendon, 1981, 1995.

Dixon, John W., Jr. *The Christ of Michelangelo: An Essay on Carnal Spirituality.* Atlanta: Scholars Press, 1994.

Dollimore, Jonathan. *Sexual Dissidence: Augustine to Wilde, Freud to Foucault.* Oxford: Clarendon, 1991.

Donaldson, Ian, ed. See Jonson, Ben.

Eilberg-Schwartz, Howard. *The Savage in Judaism: An Anthropology of Israelite Religion and Ancient Judaism.* Bloomington: Indiana University Press, 1990.

Eliot, T.S. "The Silurist." *Dial* 83 (1927): 260–61.

——. *The Complete Poems and Plays, 1909–1950.* New York: Harcourt, 1971.

Engle, Lars. *Shakespearean Pragmatism: Market of His Time.* Chicago: University of Chicago Press, 1993.

Enterline, Lynn. *The Tears of Narcissus: Melancholia and Masculinity in Early Modern Writing.* Stanford: Stanford University Press, 1995.

——. *The Rhetoric of the Body from Ovid to Shakespeare.* Cambridge Studies in Renaissance Literature and Culture, no. 35. Cambridge: Cambridge University Press, 2000.

Erickson, Peter. *Patriarchal Structures in Shakespeare's Drama.* Berkeley: University of California Press, 1985.

Ezenwa-Ohaeto. *Chinua Achebe: A Biography.* Bloomington: Indiana University Press, 1997.

Fagles, Robert, trans. See Homer.

Fairclough, H. Rushton, trans. See Virgil.

Feeney, D.C. "History and Revelation in Vergil's Underworld." *Proceedings of the Cambridge Philological Society* 32 (1986): 1–24.

——. *Literature and Religion at Rome: Cultures, Contexts, and Beliefs.* Cambridge: Cambridge University Press, 1998.

Fields, Karen E. "Foreword." In Jay ix–xvii.

Fike, Francis. "Ben Jonson's 'On My First Sonne.'" *The Gordon Review* 11 (1969): 205–20.

Fish, Stanley. "Author-Readers: Jonson's Community of the Same." In *Representing the English Renaissance,* edited by Stephen Greenblatt, 231–63. Berkeley: University of California Press, 1988.

Fitzgerald, Robert, trans. See Virgil.

Florio, John, trans. See Montaigne.

Forster, John. *The Life of Charles Dickens.* Edited and annotated with an introduction by J.W.T. Ley. London: Palmer, 1928.

Foucault, Michel. "What Is an Author?" In *Language, Counter-Memory, Practice: Selected Essays and Interviews by Michel Foucault,* 113–38. Edited by Donald F. Bouchard, translated by Donald F. Bouchard and Sherry Simon. Ithaca: Cornell University Press, 1977.

Fowler, Don. "Virgilian Narrative: Story-telling." In Martindale 259–70.

Foxe, John. *Actes and Monuments.* 1576 (Short Title Catalogue no. 11224).

——. *The Acts and Monuments of John Foxe.* Edited by Josiah Pratt. 8 vols. 4th ed., rev. London: Religious Tract Society, 1877.

Freud, Sigmund. "Mourning and Melancholia." In *The Standard Edition of the Complete Psychological Works,* 14:239–51. Translated by James Strachey. London: Hogarth, 1955.

——. *Beyond the Pleasure Principle.* Translated and edited by James Strachey. New York: Norton, 1961.

——. *Dora: An Analysis of a Case of Hysteria.* Edited by Philip Rieff. New York: Collier, 1963.

——. *New Introductory Lectures on Psychoanalysis.* Translated and edited by James Strachey. New York: Norton, 1965.

——. *The Interpretation of Dreams.* Translated and edited by James Strachey. New York: Avon, 1971.

Frye, Northrop. *T. S. Eliot.* London: Oliver and Boyd, 1963.

Frymer-Kensky, Tikva. "The Patriarchal Family Relationships and Near Eastern Law." *Biblical Archaeologist* 44 (1981): 201–14.

Gager, Valerie L. *Shakespeare and Dickens: The Dynamics of Influence.* Cambridge: Cambridge University Press, 1996.

Gallagher, Catherine. *The Industrial Reformation of English Fiction: Social Discourse and Narrative Form, 1832–1867.* Chicago: University of Chicago Press, 1985.

Gallagher, Lowell. "The Place of the Stigmata in Christological Poetics." In McEachern and Shuger 93–115.

Gallop, Jane. *Reading Lacan.* Ithaca: Cornell University Press, 1985.

Gillis, Daniel. *Eros and Death in the "Aeneid."* Rome: L'Erma di Bretschneider, 1983.

Girard, René. *Violence and the Sacred.* Translated by Patrick Gregory. Baltimore: Johns Hopkins University Press, 1977.

Gould, Cecil. "Michelangelo, *Pietà.*" In *International Dictionary of Art and Artists,* edited by James Vinson, 2:214. Chicago: St. James, 1990.

Green, Alberto R. W. *The Role of Human Sacrifice in the Ancient Near East.* American Schools of Oriental Research Dissertation Series, no. 1. Missoula: Scholars Press, for the American Schools of Oriental Research, 1975.

Greenblatt, Stephen. *Renaissance Self-Fashioning: From More to Shakespeare.* Chicago: University of Chicago Press, 1980.

——. *Shakespearean Negotiations: The Circulation of Social Energy in Renaissance England.* Berkeley: University of California Press, 1988.

——. "Remnants of the Sacred in Early Modern England." In de Grazia, Quilligan, and Stallybrass 337–45.

Greene, Thomas. "Ben Jonson and the Centered Self." *Studies in English Literature* 10 (1970): 325–48.

Greenough, J. B., et al., eds. *Allen and Greenough's New Latin Grammar for Schools and Colleges.* Rev. ed. 1888. Boston: Ginn, 1931.

Griffin, Jasper. "Introduction." In *The Oxford History of the Roman World,* edited by John Boardman, Jasper Griffin, and Oswyn Murray. 1988. Oxford: Oxford University Press, 1991, 1–10.

Gross, Kenneth. *The Dream of the Moving Statue.* Ithaca: Cornell University Press, 1992.

Grossman, Marshall. "'In Pensive trance, and anguish, and ecstatic fit': Milton on the Passion." In *A Fine Tuning: Studies of the Religious Poetry of Herbert and Milton,* edited by Mary A. Maleski, 205–20. Binghamton: Medieval and Renaissance Texts and Studies, 1989.

——. *The Story of All Things: Writing the Self in English Renaissance Narrative Poetry.* Durham, N.C.: Duke University Press, 1998.

Haller, William. *Foxe's Book of Martyrs and the Elect Nation.* London: Cape, 1963.

Hamerton-Kelly, Robert G., ed. *Violent Origins: Walter Burkert, René Girard, and Jonathan Z. Smith on Ritual Killing and Cultural Formation.* Stanford: Stanford University Press, 1987.

Harbage, Alfred B. *A Kind of Power: The Shakespeare–Dickens Analogy.* Jayne Lectures for 1974. Memoirs of the American Philosophical Society, vol. 105. Philadelphia: American Philosophical Society, 1975.

Hardie, Philip. *The Epic Successors of Virgil: A Study in the Dynamics of a Tradition.* Roman Literature and Its Contexts. Cambridge: Cambridge University Press, 1993.

——. "Virgil and Tragedy." In Martindale 312–26.

——, ed. *Virgil: Aeneid, Book IX.* Cambridge: Cambridge University Press, 1994.

Hardwick, Charles. *A History of the Articles of Religion.* 3d ed. Edited by F. Procter. London: G. Bell and Sons, 1895.

Harrison, E. L. "Divine Action in *Aeneid* Book Two." In S. J. Harrison, ed., *Oxford Readings* 46–59.

Harrison, S. J. *Vergil: Aeneid 10.* With introduction, translation, and commentary. Oxford: Clarendon, 1991.

——, ed. *Oxford Readings in Virgil's "Aeneid."* Oxford: Oxford University Press, 1990.

Hartt, Fredric. *Michelangelo: The Complete Sculpture.* London: Thames and Hudson, 1969.

Heinze, Richard. *Virgil's Epic Technique.* Translated by Hazel and David Harvey and Fred Robertson. 1903. Berkeley: University of California Press, 1993.

Helgerson, Richard. *Self-Crowned Laureates: Spenser, Jonson, Milton, and the Literary System.* Berkeley: University of California Press, 1983.

——. *Forms of Nationhood: The Elizabethan Writing of England.* Chicago: University of Chicago Press, 1992.

Herford, C. H., and Percy and Evelyn Simpson, eds. See Jonson, Ben.

Hirsh, James, ed. *New Perspectives on Ben Jonson.* Madison, N.J.: Fairleigh Dickinson University Press, 1997.

Homer. *The Iliad.* Translated with an introduction by Richmond Lattimore. 1951. Chicago: Phoenix Books of University of Chicago Press, 1961.

——. *The Iliad.* Translated by Robert Fagles. New York: Viking Penguin, 1990.

Hopkins, Jasper. *Nicholas of Cusa's Dialectical Mysticism: Text, Translation, and Interpretive Study of De Visione Dei.* Minneapolis: Banning, 1985.

Innes, C. L. "Language, Poetry, and Doctrine in *Things Fall Apart.*" In Innes and Lindfors 111–25.

Innes, C. L., and Bernth Lindfors, eds. *Critical Perspectives on Chinua Achebe.* Washington, D.C.: Three Continents, 1978.

Irigaray, Luce. *This Sex Which Is Not One.* Translated by Catherine Porter with Carolyn Burke. Ithaca: Cornell University Press, 1985.

James, E. O. *Sacrifice and Sacrament.* London: Thames and Hudson, 1962.

James, Heather. *Shakespeare's Troy: Drama, Politics, and the Translation of Empire.* Cambridge: Cambridge University Press, 1997.

Jay, Nancy. *Throughout Your Generations Forever: Sacrifice, Religion, and Paternity.* Chicago: University of Chicago Press, 1992.

Johnson, W.R. "Aeneas and the Ironies of *Pietas.*" *Classical Journal* 60 (1965): 360–64.

——. *Darkness Visible: A Study of Virgil's "Aeneid."* Berkeley: University of California Press, 1976.

——. "The Figure of Laertes: Reflections on the Character of Aeneas." In Bernard 85–105.

Jonson, Ben. *Ben Jonson.* Edited by C.H. Herford and Percy and Evelyn Simpson. 11 vols. Oxford: Oxford University Press, 1925–52.

——. *Ben Jonson.* Edited by Ian Donaldson. New York: Oxford University Press, 1985.

Kantorowicz, Ernst H. *The King's Two Bodies: A Study in Medieval Political Theology.* Princeton: Princeton University Press, 1957.

Kastan, David Scott. "'The noyse of the new Bible'": Reform and Reaction in Henrician England." In McEachern and Shuger 46–68.

Kastan, David Scott, and Peter Stallybrass, eds. *Staging the Renaissance: Reinterpretations of Elizabethan and Jacobean Drama.* New York: Routledge, 1991.

Kay, W. David. "The Christian Wisdom of Ben Jonson's 'On My First Sonne.'" *Studies in English Literature* 11 (1971): 125–36.

Kennedy, Duncan F. "Virgilian Epic." In Martindale 145–53.

Kerrigan, William. *Hamlet's Perfection.* Baltimore: Johns Hopkins University Press, 1994.

Knott, John R. *Discourses of Martyrdom in English Literature, 1563–1694.* Cambridge: Cambridge University Press, 1993.

Kristeva, Julia. *Powers of Horror: An Essay on Abjection.* Translated by Leon S. Roudiez. New York: Columbia University Press, 1982.

Kyd, Thomas. *The Spanish Tragedy.* Edited by Phillip Edwards. The Revels Plays. Cambridge: Harvard University Press, 1959.

Lacan, Jacques. "Desire and The Interpretation of Desire in *Hamlet.*" Translated by James Hulbert. *Yale French Studies* 55/56 (1977): 11–52.

——. *The Four Fundamental Concepts of Psychoanalysis.* Edited by Jacques-Alain Miller. Translated by Alan Sheridan. 1978. New York: Norton, 1981.

——. "The Meaning of the Phallus." In *Feminine Sexuality: Jacques Lacan and the Ecole Freudienne,* edited by Juliet Mitchell and Jacqueline Rose. Translated by Jacqueline Rose. New York: Norton, Pantheon, 1985.

——. "Introduction to the Names-of-the-Father Seminar." Translated by Jeffrey Mehlman. In *Television/A Challenge to the Psychoanalytic Establishment,* edited by Joan Copjec, 81–95. New York: Norton, 1990.

Lander, Jesse. "'Foxe's' *Books of Martyrs:* Printing and Popularizing the *Acts and Monuments.*" In McEachern and Shuger 69–92.

Laplanche, J., and J.-B. Pontalis. *The Language of Psychoanalysis.* Translated by Donald Nicholson-Smith with an introduction by Daniel Lagache. New York: Norton, 1973.

Larsen, Janet L. *Dickens and the Broken Scripture.* Athens: University of Georgia Press, 1985.

Lattimore, Richmond, trans. See Homer.

Lauinger, Ann. "'It makes the father, lesse, to rue': Resistance to Consolation in Jonson's 'On my first Daughter.'" *Studies in Philology* 86 (1989): 219–34.

Lee, M. Owen. *Fathers and Sons in Virgil's "Aeneid": Tum Genitor Natum.* Albany: State University of New York Press, 1979.

Leinwand, Theodore. *Theatre, Finance, and Society in Early Modern England.* Cambridge: Cambridge University Press, 1991.

Lesser, Wendy. "From Dickens to Conrad: A Sentimental Journey." *English Literary History* 52 (1985): 185–208.

Levenson, Jon D. *The Death and Resurrection of the Beloved Son: The Transformation of Child Sacrifice in Judaism and Christianity*. New Haven: Yale University Press, 1993.

Levin, Harry. *The Question of Hamlet*. New York: Oxford University Press, 1959.

Lévi-Strauss, Claude. *Totemism*. Translated by Rodney Needham. Boston: Beacon, 1962.

Levy, Anita. *Reproductive Urges: Popular Novel-Reading, Sexuality, and the English Nation*. Philadelphia: University of Pennsylvania Press, 1999.

Lewis, C. S. "Virgil and the Subject of Secondary Epic." In Commager 62–67.

Loades, David, ed. *John Foxe and the English Reformation*. Brookfield, Vt.: Scolar, 1997.

Loewenstein, Joseph. "The Script in the Marketplace." *Representations* 12 (1985): 101–14.

———. "Plays Agonistic and Competitive: The Textual Road to Elsinore." *Renaissance Drama*, n.s., 19 (1988): 63–96.

———. *Ben Jonson and Possessive Authorship*. Cambridge: Cambridge University Press, forthcoming.

Lukacher, Ned. *Primal Scenes: Literature, Philosophy, Psychoanalysis*. Ithaca: Cornell University Press, 1986.

Lupton, Julia Reinhard. *Afterlives of the Saints: Hagiography, Typology, and Renaissance Literature*. Stanford: Stanford University Press, 1996.

Lyne, R. O. A. M. *Words and the Poet: Characteristic Techniques of Style in Vergil's "Aeneid."* Oxford: Clarendon, 1989.

Mack, Burton. "Introduction: Religion and Ritual." In Hamerton-Kelley 1–70.

Mackail, J. W., ed. *The Aeneid*. Oxford: Clarendon, 1930.

Mannyng of Brunne, Robert. *Handlyng Synne*. Edited by Idelle Sullens. Binghamton, N.Y.: Medieval and Renaissance Texts and Studies, 1983.

Marcus, Leah S. *Childhood and Cultural Despair: A Theme and Variations in Seventeenth-Century Literature*. Pittsburgh: University of Pittsburgh Press, 1978.

Marlowe, Christopher. *Dido Queen of Carthage* and *The Massacre at Paris*. Edited by H. J. Oliver. The Revels Plays. London: Methuen, 1968.

Marotti, Arthur F. "Southwell's Remains: Catholicism and Anti-Catholicism in Early Modern England." In Cedric C. Brown and Marotti 37–65.

Marotti, Arthur F., and Michael D. Bristol, eds. *Print, Manuscript, and Performance: The Changing Relations of the Media in Early Modern England*. Columbus: Ohio State University Press, 2000.

Martindale, Charles, ed. *The Cambridge Companion to Virgil*. Cambridge: Cambridge University Press, 1997.

Matalene, H. W. "Patriarchal Fatherhood in Ben Jonson's Epigram 45." In *Traditions and Innovations: Essays on British Literature of the Middle Ages and the Renaissance*, edited by David G. Allen and Robert A. White, 102–12. Newark: University of Delaware Press, 1990.

Maus, Katharine Eisaman. *Ben Jonson and the Roman Frame of Mind*. Princeton: Princeton University Press, 1984.

———. "Horns of a Dilemma: Jealousy, Gender, and Spectatorship in English Renaissance Drama." *English Literary History* 54 (1987): 561–83.

———. "A Womb of His Own: Male Renaissance Poets in the Female Body." In *Sexuality and Gender in Early Modern Europe: Institutions, Texts, Images*, edited by James Grantham Turner, 266–88. Cambridge: Cambridge University Press, 1993.

———. *Inwardness and Theater in the English Renaissance*. Chicago: University of Chicago Press, 1995.

McDougal, Russell. "Okonkwo's Walk: The Choreography of Things Falling Apart."

*World Literature Written in English* 26.1 (1986); rpt. in Solomon I. Iyasere, ed., *Understanding "Things Fall Apart": Selected Essays and Criticism* (Troy, N.Y.: Whitston, 1998), 106–18.

McEachern, Claire, and Debora Shuger, eds. *Religion and Culture in Renaissance England.* Cambridge: Cambridge University Press, 1997.

McGrew, Robert E. "Tuberculosis." *Encyclopedia of Medical History.* New York: McGraw-Hill, 1985.

Metzger, Bruce M., and Roland E. Murray, eds. *The New Oxford Annotated Bible with the Apocryphal/Deuterocanonical Books.* New Revised Standard Version. New York: Oxford University Press, 1991.

Miller, David Lee. "Spenser and the Gaze of Glory." In *Edmund Spenser's Poetry,* edited by Hugh Maclean and Anne Lake Prescott, 756–64. Norton Critical Edition. New York: Norton, 1993.

——. "Writing the Specular Son: Jonson, Freud, Lacan, and the (K)not of Masculinity." In *Desire in the Renaissance: Psychoanalysis and Literature,* edited by Regina Schwartz and Valeria Finucci, 233–60. Princeton: Princeton University Press, 1994.

——. "The Earl of Cork's Lute." In *Spenser's Life and the Subject of Biography,* edited by Judith Anderson, Donald Cheney, and David Richardson, 146–71. Massachusetts Studies in Early Modern Culture. Amherst: University of Massachusetts Press, 1996.

——. "The Father's Witness: Patriarchal Images of Boys." *Representations* 70 (spring 2000): 114–40.

Miola, Robert S. "Virgil in Shakespeare," in Bernard 241–58.

——. *Shakespeare and Classical Tragedy: The Influence of Seneca.* Oxford: Clarendon, 1992.

Montagu, Ashley. *The Anatomy of Swearing.* New York: Macmillan, 1967.

Montaigne, Michel de. *The Essayes.* Translated by John Florio. 3 vols. London: Dent, 1928.

Montrose, Louis A. "Spenser's Domestic Domain: Poetry, Property, and the Early Modern Subject." In de Grazia, Quilligan, and Stallybrass 83–130.

Mueller, Janel M. "Pain, Persecution, and the Construction of Selfhood in Foxe's *Acts and Monuments.*" In McEachern and Shuger 161–87.

Mullaney, Steven. *The Place of the Stage: License, Play, and Power in Renaissance England.* Chicago: University of Chicago Press, 1988.

——. "Mourning and Misogyny: *Hamlet, The Revenger's Tragedy,* and the Final Progress of Elizabeth I, 1600–1607." *Shakespeare Quarterly* 45 (1994): 139–62.

——. "Reforming Resistance: Class, Gender, and Legitimacy in Foxe's *Book of Martyrs.*" In Marotti and Bristol 235–51.

Newmyer, Stephen Thomas. *The Silvae of Statius: Structure and Theme.* Leiden: Brill, 1979.

Newsome, Robert. "Embodying *Dombey*: Whole and in Part." In *Dickens Studies Annual* 18, edited by Michael Timko, Fred Kaplan, and Edward Guiliano, 197–219. New York: AMS, 1989.

Newton, Richard C. "Jonson and the (Re-)Invention of the Book." In Summers and Pebworth 31–55.

Nicholson, Eirwen. "Eighteenth-Century Foxe: Evidence for the Impact of the *Acts and Monuments* in the 'Long' Eighteenth Century." In Loades 143–77.

Nietzsche, Friedrich Wilhelm. *Untimely Meditations.* Edited by Daniel Breazeale. Translated by R. J. Hollingdale. Cambridge: Cambridge University Press, 1977.

Nunokawa, Jeff. *The Afterlife of Property: Domestic Security and the Victorian Novel.* Princeton: Princeton University Press, 1994.

O'Hara, James J. *True Names: Vergil and the Alexandrian Tradition of Etymological Wordplay.* Ann Arbor: University of Michigan Press, 1996.

——. "Virgil's Style." In Martindale 241–58.

Oliensis, Ellen. "Sons and Lovers: Sexuality and Gender in Virgil's Poetry." In Martindale 294–311.

Orgel, Stephen. *The Illusion of Power: Political Theater in the English Renaissance.* Berkeley: University of California Press, 1975.

——. "The Poetics of Incomprehensibility." *Shakespeare Quarterly* 42 (1991): 431–37.

——. *Impersonations: The Performance of Gender in Shakespeare's England.* Cambridge: Cambridge University Press, 1996.

——, ed. *The Winter's Tale.* Oxford World Classics. New York: Oxford University Press, 1996.

Ovid [P. Ovidius Naso]. *The Art of Love and Other Poems.* Rev. ed. Translated by J. H. Mozley. Loeb Classical Library. 1939. Cambridge: Harvard University Press, 1947.

——. *The Art of Love.* Translated by Rolfe Humphries. Bloomington: Indiana University Press, 1957.

Parry, Adam. "The Two Voices of Virgil's *Aeneid.*" In Commager 107–23.

Paster, Gail Kern. *The Body Embarrassed: Drama and the Disciplines of Shame in Early Modern England.* Ithaca: Cornell University Press, 1993.

Patten, Robert L. *Charles Dickens and His Publishers.* Oxford: Clarendon, 1978.

Petrini, Mark. *The Child and the Hero: Coming of Age in Catullus and Vergil.* Ann Arbor: University of Michigan Press, 1997.

Pickering, Samuel, Jr. *The Moral Tradition in English Fiction, 1785–1850.* Hanover, N.H.: University Press of New England, 1976.

Pigman, G. W., III. *Grief and the English Renaissance Elegy.* Cambridge: Cambridge University Press, 1985.

Pontalis, J. B. "On Deathwork in Freud, in the Self, in Culture." In *Psychoanalysis, Creativity, and Literature: A French-American Inquiry,* edited by Alan Roland. New York: Columbia University Press, 1978.

Pope, Norris. *Dickens and Charity.* New York: Columbia University Press, 1978.

Putnam, Michael C. J. "Daedalus, Virgil, and the End of Art." *American Journal of Philology* 108 (1987): 173–98.

——. *Virgil's "Aeneid": Interpretation and Influence.* Chapel Hill: University of North Carolina Press, 1995.

Qualls, Barry V. *The Secular Pilgrims of Victorian Fiction: The Novel as Book of Life.* Cambridge: Cambridge University Press, 1982.

Quint, David. *Epic and Empire: Politics and Generic Form from Virgil to Milton.* Princeton: Princeton University Press, 1993.

Reed, Henry. "Chard Whitlow." In *Parodies, An Anthology from Chaucer to Beerbohm—and After,* edited by Dwight MacDonald. New York: Random House, 1960.

Richmond, Legh. *Annals of the Poor, or Narratives of The Dairyman's Daughter, the Negro Servant, and the Young Cottager.* New York: American Tract Society, n.d.

Riggs, David. *Ben Jonson: A Life.* Cambridge: Harvard University Press, 1989.

Rose, Jonathan. "Reading the English Common Reader: A Preface to a History of Audiences." *Journal of the History of Ideas* 53.1 (1992): 47–70.

——. *The Intellectual Life of the British Working Classes.* New Haven: Yale University Press, 2001.

Ruskin, John. "Fiction, Fair and Foul—1." In *The Works of John Ruskin,* 34: 265–302. 39 vols. Edited by E. T. Cook and Alexander Wedderburn. New York: Longmans, Green, 1903–12.

Sacks, Peter M. *The English Elegy: Studies in the Genre from Spenser to Yeats.* Baltimore: Johns Hopkins University Press, 1985.

Sackville, Thomas. "Induction." In *The Mirror for Magistrates,* edited by Lily B. Campbell. 1938. New York: Barnes and Noble, 1960.

Scarry, Elaine. *The Body in Pain: The Making and Unmaking of the World*. New York: Oxford University Press, 1985.

Schur, Max. *Freud: Living and Dying*. New York: International Universities Press, 1972.

Scodel, Joshua. *The English Poetic Epitaph: Commemoration and Conflict from Jonson to Wordsworth*. Ithaca: Cornell University Press, 1991.

Shakespeare, William. *The Riverside Shakespeare*. Edited by G. Blakemore Evans et al. 2d ed. Boston: Houghton Mifflin, 1997.

Shuger, Debora Kuller. *The Renaissance Bible: Scholarship, Sacrifice, and Subjectivity*. Berkeley: University of California Press, 1994.

Silberman, Lauren. "To Write Sorrow in Jonson's 'On My First Sonne.'" *John Donne Journal* 9 (1990): 149–55.

Smith, David R. *Masks of Wedlock: Seventeenth-Century Dutch Marriage Portraiture*. Ann Arbor, Mich.: UMI Research, 1982.

Smith, Jonathan Z. "The Domestication of Sacrifice." In Hamerton-Kelly 191–205.

Southwell, Robert. *The Poems of Robert Southwell, S.J.* Edited by James H. McDonald and Nancy Pollard Brown. Oxford: Clarendon, 1967.

Spenser, Edmund. *The Faerie Queene*. Edited by A. C. Hamilton. New York: Longman, 1977.

——. *The Yale Edition of the Shorter Poems of Edmund Spenser*, edited by William A. Oram et al. New Haven: Yale University Press, 1989.

Spicer, Joneath. "The Renaissance Elbow." In *A Cultural History of Gesture from Antiquity to the Present Day*, edited by Jan Bremmer and Herman Roodenburg, 84–128. Ithaca: Cornell University Press, 1992.

Spilka, Mark. "On the Enrichment of Poor Monkeys by Myth and Dream; or, How Dickens Rousseauized and pre-Freudianized Victorian Views of Childhood." In *Sexuality and Victorian Literature*, edited by Don Richard Cox, 161–79. Knoxville: University of Tennessee Press, 1984.

Sprengnether, Madelon. *The Spectral Mother: Freud, Feminism, and Psychoanalysis*. Ithaca: Cornell University Press, 1990.

Statius. *Statius*. With an English translation by J. H. Mozley. 2 vols. 1928. Cambridge: Harvard University Press, 1955.

Steinberg, Leo. *The Sexuality of Christ in Renaissance Art and Modern Oblivion*. New York: Pantheon, 1983.

Stock, A. G. "Yeats and Achebe." In Innes and Lindfors 86–92.

Stoller, Robert. *Presentations of Gender*. New Haven: Yale University Press, 1985.

Suetonius. *Suetonius*. With an English translation by J. C. Rolfe. Rev. ed. 2 vols. Cambridge: Harvard University Press, 1998.

Summers, Claude J., and Ted-Larry Pebworth, eds. *Classic and Cavalier: Essays on Jonson and the Sons of Ben*. Pittsburgh: University of Pittsburgh Press, 1982.

Suzuki, Mihoko. *Metamorphoses of Helen: Authority, Difference, and the Epic*. Ithaca: Cornell University Press, 1989.

Swain, A. E. H. "Figures of Imprecation." *Englische Studien* 24 (1898): 6–71.

Tarrant, R. J. "Poetry and Power: Virgil's Poetry in Contemporary Context." In Martindale 169–87.

Tillotson, Kathleen. *Novels of the Eighteen-Forties*. Oxford: Clarendon, 1954.

Traub, Valerie. *Desire and Anxiety: Circulations of Sexuality in Shakespearean Drama*. New York: Routledge, 1992.

Trimpi, Wesley. "BEN IONSON his best piece of *poetrie*." *Classical Antiquity* 2:1 (April 1983): 149–50.

van den Berg, Sara. "Ben Jonson and the Ideology of Authorship." In Brady and Herendeen 111–37.

Vickers, Brian, ed. *Shakespeare: The Critical Heritage.* London: Routledge, 1974.

Virgil [P. Vergili Maronis]. *Virgil.* Translated by H. Rushton Fairclough. Rev. ed. 2 vols. Loeb Classical Library. Cambridge: Harvard University Press, 1940.

——. *Aeneidos,* in *Opera,* edited by R. A. B. Mynors. Oxford: Clarendon, 1969.

——. *The Aeneid of Virgil, Books 1–6.* Edited by R. D. Williams. 1972. New York: St. Martin's, 1975.

——. *The Aeneid of Virgil, Books 7–12.* Edited by R. D. Williams. 1973. New York: St. Martin's, 1977.

——. *The Aeneid.* Translated by Robert Fitzgerald. 1981. New York: Vintage, 1990.

Wagenvoort, Hendrik. *Pietas: Selected Studies in Roman Religion.* Studies in Greek and Roman Religion, edited by H. S. Versnel with F. T. Van Straten, vol. 1. Leiden: Brill, 1980.

Walder, Dennis. *Dickens and Religion.* London: Allen and Unwin, 1981.

Weinberger, Martin. *Michelangelo: The Sculptor.* New York: Columbia University Press, 1967.

Welsh, Alexander. *The City of Dickens.* Oxford: Clarendon, 1971.

Williams, R. D., ed. See Virgil.

Wilson, Edmund. *Axel's Castle: A Study in the Imaginative Literature of 1870–1930.* 1931. New York: Scribner's, 1969.

Wiltshire, Susan Ford. *Public and Private in Virgil's "Aeneid."* Amherst: University of Massachusetts Press, 1989.

Winner, Jack D. "The Public and Private Dimensions of Jonson's Epitaphs." In Summers and Pebworth 107–19.

Wofford, Susanne Lindgren. *The Choice of Achilles: The Ideology of Figure in the Epic.* Stanford: Stanford University Press, 1992.

Woods, Susanne. "Aemilia Lanyer and Ben Jonson: Patronage, Authority, and Gender." *Ben Jonson Journal* 1(1994): 15–30.

Žižek, Slavoj. *The Sublime Object of Ideology.* London: Verso, 1989.

# Index